# English in the World

# English in the World
## Global Rules, Global Roles

**Edited by Rani Rubdy and
Mario Saraceni**

continuum

**Continuum**

| | |
|---|---|
| The Tower Building | 80 Maiden Lane |
| 11 York Road | Suite 704 |
| London SE1 7NX | New York, NY 10038 |

www.continuumbooks.com

© Rani Rubdy, Mario Saraceni and contributors 2006

**British Library Cataloguing-in-Publication Data**
A catalogue record for this book is available from the British Library.

ISBN-10:  HB: 0-8264-8905-2
          PB: 0-8264-8906-0
ISBN-13:  HB: 978-0-8264-8905-0
          PB: 978-0-8264-8906-7

Typeset by YHT Ltd, London
Printed and bound in Great Britain by Biddles Ltd., King's Lynn, Norfolk

# Contents

# About the contributors

**Tom McArthur** is the editor of the quarterly journal *English Today: The International Review of the English Language*. He has published 15 books on aspects of language, including *The English Languages* (Cambridge University Press) and was general editor of *The Oxford Companion to the English Language* (Oxford University Press).

**Jennifer Jenkins** is Senior Lecturer in Applied Linguistics at King's College, London, where she directs and teaches on the MA in ELT and Applied Linguistics. She is the author of *The Phonology of English as an International Language*, published by Oxford University Press, and *World Englishes*, published by Routledge.

**Barbara Seidlhofer** is Professor of English and Applied Linguistics at Vienna University. She is editor of *Controversies in Applied Linguistics*, co-editor of *Principle and Practice in Applied Linguistics*, and co-editor of *Pronunciation*, all published by Oxford University Press.

**Luke Prodromou** is a freelance teacher, trainer and textbook writer based in Greece. He has trained teachers and trainers in many European countries and Latin America. He has taught courses on behalf of Pilgrims, Bell School, NILE (Norwich), ESADE (Barcelona) and the University of Edinburgh. He is currently engaged in PhD research at the University of Nottingham into non-native spoken English.

**Andy Kirkpatrick** is Professor of Language Education at Curtin University of Technology, Perth, Australia. He is co-author with Ron and Suzanne Scollon of *Contrastive Chinese-English Discourse: A Critical Appraisal*, (Foreign Language Teaching and Research Press, Beijing) and, with Nobuyuki Honna and Sue Gilbert, *English Across Cultures* (Sanshusha Press, Tokyo). He edited the volume *Englishes in Asia: Communication, Identity, Politics and Education* (Language Australia). He is co-editor of the *English Australia Journal*.

**Peter K. W. Tan** is a Senior Lecturer in the Department of English Language and Literature, National University of Singapore, where he teaches modules on the history of English, stylistics and discourse analysis. His publications have been in the broad area of hybridity as manifested in the non-Anglo Englishes – including their use on the Internet, in literary texts and in naming practices – and include associated pedagogical issues. He has published extensively, especially in the area of Singaporean and Malaysian English.

**Vincent B Y Ooi** is Associate Professor in the Department of English Language and Literature at the National University of Singapore. His research interests include linguistic computing, lexicology and computer-mediated communication, with a particular focus on non-Anglo Englishes and their relation to Anglo ones. He teaches modules on lexicology and lexicography, language and the Internet, and computer corpus linguistics.

**Andy Chiang** is an Assistant Professor in the Department of Statistics and Applied Probability, National University of Singapore, where he teaches statistics and biostatistics. He has a keen research interest in the use of statistical methods in experimental and social sciences. He is an associate editor for *The American Statistician*.

**Sandra McKay** is Professor of English in the English Department of San Francisco State University. Her interest in English as an international language developed from her extensive work in teacher education in countries such as Chile, Hong Kong, Hungary, Latvia, Morocco, Japan, Singapore, South Africa and Thailand. Her books include *Teaching English as an International Language: Rethinking Goals and Approaches* Oxford University Press, (2002, winner of the Ben Warren International Book Award), *New Immigrants in the US: Readings for Second Language Educators* (edited with Sau-ling Wong, 2000, Cambridge University Press) and *Sociolinguistics and Language Teaching* (edited with Nancy Hornberger, Cambridge University Press, 1996).

**Anthea Fraser Gupta** is a sociolinguist whose main area of research since 1975 has been Singaporean English, about which she has published a large number of articles, chapters and the book *The Steptongue: Children's English in Singapore* (Multilingual Matters). She also has an interest in language planning and education. From 1990 to 1996 she worked with the speech-language therapists of Singapore on studies relating to the development of norms of language acquisition in Singapore, and on the practice of speech-language therapy in that country. In September 1996 she took up a permanent post in Modern English Language in the School of English at the University of Leeds. She has taught in a number of different areas over the years, including sociolinguistics, phonetics, syntax, the history of English, and stylistics.

**Nicos C. Sifakis** is a Lecturer in the School of Humanities of the Hellenic Open University. He holds a PhD in Language and Linguistics from the University of Essex, UK. He has been a distance education writer and researcher since 1998. He is also co-founder and coordinator (2000–04) of the ESP/EAP SIG of TESOL Greece. His articles have appeared in various international refereed journals, including *Language and Education*, *ESP Journal* and *System*.

**Brian Tomlinson** is a Reader in Language Learning and Teaching at Leeds Metropolitan University. He is editor of *Materials Development in Language Teaching* (Cambridge University Press) and *Developing Materials for Language Teaching* (Continuum), and co-author of *Discover English* (Heinemann). He is the founder and president of the Materials Development Association (MATSDA).

**T. Ruanni F. Tupas** is a Lecturer with the Centre for English Language Communication, National University of Singapore. He previously taught Applied Linguistics and Composition at the University of the Philippines and at Virginia Polytechnic Institute and State University, USA. He has published internationally refereed papers on the politics of language in Southeast Asia, especially the Philippines and Singapore. He is currently a member of the Executive Committee and the Sub-committee on Research and Publications of the Singapore Association for Applied Linguistics.

**Michael Joseph** and **Esther Ramani** are Senior Lecturers at the University of the North in South Africa. They hold PhD degrees in Applied Linguistics from the Indian Institute of Science in Bangalore, southern India. They are currently developing new programmes for underprepared students from rural backgrounds aspiring to a tertiary education. However, their main professional interest is in the maintenance and promotion of indigenous languages. In South Africa they have developed the first bilingual undergraduate degree in which an African language (Sesotho sa Leboa) is being offered as a medium of instruction.

**Suresh Canagarajah** is an Associate Professor at the City University of New York (CUNY). His research articles have appeared in *TESOL Quarterly, College Composition and Communication, Language in Society, Written Communication, World Englishes, Journal of Multilingual and Multicultural Development*, and *Multilingua*. His books, *Resisting Linguistic Imperialism in English Teaching* (Oxford University Press 1999) and *Geopolitics of Academic Literacy and Knowledge Construction* (University of Pittsburgh Press 2002) have won several awards. His other publications include *Critical Academic Writing and Multilingual Students* (University of Michigan Press 2002) and a collection of articles by international scholars on responses to globalization, *Reclaiming the Local in Language Policy and Practice* (Erlbaum 2005). He is currently editor of *TESOL Quarterly.*

# Introduction

## An intricate scenario: the use of English around the world

English is today a truly global language. This has become something of an understatement if one considers the dramatic expansion in the roles of English as a language of international communication in trade, diplomacy, sport, science, technology and countless other fields, in a growing number of regions and cultural contexts. More recently, revolutions in transport, technology, commerce and communications, including satellite broadcasting and the Internet, have all further reinforced the global pre-eminence of English.

The global spread of English, its causes and consequences, have long been a focus of critical discussion. One of the main concerns has been that of standardization. This is also because, unlike other international languages such as Spanish and French, English lacks any official body setting and prescribing the norms of the language. This apparent linguistic anarchy has generated a tension between those who seek stability of the code through some form of convergence and the forces of linguistic diversity that are inevitably set in motion when new demands are made on a language that has assumed a global role of such immense proportions.

One consequence of the global predominance that English has gained over the last few decades is that today non-native speakers of English far outnumber its native speakers (Graddol 1997, Crystal 2003). The number of people learning English in China, for example, is greater than the total number of speakers of English in the USA (Taylor 2002, cited in Jiang 2003, 3). This has led to a shift in the numerical balance of power between native and non-native speaker groups. Also, because the range and variety of contexts in which English is used has increased exponentially, this has reduced the importance of the canonical context of native speakers speaking with non-native speakers, as more and more non-native speakers find reasons to communicate with each other using the language.

Indeed, the issue of language diversity is an extremely complex one. Scholars are faced with a number of challenging questions: What is standard English? What are varieties of English? How can variation be described? Variation does not follow clear and identifiable patterns, and in order to answer these questions, one inevitably has to deal with intersecting parameters such as identity, power, gender, class and regional location.

## Towards simplification: the teaching and learning of English

While an exhaustive description of the use of English is a futile pursuit, with regard to the teaching and learning of English in the classroom such complexities have necessarily to be reduced to manageable models. The language of the classroom tends to be rather static and disregardful of variation in style and register and, more conspicuously, of regional variation. One of the main issues in the pedagogy of English is indeed the choice of an appropriate model for the teaching of English as a foreign or second language. Here 'model' refers to regional variation, which is the main focus in the whole volume. In this sense, the choice is seen as lying between three principal 'rival' systems: Standard English (usually Standard British or Standard American English), World Englishes, and EIL/ELF (English as an International Language/English as a Lingua Franca).

### Standard English

'Standard' English (without delving into the details of what this expression may mean) remains the most popular model. Being a written variety, mainly designed for institutional purposes (education, administration, business, etc.) it is not only considered well-suited to written communication (Widdowson 1994), but users are expected to conform to its conventions, particularly with reference to grammar and lexis (Gupta, this volume). Even governments that are wary of the adoption of Anglo-American values through the learning of English tend to be convinced that it is native-speaker models which should be taught in the classroom. This, despite the fact that for a majority of learners and teachers it is actually disempowering, as Kirkpatrick argues here. In many cases, this is in fact not a real choice but the result of a lack of alternatives. The vast majority of teaching materials are based on British and/or American English, and for most teachers around the world this is fairly unproblematic.

More recently, the changed world-English landscape has led to the questioning of the application of British and American standards to these settings, and a recognition that the native speaker of English should no longer be the measure against which non-native speaker performance is judged. The notion of a monolithic, unadaptable linguistic medium owned by its original speakers and forever linked to their rules has been rejected as naïve and untenable (Seidlhofer and Jenkins 2003, 141). Thus, this model has been the object of much criticism in the last few decades. First of all, in view of the very fact that it is effectively a choice imposed from the outside, the selection of British or American English has been widely criticized as the expression of a form of linguistic imperialism (Phillipson 1992, Pennycook 1994, Canagarajah 1999). In addition, because they privilege native speakers of English as innately superior, as both language users and teachers, the model has also been questioned for its exclusive orientation from an ideological point of view. McKay (2002, and this volume), for instance, shows how if the EIL language curriculum is to be specifically designed to engage the L2 students' reality and activate their learning within this context, the special advantage of the native-speaker teacher disappears.

## World Englishes

In several countries of the Outer Circle, such as Nigeria, India, the Philippines and Singapore, where English has taken a firm hold as a major language, local forms of English have emerged as a result of 'nativization' processes which are fast becoming institutionalized. These new varieties of English, or World Englishes, are felt to be more appropriate models, particularly in view of their endonormative potential (Kachru 1982, Kachru 1992). Unlike native speaker models, they are not imposed from the outside. This perception is, however, sometimes at odds with the official policy of using and teaching an internationally comprehensible variety: a good example is Singapore.

Concern has also been expressed about the uncontrolled spread of nativized forms of English on the grounds of linguistic fragmentation. Arguably, if everyone communicates in their local varieties, the language will diverge to the point of mutual incomprehensibility, thus cancelling out its value as a lingua franca. The resultant product would be not different dialects of English but different mutually unintelligible languages, much like the splitting up over time of Classical Latin into the vernacular Romance languages. This argument has to do with considerations of the functional efficiency of the language (Milroy and Milroy 1999). Thus Jenkins comments in relation to phonological variation (this volume), 'if the policy of pluricentricity is pursued unchecked, in effect a situation of "anything goes", with each expanding circle L1 group developing its own English pronunciation norms, there is a danger that these varieties will move further and further apart until a stage is reached where pronunciation presents a serious obstacle to lingua franca communication' (p.35). Others have pointed out that there are strong centripetal forces at work, such as the Internet, the international press and media, the publishing industry, tourism and air travel, multinational corporations and the like, which reinforce the need for a mutually comprehensible form of English and exert an informal regulatory function – 'a sort of linguistic thermostat' (Maley 2002, 46).

## English as an International Language or English as a Lingua Franca

The changing patterns in the 'ownership' of English have produced demographic changes in English usage around the world. The data reflecting this usage is sufficiently rich and varied to warrant the generation of hypotheses about a particular kind of international communication which has English as a shared code used mainly by non-native speakers to communicate with one another. Interactions of this type, as they are envisaged, are specifically premised on the goal of information exchange among business people and international travellers, often in influential networks. Accordingly, the language used in such international communication settings has been termed English as an International Language (EIL) or English as a Lingua Franca (ELF) (for example, Seidlhofer and Kirkpatrick in this volume), and it has been argued that this is a suitable model because it liberates L2 speakers from the imposition of native speaker norms as well as the cultural baggage of World English models.

Since proposals for a pedagogical model inevitably hinge on the decision makers' political and/or ideological persuasions, one way of formulating the issue is by posing the question: Is the decision to be made more closely oriented to a monolithic, undifferentiated framework, or to one that embraces a 'polymodel' approach? The former provides an option characterized by uniformity and stability (Kirkpatrick, this volume). The latter betrays the influence of a multitude of source languages, characterized by non-conformity to what are considered standard English norms. Another way of formulating the issue is to view it as a dichotomy between what seems a Eurocentric vision versus a pluricentric one (Leitner 1992).

## The debate

The collection of papers in this volume is intended as a contribution to this entire debate on norms. Its aims are to (1) bring together different theoretical perspectives that reflect the debate, and (2) to provoke exploration of possible pedagogical solutions that may be both valid and viable for adoption in international contexts. The question being addressed then is: What forms would be appropriate for successful interaction among international L2 speakers of English today, and what would be the implications for classroom practice? It is felt that an exchange of views on this controversial issue between proponents of World Englishes and those of EIL/ELF will be a productive and stimulating one.

Because of the particular function that it serves, EIL/ELF has been described (Jenkins 2000, Seidlhofer 2001) in ways which characterize it as significantly different from 'standard' English as used among native speakers. It has been proposed as a synthetic form which combines features of standard English with those most commonly shared by speakers of all non-native varieties of the language, whether they be Europeans, people from the Middle East or Asians. Such proposals primarily seek to establish, on the basis of findings from empirical research, a Lingua Franca core. The underlying assumption is that students of English as a foreign language are better served if they are taught EIL/ELF, and spared the unnecessary imposition of the native speaker's norms of English.

Thus Jenkins' framework of English accents (2000, and this volume) reverses the imposition of an ENL (English as a Native Language) norm on non-native-speaker learners, and takes a sociolinguistically-oriented view of L2 divergences as differences, not deficiencies.

This perspective allows her to redefine pronunciation errors not in terms of proximity to ENL norms but the degree to which intelligibility in ELF communication is affected. Only where an item is core are violations of it to be considered an ELF pronunciation error, but where it is non-core, divergences are instead viewed as (L2) regional variation. Thus local diversity in specific linguistic contexts is catered for. However, the criterion of mutual intelligibility becomes suspect, particularly when its loss or absence is implicitly linked with violations of ENL norms. That such an implicit relationship underpins the ELF framework becomes evident in Seidlhofer's recent discussion of Jenkins' work. Seidlhofer notes that Pragmatics is 'less constrained and thus less manageable in research; unlike the case for pronunciation features, violations of ENL pragmatic norms rarely lead to loss of intelligibility' (Seidlhofer 2004, 217). There is a potential for some kind of circularity here, and intelligibility is not entirely separated from ENL norms.

What is significant about the EIL/ELF perspective is the calling into question of the absolute prescriptive validity of ENL norms, and its attempt to address the pedagogical concerns of international L2 learners of English by proposing an alternative system based on the findings of solid empirical research. The attempt to codify ELF is at present being further supported by research initiatives in lexico-grammar (Seidlhofer 2002a, 2002b) and consolidated by references to computer-based data from the ICE (International Corpus of English) and the VOICE (Vienna–Oxford International Corpus of English).

Nevertheless, so long as the underlying tacit assumption is that once the Lingua Franca core is systematically codified, it can then be used as a model for teaching and learning this form of English in the classroom, the question that arises is whether one form of prescription is not being (unwittingly or even wittingly) replaced by another. It is true that its proponents have gone out of their way to deny any prescriptive designs, and have emphasized the purely descriptive nature of their interest as a preliminary basis for systematically codifying ELF. Still, what underlies this pursuit of 'commonalities' or salient features in the ELF data is the hope that pedagogic decisions would be informed by these findings (though 'not determined by' them, as Seidlhofer citing Widdowson is at pains to emphasize, this volume). Critics of the EIL/ELF perspective may interpret this search for generalizations among international forms of English usage as a desire to regulate at some level what goes into the teaching and learning of English as an international language. But by their very definition these forms are likely to be very diverse, having come into being through their use for a diversity of intercultural interactions and purposes, and bearing the influence of multiple source languages. So although the proponents of ELF claim that they are happy to allow 'learners and users of English to decide which kind of English they need and want' (Seidlhofer, this volume), the question that arises is: Once the core features are established, are these likely to assume the character and force of a new dogma, particularly if the findings they are based on bear the stamp of visibly high-tech undertakings of international standing as represented by the ICE and VOICE corpora?

Another significant factor in all matters of language use and language learning is that of culture. In many Outer Circle countries (e.g. areas of South-East Asia, the Indian subcontinent, a number of African countries, parts of the Caribbean) there exist distinct varieties of English which are used intra-nationally, and reflect many features of inter-cultural interaction that resonate with the local setting. Besides, these varieties are lexico-grammatically as sophisticated and function-ally as viable as any of the traditionally recognized Inner Circle varieties of English. The proponents of EIL/ELF contend that whereas in the Outer Circle countries English can be said to have become localized to meet domestic, intra-national purposes, and show sufficient shared features within the region or speech community to warrant the possibility of their own norms, English as a globalized means of international communication is expected to transcend all communal and cultural boundaries.

Since much of the discussion of English as a Lingua Franca focuses on the situation in the Expanding Circle, where it is meant to function as a means of intelligible communication between speakers for whom English is neither a first language nor an institutionalized second language, cultural identity is obviously not such a crucial element as is usually the case in discussions of Outer Circle speakers. Though culture is not totally ignored, as Tan et al. point out (this volume), given that English is not the first language of its speakers in these contexts, there is a tacit justification perhaps for not taking fully on board the cultural norms of Expanding Circle speakers. Similarly, not being subject to forces of standardization, by virtue of it being no-one's first language, and being exposed to a range of local native-language influences within the Expanding Circle, the accelerated processes of change generated in English as an international language are by and large looked upon by proponents of LFC as processes of destandardization (Seildlhofer 2004, 212). Seidlehofer, for instance notes

> Many interactions in English are between participants who do not control standard grammar and whose lexis and pronunciation do not conform to any recognized norm ... Nonstandard, unedited English is becoming more and more visible. (*ibid*, citing Melchers and Shaw 2003, 195)

Apparently, concerns such as this are a further justification for reducing or restricting variation, containing diversity through the proposal for a 'common core'. In sum, critics of ELF may take the view that inter-cultural communication and cultural identity are to be made a necessary casualty as a part of this process. If we take this view to its logical conclusion, this would involve, as Tan et al. argue in this volume with reference to Singaporean learners as an exemplar, getting students to deliberately employ a variety different from all the real encounters available to them outside the classroom – i.e. adopting as reality something that goes against their own experience of the world. Thus, notwithstanding the sound and impressive quality of the empirical research on which descriptions of ELF are based, its eventual codification with a view to applying it as a framework for teaching English globally appears problematic and controversial.

First, it is doubtful whether such a monomodel, serving the entire community of international L2 speakers, can be created on this basis (Prodromou 2003, and this volume). Second, even if we posit not one but several Lingua Franca models, one for Europe, another for South Asia, yet another for the ASEAN countries, crucially this would not only work at cross-purposes with the notion of a 'core', but does not seem to be reflecting the reality of the actual contexts of use. For instance, in a separate piece of research, Kirkpatrick and Saunders (2005) have shown that educated Singaporean English, taken as an example of ASEAN lingua franca English, is highly intelligible to educated speakers of a wide range of varieties despite an extremely wide range of variation. They conclude, albeit on the basis of their limited data, that rather than being a systematic code, ASEAN lingua franca English comprises a number of separate systems with high degrees of variation and error, making it questionable whether it might be described as a system that could be codified and used as a model for the ASEAN English language classroom. What their findings suggest is that a tolerance for variation, and a focus on mutual cooperation and intelligibility, could become key principles of language teaching. The conclusion they draw is that language teachers and learners would need to understand that variation from the norm in lingua franca communication is itself likely to be 'the norm'.

Furthermore, regardless of the benefits of positing a uniform Lingua Franca core, some scholars believe that to suggest that all EIL learners should learn only the LFC, is to shortchange students who may have quite legitimate aspirations towards acquiring some of the other Englishes, including the standard variety. From this perspective, the language users and learners themselves should have the prerogative of self-determination. Thus for Tomlinson (this volume), for any group of applied linguists, language planners or curriculum developers to undertake this task is tantamount to arrogance. Prodromou likewise maintains that while an empirically based and coherently codified description of the 'successful bilingual with intercultural communicative competence' (Alptekin 2002) might present a valid alternative to native norms, its purpose would be far from being served if the grammatical acceptability bar of ELF were to be lowered to an extent where it ceased to meet the aspirations of countless non-native learners who have reached a high level of proficiency both in grammar and vocabulary. ELF speakers who are not native speakers of English will, nevertheless, be meeting and interacting with native speakers as well as non-native speakers, who will also have been exposed to canonical grammar and lexis, and while it is right for ELF not to be determined by the latter, it would not be right to exclude them either.

The possibility of imposing a single model or template on the diverse contexts in which English is taught worldwide is anathema for Canagarajah too (this volume), who maintains that it is time we orientate to English as a hybrid, multinational language that constitutes diverse norms and systems, represented by the global community of English speakers. While there are subtle differences, this hybrid system is also characterized by underlying similarities. What is more, the global community of English speakers in many post-colonial contexts have already developed strategies which they employ skilfully to negotiate their differences through natural processes of interaction in communication. This is different from current proposals of LFC in that it is not artificially constructed or externally imposed, but develops from within. Allaying fears that hybridity will breed fragmentation, Canagarajah puts his faith in the power of human agency when he asserts, 'Creating an appreciation of differences and a readiness to negotiate diversity will see to it that this hybrid system of World Englishes bridges communities rather than fragments them' (p.208).

Yet others like Joseph and Ramani (this volume) call for the development of a counter-culture which goes beyond the mere recognition of the hegemony of English in a rapidly globalizing world and is willing to problematize the relation between indigenous languages and English. They seek a radically new form of globalism which values and upholds diversity and offers practitioners a 'politics of the possible', enabling them to become involved in a form of 'professional activism' (Prabhu 1987).

In the end, the validity of the EIL/ELF proposal will probably depend upon whether or not it chooses to embrace a polymodel approach to the teaching of English or a monolithic one, whether it leads to the establishing and promoting of a single (or a limited form of) Lingua Franca Core for common use among speakers in the Outer and Expanding Circles, possibly stripped of any cultural influences, or whether it will be flexible enough to manifest the cultural norms of all those who use it along with the rich tapestry of linguistic variation in which they are embedded.

An alternative viewpoint to EIL/ELF, which has been around for some time now, is one which acknowledges the polymorphous nature of the English language worldwide, identifying such different varieties under a World Englishes paradigm. The emphasis, in this case, is not on prescribing either a reduced or extended form of standard English, but on questioning the very concept of 'standard', and on advocating a pluricentric model rather than a monolithic one (Kachru 1994, Canagarajah 1999).

In this view, for both teaching and learning, the implication is that importance is not given so much, or exclusively, to the accurate application of a set of prescribed rules with the aim of achieving international intelligibility, but to tolerance for diversity and appro-priacy of use in specific sociolinguistic contexts. This view acknowledges that there are varieties of English which have developed to perform specific tasks in specific communicative situations. Such a view prioritizes the process of cross-cultural comprehensibility between learners as a communicative goal in itself (Alptekin 2002) over notions of accuracy and standards, and is compatible with the pedagogical proposals suggested by McKay, Prodromou, Sifakis and Tomlinson in the present volume. These scholars agree on the need to be sensitive to the multilingual and multicultural realities of their learners and of empowering them to cope with the variety of Englishes, both non-native and native, they will encounter in the world outside their classroom walls. It also accords well with Tan et al.'s suggestion that the answer is perhaps not an over-focus on the code but an encouragement to teachers and learners and English language users the world over to develop a willingness and adaptability to manipulate the code to fit different contexts and sensibilities. This practice of negotiating their differences in actual interactions of communication, which transcends linguistic standardization (Sifakis, this volume), is in harmony with the kind of adaptable and flexible approach suggested by Kirkpatrick for speakers of English in the Expanding Circle, and is attuned to Prodromou's as well as Canagarajah's conception of global English as a *process* which reflects the interface between context and language choice.

These ideas are clearly at variance with the suggestion that there should be one common core variety which is both multifunctional and able to be taught to all L2 non-native speakers. From the above point of view, then, EIL/ELF might conceivably be seen as introducing a form of neo-standardization in the guise of a universal pedagogical solution for L2 speakers of English.

Oddly, this debate problematizing the norms and standards for EIL has generally been confined to scholarly arenas. The real consumers, the learners and teachers, are seldom consulted about which model of English they would prefer to use (Tomlinson, this volume, Prodromou, this volume), or what they feel about the system that is actually being used in their classrooms (an exception to this is Timmis 2002). For this reason Ruanni's paper in this volume is a rare articulation of their predicament, giving voice to the dilemmas faced by teachers (and their learners) within a Philippino context in their attempts to reconcile the conflicting interests represented by the need to provide access to standard English and an authentic grounding in the local culture. Ruanni points out the limitations that exist in the perspectives of both the World Englishes and English as an International Language in helping teachers make appropriate decisions when confronted with such hard choices, so long as such aspects of pedagogical choice remain integral to local and/or global power structures and measures of success in formal education.

The diversity of views on the subject clearly indicates that a debate is timely in order to sharpen our perceptions and clarify thinking about this important global phenomenon. Such a debate should also lead to a better understanding of the pedagogical implications involved. The papers in this volume are intended to reflect a strong and urgent sense of the issues outlined above. The power that English and speakers of English wield today makes it imperative that many of the controversial aspects relating to English as an international language be addressed. Identifying concerns that are particularly interesting or contentious from either point of view (EIL/ELF or World Englishes) will not only help advance further thinking among the scholarly community, but also yield important pedagogical insights that can feed into teachers' and learners' classroom experience. Hopefully, it will also activate them to contribute to the debate by voicing their own perspectives.

## References

Alptekin, C. 2002. 'Towards intercultural communicative competence in ELT'. *ELT Journal*. 56/1, 57–64.

Canagarajah, A. 1999. *Resisting Linguistic Imperialism in English Teaching*. Oxford: Oxford University Press.

Crystal, D. 2003. *English as a Global Language* (2nd edn). Cambridge: Cambridge University Press.

Graddol, D. 1997. *The Future of English? A Guide to Forecasting the Popularity of the English Language in the 21st Century*. London: BC.

Jenkins, J. 2000. *The Phonology of English as an International Language*. Oxford: Oxford University Press.

Jiang, Y. 2003. 'English as a Chinese language'. *English Today*. 19/2, 3–8.

Kachru, B. 1982/1992. 'Models for non-native Englishes'. In B. Kachru (ed.). 1992.

Kachru, B. (ed.) 1992. *The Other Tongue. English Across Cultures*. 2nd edition, Urbana, IL: University of Illinois Press.

Kachru, B. 1994. 'The speaking tree: A medium of plural canons'. In J. E. Alatis (ed.), *Educational linguistics, cross-cultural Communication and Global Interdependence*, Washington, DC: Georgetown University Press. 1–17.

Kirkpatrick, A. 2004. 'English as an ASEAN lingua franca: implications for language teaching'. Paper presented at the IAWE Conference, Syracuse University, 16–18 July 2004.

Kirkpatrick, A. and N. Saunders 2005. 'Singaporean English in an Australian university: intelligibility and attitudes'. In D. Deterding, A. Brown, and Low Eeling (eds), *English in Singapore: pronunciation research on a corpus*. Singapore: McGraw Hill.

Leitner, G. 1992. 'English as a pluricentric language'. In M. Clyne (ed.), *Pluricentric Languages*. Berlin: Mouton-de Gruyter. 178–237.

Maley, A. 2002. 'Teaching English in India: for whom the bell tolls'. In S. C. Chaudhary (ed.), *Teaching English in Non-native Contexts*. Chennai: Orient Longman.

McKay, S. L. 2002. *Teaching English as an International Language: Rethinking Goals and Approaches*. Oxford: Oxford University Press.

Melchers, G. and P. Shaw, 2003. *World Englishes*. London: Arnold.

Milroy, J. and L. Milroy 1999. *Authority in Language: Investigating Standard English*. 3rd edn. London: Routledge.

Pennycook, A. 1994. *The Cultural Politics of English as an International Language*. Harlow: Longman.

Phillipson, R. 1992. *Linguistic Imperialism*. Oxford: Oxford University Press.

Prabhu, N. S. 1987. *Second Language Pedagogy*. Oxford: Oxford University Press.

Prodromou, L. 2003. 'In search of SUE: the successful user of English'. *Modern English Teacher*, 12/2, 5–15.

Seidlhofer, B. 2001. 'Closing a conceptual gap: The case for a description of English as a lingua franca'. *International Journal of Applied Linguistics* 11/2, 133–58.

Seidlhofer, B. 2002a. 'The case for a corpus of English as a lingua franca'. In G. Aston and L. Burnard (eds), *The roles of corpora of contemporary English in langue description and language pedagogy*. Bologna: Cooperativa Libaria Universitaria Editrice Bologna. 70–85.

Seidlhofer, B. 2002b. 'Habeas corpus and divide et impera: "Global English" and applied linguistics'. In K. Spelman Miller and P. Thompson (eds), *Unity and Diversity in Language Use*. London: Continuum. 198–217.

Seidlhofer, B. and J. Jenkins. 2003. 'English as a lingua franca and the politics of property'. In C. Mair (ed.), *The Politics of English as a World Language: New Horizons in Post-colonial Cultural Studies*. Amsterdam: Rodopi. 139–54.

Seidlhofer, B. 2004. 'Research perspectives on teaching English as a lingua franca'. *Annual Review of Applied Linguistics*, 24, 209–39.

Timmis, I. 2002. Native-speaker norms and International English: a classroom view. *ELT Journal*. 56/2, 240–49.

Widdowson, H. 1994. 'The ownership of English'. *TESOL Quarterly* 28/2, 377–89.

# Part I:  Conceptualizing EIL

A major part of the literature concerned with English as a world language is characterized, in dealing with its subject matter, by tensions between opposites – unity vs diversity, monocentrism vs pluricentrism, native speaker vs non-native speaker, description vs prescription, centre vs periphery, and so on. The present volume is no exception: global roles and global rules are, in many ways, antagonistic notions. In the first part of this collection such tensions are epitomized perfectly well. These stem from the necessity, shared by all contributors, to define the core issues they deal with and to try and find answers to fundamental questions.

In this sense, the opening interview with Tom McArthur provides an overview of such fundamental questions. Tom McArthur became interested in English as a world language in the 1960s in India and, since then, this has been his main academic interest. In an informal and passionate style, he shares his views about various linguistic, ideological and pedagogical aspects of 'the English languages', such as the directions that the English language is – and will be – taking, the relationship between English and power and the problems involved in dealing with different varieties of English in educational settings. Particularly interesting is his idea of three distinct models of English: 'the English language', 'the English language complex' and 'the English languages', each describing a different set of communicative and social roles.

As the international lingua franca, English has broken free from ownership by the citizens of a few countries. However, this 'freedom' is accompanied by a certain amount of anxiety. Principally: if let loose, will English fragment into a number of mutually unintelligible varieties? This preoccupation has been repeatedly expressed in the last two decades although, interestingly, no-one seems to have provided universally accepted answers.

Jennifer Jenkins, the author of the first paper in this volume, is particularly concerned with the issue of (un)intelligibility among speakers of English around the world. While previous approaches (cf. Quirk et al. 1985) had tended to identify a common core among varieties of English, in a subtractive mode, Jenkins seeks to discriminate features of phonological variation according to their impact on mutual intelligibility. Based on empirical research (Jenkins 2000), Jenkins has differentiated between aspects of variation which impede mutual intelligibility (core) and those which do not (non-core). These are accepted and added to the description of English as a Lingua Franca (ELF). In doing this, she decidedly rejects the idea that native-speaker models should be the ideal target for learners of English, aspiring, as she does, towards 'global intelligibility and local diversity'.

One of the central issues in this whole collection is the difference between description and prescription. However, description and prescription are perhaps two faces of the same coin. Sophisticated language description, helped by corpora, is extremely useful, as it offers invaluable insights into authentic language use. At the same time, a certain amount of prescription is unavoidable in language education and it is the natural step which follows an otherwise sterile description.

Barbara Seidlhofer, in the second paper in this collection, makes a strong case for the necessity to describe ELF empirically. In directly challenging some of the claims made for the proposal in this volume, she argues that a corpus-based description of ELF is of fundamental importance in order to provide L2 users of English around the world with a model alternative to that based on native-speaker norms. The Vienna–Oxford International Corpus of English (VOICE) was set up precisely for that purpose and Seidlhofer envisages that the data that it is producing are, on the lexico-grammatical level, similar to those found by Jenkins on the phonological level. That is, some common aspects of variation within ELF – such as the omission of the inflectional morpheme -s in the third person singular verb forms – do not cause problems of intelligibility and may not necessarily be considered errors.

In his chapter Luke Prodromou provides a critique of Barbara Seidlhofer's research and argues that the kinds of lexico-grammatical simplifications found therein may well be at odds with what successful bilingual users of English actually do or aspire to do. Successful users of English are very unlikely to want to settle for an imperfect or crippled lexico-grammatical repertoire of the language. It is a well-known fact, for example, that the grammar of English is something that successful learners master well and, according to Prodromou, it would be a mistake to disregard this. Drawing on his own corpus data, Prodromou focuses his attention on another aspect of language competence, namely that of idiomaticity. While lexico-grammar is generally unproblematic for successful language learners, idiomaticity is not. Its importance in assessing 'native-like' proficiency, therefore, should be seriously reconsidered.

In the fourth paper, Andy Kirkpatrick considers the roles of three different potential models of English in the context of English language teaching in East Asia and Australasia: (a) an exonormative 'idealized' standard of English, such as British RP or General American, (b) a nativized regional variety of English, such as Philippino or Singaporean, and (c) a lingua franca model. The writer seeks to define and identify the current roles of each, with a particular focus on the issues surrounding the definition and identification of a lingua franca model. He then discusses the advantages and disadvantages of adopting each as the model for English language teaching, on the basis of factors such as learners' sense of identity, the necessity for international communication, the position of various stakeholders (including governments, international language teaching organizations, publishers, teachers and learners), the perceived relative 'superiority' of one model over the others, the relative feasibility and practicability of adopting each model, and the possible future roles of each of the models.

Peter Tan, Vincent Ooi and Andy Chiang offer their views on English as a Lingua Franca, especially as it pertains to what they call 'non-Anglo English' contexts. Tracing back the origin of the term Lingua Franca, they note how the modern sense assigned to the English language is somewhat different. In particular, they argue that an ELF model could ultimately be counter-productive as it would add a new set of norms alongside existing ones. That is, if ELF is different from established standard varieties such as British and American English as well as from other local nativized Englishes (e.g. Singaporean English), then its adoption in the classroom would actually complicate things further, as learners would have to cope with externally prescribed norms, different from the kinds of English they are exposed to in their daily lives.

Finally, Anthea Fraser Gupta's paper endorses the continued importance of holding standard English as a reference point. This is especially crucial for EFL teachers if appropriate levels of proficiency are to be attained in the written skill in particular. Gupta's arguments echo an earlier well-publicized debate between Sir Randolf Quirk, a champion of Standard English, and Braj Kachru, who is responsible for spearheading World Englishes. However, her view of Standard English is that of an externally imposed prescriptive set of norms, but one which derives from a meticulous observation of actual language usage. Indeed, Gupta's advocacy of Standard English is not restricted to British or American standards. On the basis of numerous examples from corpus data she shows that not only are there standards being adhered to among non-native varieties of educated speakers, particularly in the written mode, but that there is also enough room for variation even within standard norms for speakers to use alternative forms without their being rated 'incorrect'.

## References

Jenkins, J. 2000. *The Phonology of English as an International Language.* Oxford: Oxford University Press.

Quirk, R., S. Greenbaum, G. Leech and J. Svartvik, 1985. *A Comprehensive Grammar of the English Language.* London: Longman.

# An Interview with Tom McArthur

*Rani Rubdy*
*Nanyang Technological University, Singapore*
*Mario Saraceni*
*University of Portsmouth, UK*

**Q1** *Can you tell us something about your own special interest with regard to English as a world language?*

**A1** It began in the 1960s in Bombay (Mumbai), when I was teaching English at Cathedral School – one of the best jobs I've ever had. I wrote articles for a sociopolitical magazine called *Opinion*, one of which I called 'World English'. Since I was discussing English in India and elsewhere, the name seemed appropriate and I rather liked it, but had no idea that one day those two words would take over my life. I can't recall why I hit on that particular phrase, and I didn't check it out in any dictionaries (having no expectation of finding it), and it was years later that I looked for it in the *OED* and found it under *world*. The citations are meagre, the first of them dated 1928, from a journal I later got to know, *American Speech*.

The current names for English in the world at large all came in a cluster in the 1980s, in a rush of books, journals and conferences. In 1983 I returned to the UK from the Université du Québec, to start a quarterly journal with Cambridge: *English Today: The international review of the English language*. At about the same time, Braj Kachru and Larry Smith started *World Englishes* in the US, but with the British publisher Pergamon – not just covering 'world English' but making it multiple: *World Englishes*. Compared with a way-out title like that, my journal's name was vanilla, patterned by Cambridge on *History Today*. But it's been useful vanilla.

**Q2** *What would you say are some 'burning issues' in the area of English as a world language today?*

**A2** The burning-est issue for me at the moment is the limits of English. How far can we take it? How far will it go? Ah, stop there, as I write. See the little green and red lines on my laptop screen, which tell

**21**

me I can't write *burning-est*. It isn't proper English. Isn't right. It's WRONG, and that's exactly why it's a burning issue. The lines are telling me there are limits and rules, all for the greater good, of course, and especially so that nobody who sees the text will think I'm illiterate. But the system can't judge or discriminate. It doesn't know about creativity, which lies out there on the far side of grammar and style. *Burning-est* came into my mind as I wrote. So why not use it, just this once, for effect?

By breaking the rule on my laptop I have reminded anyone who reads this that a particular rule exists. But why *not* 'break the rules' from time to time, judiciously and maybe to show why rules aren't always enough? Poets do that – and get away with it. Computer grammar and spell(ing) checkers don't know about poets. But should experts on English as a world language get away with it too? My email address is <scotsway@aol.com>. Tell me whether I can write burning-est or not. I could publish the comments in *English Today*.

The Greeks had a name for a word that happens just once: a *hapax legomenon* (roughly translated, a 'once-say'; better maybe, 'a one-off'). Small children create them all the time, and nobody minds: how cute. But in EFL/ESL/EIL terms something like *burning-est* can be alarming: 'Native-speakers shouldn't say or write such things. It isn't fair. It confuses foreign learners. We might think this is a *real* word.' But doing things like that confuses more than foreign learners. In such matters I take Lewis Carroll as my guide: a mathematician and word-maker who did English a world of good. He and Alice stretched the language every-which-way, making it mimsy and frabjous, so that the momraths DID finally outgrabe. You won't find all these words in the *OALDCE*. *Mimsy* ('rather feeble and prim or over-restrained'), *frabjous* ('delightful, joyous'), but not *momrath* or *outgrabe*, are in the *New Oxford Dictionary of English* (1998), which describes itself as 'the foremost authority – the most comprehensive coverage of current English', and who would dare dispute the claim? But you won't find 'burning-est' there, but it would turn up in a later edition if you all start spreading it and it gets into print. Usage, after all, is king.

So am I or am I not writing English 'properly'? Am I being unfair to any non-native user who reads this? Were Lewis and his Alice being unfair? Are all the the wordsmiths and poets and non-standard users of English being uncooperative, by failing to fit what they say and write into an ELT standard – by failing to stick to the core vocabulary that foreign learners learn and that many teachers and others have advocated?

So, creativity for me is a burning issue. I think that learners of any kind need to make a target language their own, need to be free to make mistakes, and learn from them – and even make what looks like a mistake but is in fact poetry. Is 'burning-est' a mistake? Is 'frabjous' fractious and 'outgrabe' outrageous? Can't be. They were made by university people, experts, the very popes of usage. But someone might say that you can't be an expert if you think you can add *-est* to an *-ing* form. *Can't*. Ah, but *did*. Assuming of course that you publish this – because until published all this stuff doesn't exist (does it)? Except locked up in my computer, unread. Where text is concerned, publishers' editors and sub-editors are the gatekeepers.

Often when learning a foreign language we are expected to conform, to play safe, because we don't (yet) know the rules. But after we've learned the language we may well continue to play safe, because we don't want people to think we make mistakes. *Of course* rules are important – but so are creativity, poetry, games, and telling and understanding jokes. Any other burning issues? Yes. (D'you wish this expert would write proper sentences, with proper subjects, verbs, and objects?) A burning issue is equal opportunity among the world's fairly fluent, fairly standard users of the 'E' in ENL, ESL, or EFL. Another burning issue is knowing when to use simpler language and when to use harder language. Plain English is useful. Very. But it may not s-t-r-e-t-c-h us enough.

**Q3** *In the past, English gained its power as the language of the global market place. In the twenty-first century its association with the information-based economy has rendered its position virtually unchallenged. Does this mean that any country will have no choice but to embrace English or be left out of the race?*

**A3** English gained in power because it was the language of a trading nation with a literature, an army, a navy, and a high opinion of itself. One of its colonies learned the lesson extremely well and set up in business on its own, becoming two centuries later 'the world's only superpower'. I don't think there is any point in dodging this issue of power. English was spread by emigration, trade, missionary expeditions, and *force*. 'Gunboat diplomacy' is as common today as ever it was. Most big languages have expanded in much the same way. English is not unusual, just large. It is a fine and fascinating language, as Shakespeare has demonstrated, but it is also a frightening language. That's the paradox. So enjoy, as they say in New York Jewish English (whose first speakers were happily unaware that *enjoy* is a transitive verb in EFL/ESL, but survived all the same).

**Q4** *Many people are concerned that the worldwide spread of English is accompanied by a form of cultural imperialism, whereby Anglophone cultures seem to impose themselves on all other cultures. What are your views about such concerns?*

**A4** 'Seem' is kind. They *do* impose themselves, but so did the Greeks and Romans and Arabs. Your 'many people' are right to be concerned, but their best defence may be to use English as the Polish universalist Ludwig Zamenhof hoped people would use his artificial language, Esperanto (which means 'Someone who hopes'). It was a wonderful dream. Many people have learned Esperanto and use it as their preferred international language, but there aren't many Esperantists, whereas around a billion people do things with English. I heard tell once of a Japanese learner of English who was told he could learn Esperanto in a tenth of the time it would take to learn English. He replied: 'Ah, that means I would waste a tenth of the time I need to learn English.' Another Japanese, Yukio Tsuda (Professor of International Communication at Nagoya University) noted not long ago ('Envisioning a Democratic Linguistic Order,' *TESL Reporter*, 33/1, Brigham Young University, Hawaii, April 2000):

> English is no doubt a lingua franca, a global language of today, but the hegemony of English is also very threatening to those who are not speakers of English.... Because English sells well, English is now one of the most important products of the English-speaking countries. So, English is not merely a medium, but a proprietary commodity to be marketed across the world.... Having to use English can result in a kind of existential crisis as well as a loss of human dignity. I, for one, as a non-English speaking person, have experienced these crises in English-speaking environments.... A democratic linguistic order is a vision which aims for democracy among all languages, rather than democracy plus English.

Tsuda has a point. English is a proprietary commodity, and big business, with franchises and products galore. I sometimes think of the profits from commercial courses in ESL and EFL as a tax the world pays for using the language. But one must be cautious here, especially as regards the cost, pain, and effort in learning any foreign language. We all experience painful moments, whatever language we are using: mother tongue or other tongue. Languages themselves are neutral, but their use may not be. I've been discussing some troublesome aspects of English here, but I should also mention that one can fall in love with it. Many people have done, including me – which, as a Scot, with my own national traditions, is saying a great deal.

In Britain many people shifted into English over the centuries, from the languages Welsh (in Wales) and Gaelic and Scots (in Ireland and Scotland), but in the process they made it their own English, not the English of England. They did this for the same reasons that now feed the worldwide English language industry. People everywhere want to do well in life. Doing well increasingly means learning and using English, much as it did in Scotland, Wales and Ireland. People will find the time, the energy and the money, and will set their children to work on this lifelong adventure from kindergarten, if they can afford it.

There are low-caste people by the million in northern India who hate English, and their feelings have nothing to do with the British or indeed the language. The British Empire is gone. These people hate English because they hate upper-caste fellow Indians who ensure that their own children learn it while ensuring that low-caste children don't. Remove this obstacle and they would learn English and get it for their children, just like so many others worldwide.

**Q5** *Are there any other negative effects of the spread of English as a lingua franca?*

**A5** One of my prime concerns is 'language death': not among the large safe systems like Putonghua in China, Spanish in Latin America, and Arabic in North Africa and West Asia, and not among upper-middle-level languages like French, German, Hausa, Japanese, Russian, Swahili, and Tamil; or lower-middle-level languages like Cantonese, Hungarian, Punjabi and Swedish. It is the small languages we need to be concerned about. Danish and Dutch are, as it were, large small languages and are all right, but the widespread Berber language in North Africa is in retreat, and Welsh survives uneasily in the UK. Formerly strong but now small and weak languages, such as Gaelic in Ireland and Scotland, are in serious danger of extinction, as are thousands of the world's really small languages, some of whose last speakers will have died between the time I write this text and the time you read it. Users of English do not set out to destroy other languages, but a large language is by its very nature a threat to small languages.

**Q6** *Within the ELT field one has the impression that British and American English are seen at the top of a worldwide lectal pyramid, while other varieties are considered at a basilectal level. The choice of British and American English as reference points appears to be pedagogically justifiable. However, the result is that speakers of other varieties are marginalized and disempowered. How can one reconcile these ideological concerns with that of pedagogical expedience?*

**A6**  You could say that the same things that I have just described in terms of the world's languages is also true of the world's 'English languages'. World English is immense and diverse, and like my own case in Scotland many people are bilingual (or bidialectal) within English. And that is as true for the US and the UK as for regions like the Caribbean and West Africa. Within English there are endangered varieties. Standard varieties of English, wherever they are, have far higher prestige, and any variety which performs 'well' on the world's stage – notably standard American and British, and increasingly standard Australian and Canadian – is, as it were, socially and culturally safe (even if some are more equal than others).

So American and British are at the top, comprising a kind of dual world standard, followed by Australia, Canada, New Zealand, the Irish Republic, South Africa, the Philippines, the Caribbean, and West and East Africa. Some people may suppose that the idealized standard forms of American or British (or British and American) are the 'best', and the others will do the job but are not so select. Other people, however, and I think increasingly, seem to be interested in a broader world standard which can be taught from any native-speaking base, as long as students are provided with examples of other varieties. This second route seems to be the way ELT is going. There is plenty of competition, but learners, it seems to me, will go to whatever territory is the most accessible and affordable: it is manifestly easier for a middle-class family in East Asia to send an adolescent to Australia than to the UK or the US. By and large, however, the level or standard of ELT is much the same around the primary English-speaking world. The rest is image (or branding).

**Q7**  *In Singapore, where English is a second language, recent campaigns to promote Standard English like the Speak Good English Movement are symptomatic of efforts to keep the English language untouched by local 'corruptions'. What are your views on initiatives of this kind?*

**A7**  The Lion City is a special case which for me at least is no longer an ESL territory. It is in the process of becoming – or may well already have become – an ENL country, created by two distinct processes: top-down from the government and bottom-up from the population at large. The multiracial young share both an acrolectal and a basilectal language culture: that is, they can use one English (Singaporean Standard English) for educational, professional and other more formal purposes, and another (often called 'Singlish', and highly controversial) for informal purposes, at times mixed with their home languages (usually a form of Chinese, Malay, or a South Indian language, pre-eminently Tamil). This makes them, like many other English-using countries, ENL and ESL. I sympathize. I grew up in Glasgow with a street Scots and a classroom English, the authorities deploring the version of street and home while promoting the rather bourgeois model favoured in school: 'Good English'. As with us, Singaporeans will no doubt find themselves ranging along a continuum from 'Good English' for high-level public purposes and 'Singlish' for fun and peer-group solidarity.

**Q8** *If English is international, it must be intelligible to speakers around the world – both native and non-native. But the fact that a number of 'new varieties' have emerged, each with its own distinct characteristics, flies in the face of this basic requirement. What is your reaction to this paradox? What is the solution?*

**A8** Many Englishes are in varying degrees opaque to speakers of English from other places. At the same time, however, English *is* manifestly international. And at the international level the opaque and the transparent constantly meet and mix, because they are part of a continuum, not neatly separated off. The idea that all English *must* be 'intelligible to speakers around the world' is an interesting one. Why must it? This is a huge language complex. It has existed for a very long time. People vary in their abilities and dispositions. And the time they can spend 'perfecting' their English (wonderful idea, 'perfecting' something like that!) is limited, whether one is native to it or learning it as a second or third language. Sometimes we ask or expect too much of the Great World English Enterprise ('GWEE' would make a rather neat acronym). I long ago reconciled myself to the fact that I won't ever know enough of the other languages I'm supposed to 'know'. If only I had the incentive with them that so many people have as regards English!

We do, however, already have a kind of world English that is widely if not universally intelligible, but one in which those acquiring it will miss something that has been said too fast or indistinctly, or will need a dictionary when reading a less familiar or rather complex text. As they say in New York, what else is new? After all, when learners of English become as good as native users they will still have to experience all the double-takes and come-agains that natives experience and that in any case they routinely experience in their own languages without worrying much about it.

The intelligibility issue *is* a paradox, but it seems to me a natural one. It is made more paradoxical by the view that a number of 'new

**27**

varieties' have been emerging recently. I don't know *any* 'new' varieties, but I have heard people call a variety several centuries old 'new', which I take to mean 'new to a person or group whose attention has just been drawn to it'. West African usage, Caribbean varieties, and South Asian kinds of English are all several hundred years old, but it may be true that some continental European varieties of English are indeed new – the outcome in recent decades of good schooling in languages and access to UK and US media and other products. The interesting thing about these varieties is that they are broadly middle-class and professional. A basilectal lingua-franca English most notice-able in southern Europe has recently drawn the attention of a number of linguists.

**Q9** *In some countries of Asia and Africa, English has become 'nativized' and begun to be considered an Asian or African language, and not one that is owned exclusively by any one speech community. For this reason some sociolinguists are of the view that it may be more realistic to recognize a plurality of standards. Given this view, if 'the English language' needs to be pluralized into 'the English languages', what does ELT stand for?*

**A9** I'm glad you raised this one. It fits my own observations over many years, as summed up in *The English Languages* (Cambridge, 1998). English is such an immense language that for me it has been essential to have at least three models. First there is English as a 'conventional' language ('the English language'), useful on a day-to-day basis but for me only the starting point for the second model ('the English language complex'), which has many varyingly distinct sub-entities, and finally to the third model of English as a continuum of recognizably distinct languages ('the Englishes', 'the English languages'), dominated by the educated standards of various countries that provide the basis (particularly through the norms of the US and UK) of a 'World Standard English'. Most learners have no interest in all of this. If, as I hope, they are lucky, they will learn an English appropriate to their needs and situation, and expand (perhaps creatively) as and when they feel the need.

One can think of it this way: If we were free to choose a language as a fairly uniform high-level lingua franca for the world (in terms of consistency and convenience), we would be crazy to choose English. It's too big. It's too varied. And, in any case, natural languages tend to be messy, which is why Zamenhof's Esperanto would have been easier and better. Indeed, Ogden and Richards' now virtually forgotten *Basic English* in the 1920/30s would have been easier. I would say, however, that most published courses of English, taken systematically under reasonable learning conditions and with an adequate and sympathetic tutor, will get people to the point where they know artificial classroom English and can move from it to real English in the world. When that transfer takes place, it is a pretty good outcome.

**Q10** *On the other hand, pedagogy tends to be ill at ease with multiple and/or flexible standards. How then can the ELT profession cope with such multiplicity of standards?*

**A10** The question is designed to provoke. I tend to be ill at ease with pedagogy that can't handle the real world. I suppose drilling according to graded syllabuses is easier than helping students develop their own coping strategies while becoming more and more accustomed to real English. Logically, and for safety's sake, we start with something well grounded and safe, and move on in increments, hoping to take most of our students with us. The further we get into the syllabus and the language, however, the more complex and diverse the material and the experience – until the classroom approximates real life. This in effect is an exercise in gradually going from the simple and artificial to the complex and real.

So, we start with a useful fake: a single idealized pronunciation model, some basic grammar and practice sentences, some everyday easy vocabulary, no idioms, no slang, no figurative language, and a few irregular verbs because the commonest verbs are irregular. Then relentlessly on towards real life. Some courses traverse years of schooling, some last for only a couple of weeks, but the principle is the same: from the known and safe to the unknown and disturbing, until that too becomes safe (with luck and hard work). If there *are* multiple standards – or variations with a broad world standard – then the sooner students learn that the better.

The print standard is dual (US and UK) and fairly stable. The spoken so-called standards are fluid, and students will generally fail to get them anyway. Maybe better that way, so that they produce a viable pronunciation of English commensurate with their mother tongue. Why shouldn't most Italians and Thais have Italianate and Thai-like accents, just as the Irish sound Irish and various South Africans sound variously South African? Let them be as intelligible as they can within their varied phonologies, just like the rest of us. I sound like a middle-class Scot who has spent a lot of time in England and Canada. As a result, a lot of people can't figure out just what I am, but that doesn't matter. They understand me.

**Q11** *According to one school of thought there is a broad category of 'international' speakers of English who use the language mainly for practical or transactional purposes. The proponents of this view maintain that the users of English as an International Language only really need a subset of the lexis, grammar and phonology of the English language rather than the full linguistic repertoire that is the preserve of the native speaker. What are your views on the matter and what do you think are the implications for English Language Teaching?*

**A11** We all only have a subset: none of us has the whole kit and caboodle (a point that this American idiom may illustrate: it may not be clear, but one can guess the meaning from the context). Some people do need only a subset of English for a specialized area, and ESP targets such areas quite well. Some people only need to be able to read technical journals and manuals, and after some basic training they pick up the rest of what they need on their own. Others may need to understand and use spoken (including rapid) English (as in emergency situations). And some may need to take at least a listening part in seminars and manage the basics of social events, without ever needing to be fluent and idiomatic. Plenty of materials have been created to help with such matters over the last 20 years or so. The English cake can be sliced in many ways. That, I suppose, is why it's now called the global lingua franca.

**Q12** *Teachers already have a hard time dealing with the differences between British and American English. If further pluralization of Englishes is to be accepted, would this not add to their difficulty, particularly where English is largely learnt as a foreign language, as, say, in Thailand? What can teachers do about this in the classroom?*

**A12** This question is intriguingly constructed, and a good one to end on. Yes, teachers already have a hard time, but what else is new (as they say in New York)? Many professionals have a hard time, as for example doctors and nurses. I've just lived through the stresses and strains of the Sars outbreak in Hong Kong, and my admiration for the territory's medical professionals in a trilingual setting (Cantonese, Putonghua and English) is profound. Language professionals, it seems to me, have to be as objective and thorough as any other professionals. There is a body of information and skills to be absorbed, but it is not static, any more than the number of diseases doctors have to deal with is static. If we are lucky, the information we have relates to language as it really is, while our skills are flexible enough across a spread of (E)LT theories and practices, to allow an experienced teacher to be selective in the same way that a surgeon or a nurse or a lawyer is selective.

**30**

As regards the American/British dichotomy, my usual advice is: focus on one, know about the other, and be prepared to deal with both (which is by and large what native speakers have to do). The mixing of American and British spoken usage (usually US entering UK and other styles) is well understood and seldom a source of anxiety. A teacher might, however, need to be involved as an editorial adviser if a maturer student needs to write towards US or UK norms. It would also make sense to know something about such other varieties as Australian and Canadian, and how they relate to British and American, especially on paper. Beyond that, of course, the teacher needs to know something about the language(s) that the students bring to the classroom. Working with Thai students, a knowledge of Thai makes sense; working with 'international' students, a useful general knowledge inevitably develops, and one begins to appreciate how mother tongue X has this effect while mother tongue Y does something quite different. Perfection targets are fine in theory, but reality gets in the way.

# Global Intelligibility and Local Diversity: Possibility or Paradox?

Jennifer Jenkins
*King's College, London*

It is by now a well-rehearsed fact that English has become an international language used most frequently as a lingua franca among its (so-called) non-native speakers from different L1 backgrounds. In response to the changed world-English landscape, a number of scholars – including, perhaps surprisingly, a few from the field of Second Language Acquisition (e.g. Cook 1999, 2002; Firth and Wagner 1997) – have argued that the (so-called) native speaker of English should no longer be the measure against which (so-called) non-native speaker performance is judged.

Meanwhile, Lowenberg (2002) likens the processes of language change employed by non-native speakers (NNSs) of English in the Expanding Circle (Kachru 1992) to those of non-native speakers (NNSs) in the Inner Circle. Examples (not Lowenberg's) from lexicogrammar include the conversion to countability of uncountable nouns such as 'staff' ('several staffs' instead of 'several members of staff'), an all-purpose question tag form such as 'isn't it' (cf. UK youth 'innit') in place of the unwieldy range of options in NS Standard English, and phrases such as 'discuss about' by analogy with 'talk about'. From phonology there is, for instance, the shift of dark /l/ to either clear /l/ or to 'w' where it occurs before a consonant or pause (as in, respectively, 'milk' and 'feel'), and that of voiceless 'th' to /f/, /s/ or /t/, whatever its position in a word. All these forms have, of course, long featured among the Indigenized Varieties of English (IVEs) of the Outer Circle. In fact it is not implausible that the only difference between English language change across the three circles is the time factor, with NNSs in both Outer and Expanding Circles speeding up the natural processes of regularization (Aitchison 1997) that occur more slowly in the Inner Circle – where currently it is perfectly acceptable to talk of 'teas' and 'coffees' instead of 'cups of tea' and 'cups of coffee' but not (yet) of 'advices' or 'furnitures'.

Another difference, though, is attitude towards such change.

Linguists surveying language change in NS English tend to regard it as a sign of creativity and innovation. They ridicule NS 'complainers' who write letters to newspapers warning of the degeneration of the English language because their fellow NSs are increasingly saying 'less' rather than 'fewer' with countable nouns, introducing direct speech with quotative 'like', and so on. On the other hand, linguists' tendency with NNS-led change, particularly in the Expanding Circle, is to label it wholesale as error regardless of how widespread its use or the degree to which it is mutually intelligible among speakers of English as a Lingua Franca (ELF). As Bamgbose points out,

> The main question with innovations is the need to decide when an observed feature of language use is indeed an innovation and when it is simply an error. An innovation is seen as an acceptable variant, while an error is simply a mistake or uneducated usage. If innovations are seen as errors, a non-native variety can never receive any recognition (1998, 1–2).

In similar vein, de Klerk (speaking of Black South African English) asks

> When does a substratal feature assert itself sufficiently to overcome the fear that if deviations are allowed, the rules will be abandoned and chaos will ensue? Is it when speakers use it often enough to silence the prescriptors? (1999, 315).

Language change leads, then, despite the range of attitudes it elicits in the process, to a degree of regularization across English varieties insofar as the language is predisposed to develop in certain ways and in accordance with language universals (Aitchison op. cit.), with the resulting forms receiving the approval of the Inner Circle's linguistic gatekeepers only if and when they enter the speech of educated NSs of English. This is not to suggest that all creativity in English leads ultimately to harmonization across its varieties. Far from it: much change results from idiosyncratic adaptations of the language by individual L1 groups in order to render English more appropriate to their own use, and leads to greater rather than less variation. The variants arising from this type of change are far less likely to find their way into Inner Circle Englishes. This, in turn, means that if current gatekeeping attitudes to NNS creativity prevail, these variants are doomed for perpetuity to the status of dialect features – by implication sub-standard – where they occur in (even codified) Outer Circle Englishes, and of L1 transfer errors where they occur in (admittedly as yet uncodified) Expanding Circle Englishes. Thus, if a German-English speaker pronounces the 'a' of the word 'charity' as /e/ or the first sound of the word 'worse' as /v/ (both of which occur in my ELF data), these are by definition pronunciation errors rather than examples of German-English accent norms.

The problem with assigning the status of error to any and every item affected by L1 transfer is that it attaches a 'contamination' metaphor to current language contact while ignoring the vast amount of previous language contact which influenced the development of English from the days of Old English onwards and resulted in much of the present-day Modern English(es) now spoken by the Inner Circle's educated NSs. In this regard, in a compelling argument about language contact involving English creoles and IVEs, Mufwene makes two points which have critical implications for the development of ELF varieties in the Expanding Circle. Firstly, he argues that both creoles and IVEs are regarded by linguists as 'illegitimate offspring' of English or 'children out of wedlock' because

> we have typically downplayed the role of contact in the case of 'native' Englishes but have routinely invoked it in the case not only of creoles but also of indigenized Englishes (2001, 107).

In other words, the claim for (so-called) native Englishes is that they have a single identifiable 'parent' and an 'ordinary', 'uncontaminated' development down the centuries, whereas the claim for (so-called) 'new' Englishes and English creoles is that they have been infected (my word) by large-scale contact with other languages and are therefore not entitled to the unmarked name 'English'. This is precisely the situation which now obtains for ELF with minor differences in the terminology employed: influence from an Expanding Circle speaker's L1 is labelled 'L1 transfer' or even 'L1 interference', and its product is 'error' to be eliminated. There is no suggestion that contact between ELF groups' L1s and English might be leading to the emergence of new English dialects, let alone bona fide standard varieties. Mufwene's second point is that

> if mutual intelligibility were ... a critical criterion, more important than sharing an identifiable ancestor, there would be more reasons for treating Modern English varieties and English creoles as dialects of the same language than for lumping the former together with Old English while excluding creoles (op. cit, 119).

Again, the same is true of Expanding Circle Englishes which, like the Gullah and Singlish examples Mufwene provides, are likely to be easier to interpret for both NNS and NS alike than the 'untainted' (my word) Old and Middle English samples he quotes to support his claim.

Let us now return briefly to the two examples of German-English pronunciation given above and consider them in the light of Mufwene's arguments. These German-influenced pronunciations, as I pointed out, would both be regarded as errors: candidates for correction and remedial work if uttered in the context of an English language classroom, and symptoms of a deficient English competence if uttered in the world outside. The same would be true, for example, of a Japanese-English speaker who pronounced 'Macdonald' as 'Macudonaludo' or 'red' as 'led', in the first case employing epenthesis (vowel addition) to separate the consonant clusters and, in the second, substituting the sound /l/ for /r/. In all these four cases, L1 transfer would be regarded as the 'culprit'. But if, on the other hand, contact with the German or Japanese L1 were to be approached not from this 'deficit' perspective (Kachru 1991), but from one which acknowledged difference from NS pronunciation norms as a sign of creativity, then a very different conclusion could be reached. These ELF pronunciations could be considered 'legitimate' (in the sense of Mufwene's first point). They would then no longer be errors but examples of German and Japanese innovation whose effect is to appropriate English in order to make it more appropriate for, respectively, German-English and Japanese-English users, both sociolinguistically (through the development of a local standard) and socio-psychologically (through the capacity to express their users' local identity).

However, all is not quite so simple. If we were talking exclusively of local use (German-English among Germans, Japanese-English among Japanese, and so on), then there would be no reason not to advocate a pluricentric approach of this kind. Each L2 regional English would be free to develop in its own way without regard to conformity to NS norms – provided, of course, that their members were not overly concerned with the derogatory attitudes of Inner Circle gatekeepers. But there is still Mufwene's second point to consider: the issue of intelligibility. And here, one has to admit that the gatekeepers have a point, albeit by default rather than intent. It is that if a policy of pluricentricity is pursued unchecked, in effect a situation of 'anything goes', with each Expanding Circle L1 group developing its own Engish pronunciation norms, there is a danger that their accents will move further and further apart until a stage is reached where pronunciation presents a serious obstacle to lingua franca communication. This would make no sense if the prime purpose of learning English in the Expanding Circle is to be able to use it in lingua franca communication with other NNSs from different-L1 backgrounds.

I am not for a moment recommending the monolithic approach still in vogue in Expanding Circle English language classrooms, where the 'choice' is one of either a British (Received Pronunciation) or North American (General American) model as the pronunciation goal. NS accents are not only sociolinguistically inappropriate for communication in which NSs are rarely involved, but also psycholinguistically and socio-psychologically unachievable for the majority of adolescent and adult learners (see Jenkins 2000, 208). Macdonaldization, whether of the British or American variety, to my mind has no place in English language classrooms of the twenty-first century unless a learner (having examined fully the facts about world Englishes) prefers for some personal reason to aim for an Inner Circle accent.

However, there still has to be sufficient common ground for lingua franca communication to achieve success, and as far as pronunciation is concerned, this means that speakers need to be confident that their accents will not prevent them from understanding the propositional content of one another's utterances (even if they then go on to misinterpret each other in the pragmatic sense). What I am suggesting is that mutual intelligibility is the most satisfactory criterion for pronunciation (and probably lexicogrammar too: see Seidlhofer 2001, this volume) in ELF contexts, but that it is something to be negotiated and developed by ELF speakers themselves rather than imposed from 'above' by NSs or their NNS admirers. This, of course, brings us full circle by casting an entirely different light on the issue of NNS variation from NS pronunciation norms or, in other words, on the issue of NNS creativity.

The problem that remains, though, is how to safeguard mutual phonological intelligibility in ELF communication as more and more ELF accent varieties emerge. My approach has been to collect extensive data from ELF interactions (always NNS–NNS from different L1s) in order to identify which L1-influenced pronunciation features impede intelligibility for a different-L1 interlocutor, and which have no effect. In other words, instead of using either NS 'ownership' to determine what is acceptable in ELF or NS intuition to determine what is intelligible in ELF, I have let the data and, therefore, the ELF interlocutors speak for themselves. It would thus constitute a serious misrepresentation of my position to suggest that I am attempting to impose a monolithic pronunciation model on ELF users. For not only is the Lingua Franca Core not a model (see below), but it also respects both ELF learners' right to choose whether or not they adopt it and the diversity of their accents (see below). Conversely, it is the near-universal focus on RP and GA in Expanding Circle English language education which is an imposition – one which I am endeavouring to reverse through my 'core' approach.

The following is a very brief summary of my findings (see Jenkins

2000, 2002 for full details). First, the core features, i.e. those found to be essential to mutual intelligibility in ELF across a wide range of L1s:

## The Lingua Franca Core (LFC)

1. Consonant sounds except for substitutions of 'th' and of dark /l/
2. Aspiration after word-initial /p/, /t/ and /k/
3. Avoidance of consonant deletion (as opposed to epenthesis) in consonant clusters
4. Vowel length distinctions
5. Nuclear (Tonic) stress production and placement within word groups (tone units)

The features which emerged from the research as not essential to mutual intelligibility in ELF and therefore designated 'non-core' for ELF pronunciation are:

## Non-core features:

1. Certain consonants (see Lingua Franca Core no.1)
2. Vowel quality
3. Weak forms
4. Features of connected speech such as elision and assimilation
5. Word stress
6. Pitch movement on the nuclear syllable (tone)
7. Stress-timed rhythm

If we return once again to the German-English and Japanese-English pronunciation examples discussed earlier, it becomes clear that in each case there is one core and one non-core item. For the German-English speaker, the substitution of the consonant sound /w/ with /v/ in the word 'worse' is core (LFC no.1) and can therefore be classed as an error. On the other hand, the production of the first vowel in the word 'charity' as the sound /e/ is non-core (Non-core no.2) and therefore not an error. The same is true respectively of Japanese-English substition of /l/ for /r/ (i.e. core) and of Japanese-English epenthesis (i.e. non-core). Pronunciation error for ELF is thus redefined: it is no longer based on proximity to NS norms but on the degree to which it affects intelligibility in ELF communication. Where an item is core it can be considered an ELF pronunciation error, but where it is non-core it is instead a matter of (L2) regional variation. By embracing the sociolinguistic facts of regional variation (e.g. they are the rule, not the exception), the core approach thus recognizes the rights of NNSs of the Expanding Circle to their own 'legitimate' regional accents rather than regarding any deviation from NS pronunciation norms as an error (as is the case in English as a Foreign Language approaches). In other words, it is an attempt to extend to Expanding Circle members the rights that have always been enjoyed in the Inner Circle and to an increasing extent in the Outer.

A 'core' approach, moreover, recognizes that the accents of bilingual NNS teachers of English who share their learners' L1 are the most appropriate – not to mention most motivating – as classroom models. Their owners not only have all the advantages outlined in the growing literature on the subject of NNS English teachers (see, for example, Braine ed. 1999), but also combine in their accents the core features for international intelligibility together with their own regional version of the non-core features for local identity and sociolinguistic appropriacy. Like Hung (2002), I look forward to the day when dictionaries of English break free from their fixation with RP and GA models and, instead, provide transcripts of words spoken with these local-but-internationally-intelligible accents.

The final word goes to Robert Phillipson who, in his discussion of my book *The Phonology of English as an International Language*, makes the following point:

> It is extremely significant that someone working with a key constituent of a language, namely its phonology, relates this explicitly to ideological debates about the role of English, and makes an explicit effort to theorize the appropriation of various types of endonormative Englishes that represent a counterweight to hegemonic Anglo-American dominated English...Her book lays some of the foundations for a pedagogy of appropriation (2002, 21).

To end where I began, global intelligibility and local diversity for English accents in lingua franca contexts are, it seems, very much the possibility – even probability – and not at all paradoxical.

## References

Aitchison, J. 1997. *The Language Web*. Cambridge: Cambridge University Press.

Bamgbose, A. 1998. 'Torn between the norms: innovations in world Englishes'. *World Englishes* 17/1, 1–14.

Braine, G. (ed.) 1999. *Non-Native Educators in English Language Teaching*. Mahwah, New Jersey: Lawrence Erlbaum.

Cook, V. 1999. 'Going beyond the native speaker in language teaching'. *TESOL Quarterly* 33/2, 185–209.

Cook, V. 2002. 'Language teaching methodology and the L2 user perspective'.

In V. Cook (ed.), *Portraits of the L2 User*. Clevedon: Multilingual Matters.

de Klerk, V. 1999. 'Black South African English: Where to from here?'. *World Englishes* 18/3, 311–24.

Firth, A. and J. Wagner 1997. 'On discourse, communication and (some) fundamental concepts in SLA research'. *Modern Language Journal* 81, 285–300.

Hung, T. 2002. '"New English" words in international English dictionaries'. *English Today* 18/4, 29–34.

Jenkins, J. 2000. *The Phonology of English as an International Language*. Oxford: Oxford University Press.

Jenkins, J. 2002. 'A sociolinguistically-based, empirically-researched pronunciation syllabus for English as an International Language'. *Applied Linguistics* 23/1, 83–103.

Kachru, B. 1991. 'Liberation linguistics and the Quirk concern'. *English Today* 25, 3–13.

Kachru, B. 1992. *The Other Tongue: English across Cultures* (2nd edn). Urbana, IL: University of Illinois Press.

Lowenberg, P. 2002. 'Assessing English proficiency in the Expanding Circle'. *World Englishes* 21/3, 431–35.

Mufwene, S. 1997. 'The legitimate and illegitimate offspring of English.' In L. Smith and M. Forman (eds) 1997. *World Englishes 2000*. Honolulu, Hawai'i: University of Hawai'i Press.

Mufwene, S. 2001. *The Ecology of Language Evolution*. Cambridge: Cambridge University Press.

Phillipson, R. 2002. 'Global English and local language policies'. In A. Kirkpatrick (ed.), *Englishes in Asia*. Melbourne: Language Australia Ltd.

Seidlhofer, B. 2001. 'Closing a conceptual gap: the case for a description of English as a lingua franca'. *International Journal of Applied Linguistics* 11/2, 133–58.

# English as a Lingua Franca in the Expanding Circle: What it Isn't

*Barbara Seidlhofer*
*University of Vienna, Austria*

## Introduction

The invitation to contribute to this volume was accompanied by a book proposal drawn up by the editors, giving the rationale and an outline of the collection of papers. It also summarized some recent developments in work on English in the world and highlighted some controversial issues that they hoped to see discussed in the contributions. Some of these developments and issues concerned the description of English as a lingua franca, especially in the Expanding Circle (Kachru 1992), and in particular the empirical work undertaken and reported on, either individually or jointly, by Jennifer Jenkins (2000, 2001, this volume) and myself (Seidlhofer 2001, 2002a, 2002b, Jenkins & Seidlhofer 2001, Seidlhofer and Jenkins 2003). While I found the book proposal very interesting, I also felt that in certain respects it misrepresented our research. Since the editors had also stressed that they hoped 'the papers w(ould) reflect a strong and urgent sense of the debate outlined', 'focusing on the more controversial aspects of EIL and identifying issues that may be particularly interesting and contentious', their invitation to me to contribute is a welcome opportunity to address some of the most pervasive misconceptions in the spirit of a constructive debate.

One such misconception is that our work ignores the 'polymorphous nature of the English language worldwide' and denies 'tolerance for diversity and appropriacy of use in specific sociolinguistic contexts'. Nothing could be further from the truth. The proposal also suggests that we are advocating direct teaching of 'prescribed rules' of a 'monolithic variety' 'to all L2 non-native speakers'. We advocate nothing of the kind. These and similar misconceptions had already been expressed before by various people, and this made the opportunity to try and summarize and react to them in this collection particularly welcome. What better way, then, to set the record straight and clarify our position(s) than by addressing these issues head-on?

The title of this essay is an apt one for the purpose. I have borrowed it from Peter Trudgill, and for a particular reason. His contribution to Bex and Watts' (1999) *Standard English: The Widening Debate* is entitled 'Standard English: what it isn't'. Trudgill is also concerned to clear up some misconceptions – as the author sees them – expressed persistently not just by the laity but by linguists themselves, and in this process discusses a number of issues of relevance to the debate about English in the World. What makes the intertextual link so apt is that so much of what Trudgill says about Standard English could equally be said about EIL. To illustrate this, I quote the beginning of the first three paragraphs of Trudgill's paper and simply replace the expressions 'Standard English' by 'English as a Lingua Franca' and 'standardized language' by 'lingua franca'. I have also added a definition of English as a Lingua Franca (henceforth ELF)[1] to replace that of Standard English. This is how the text now reads:

> There is a reasonably clear consensus in the sociolinguistics literature about the term *lingua franca*: a *lingua franca* is '*a "contact language" between persons who share neither a common native tongue nor a common (national) culture, and for whom English is the chosen* foreign *language of communication*' (Firth 1996, 240).

It is therefore somewhat surprising that there seems to be considerable confusion in the English-speaking world, even amongst linguists, about what English as a Lingua Franca is...

In this chapter, I therefore attempt a characterization of *English as a Lingua Franca*. It should be noted that this is indeed a characterization rather than a strict definition – language varieties do not readily lend themselves to definition as such. We can describe what Chinese is, for example, in such a way as to make ourselves very well understood on the issue, but actually to define Chinese would be another matter altogether. The characterization will also be as much negative as positive – a clearer idea of what ELF is can be obtained by saying what it is not as well as by saying what it is (modified version of Trudgill 1999, 117f., changes italicized).

In what follows, I will concentrate on my own project: Jenkins, as will be clear from her own contribution to this volume, can speak for herself. Her paper also conveniently provides some of the theoretical background to our shared ELF thinking.

## Misconception 1: ELF research ignores the polymorphous nature of the English language worldwide

It is precisely the observation of the polymorphous nature of the English language worldwide that prompted the wish to capture this richness and diversity in the corpus I have been compiling at the University of Vienna, the Vienna–Oxford International Corpus of English (VOICE)[2]. For in order to be able to acknowledge this polymorphous nature you need to be able to perceive it, and in order to perceive it, you need to document it. One of the most impressive insights of corpus-based studies of native-speaker language use has been precisely that these native speakers' intuitions are unreliable and do not enable them to say with any precision how they really use the language, and this is why corpora are needed which can be analysed for patterns of attested language use. In the case of ELF, the problem is aggravated by the fact that there cannot even be any native speaker intuitions about ELF because, by definition, nobody speaks ELF natively. So what we really have are impressions of ELF rather than intuitions. It would seem that this makes a broad empirical base on which to substantiate, or indeed contradict, these impressions particularly necessary.

A considerable amount of descriptive work has fairly recently been undertaken not only on Inner Circle but also on Outer Circle varieties of English – must notably within the framework of ICE, the International Corpus of English. ICE components available at the time of writing are those of East Africa, Great Britain, India, New Zealand, Philippines (written only) and Singapore (see http://www.ucl.ac.uk/english-usage/ice/). This descriptive research makes it possible to actually look at the many different forms the English language is used in, and thus enables us to notice, acknowledge and, if we like, to celebrate the diversity thus documented. Now it stands to reason that English in the Expanding Circle must contribute quite naturally to this diversity. This diversity, however, is generally not accepted as having its own validity: because English in the Expanding Circle is usually learnt as a foreign language, it has been expected to conform to Inner Circle norms. If, however, it can be demonstrated that Expanding Circle speakers are using English successfully but in their own way, which sometimes may and sometimes may not conform to Inner Circle English, then this surely is a contribution to the acknowledgment of the polymorphous nature of English worldwide.

## Misconception 2: ELF work denies tolerance for diversity and appropriacy of use in specific sociolinguistic contexts

In view of what I just said above, it is difficult to see how this misconception can arise. The thrust of my empirical ELF work is precisely to capture as much of the diversity there is, and to investigate how ELF is used appropriately, albeit often not in conformity with ENL norms, in the specific sociolinguistic contexts in which speakers in the Expanding Circle decide to make use of English – precisely in forms that serve 'to perform specific tasks in specific communicative situations' (cf. book proposal). The empirical work that Jennifer Jenkins has already undertaken on the phonology of EIL has enabled her to demonstrate that certain 'deviations' from ENL phonemic realizations – the ones she identified as 'non-core' – should not be considered pronunciation errors but manifestations of (L2) regional variation, which allows the speakers' identities to 'shine through' while still ensuring mutual intelligibility. If – and this is of course an empirical question which cannot be answered yet – similar features should be found in ELF lexicogrammar, e.g. through VOICE, these insights are surely likely to help enhance rather than deny tolerance for diversity.

Jenkins and I have always made the point that in this respect it is precisely the work on Outer Circle varieties that has led the way for ELF research: there is hardly a paper by her or me that does not have references to Bamgbose, Kachru, Mufwene, Sridhar, etc. – see also Jenkins (2003). Bamgbose (1998) in particular has demonstrated the importance of codification as a prerequisite for acceptance:

> ... as long as non-native English norms remain uncodified, they cannot become a point of reference for usage and acceptance.

> Crucial to the entrenchment of innovations and non-native norms is codification. Without it users will continue to be uncertain about what is and what is not correct and, by default, such doubts are bound to be resolved on the basis of existing codified norms, which are derived from an exonormative standard. Codification is therefore the main priority of the moment, and it is to be hoped that research and collaboration in the future will be directed towards this objective. (Bamgbose 1998, 5, 12)

Quite simply, the point is that you need to be able to *show* what it is you want people to accept. Otherwise the debate about non-native Englishes, whether in the Outer or in the Expanding Circle, will remain stuck in empty preaching and ideologizing, in vague programmatic talk on a meta-level that does not impinge on people's daily lives, and especially not on the lives of students and teachers.

But it would not do to simply look at features of the language code: what is likely to emerge, and strongly suggests itself from the relatively small ELF samples investigated so far, is that what ELF speakers draw on to a high degree is their awareness of the intercultural and bi- or multi-lingual nature of the communication they are engaged in, and that they employ very effective strategies in order to successfully communicate across cultures. As long ago as 1987, Karlfried Knapp outlined what could be termed 'maxims' of a kind of neo-Gricean cooperative principle for intercultural communication:

> Expect differences in ways of interacting. [...]
> Expect uncertainty. [...]
> Expect misunderstandings. [...]

The analysis of ELF corpora will afford us a better understanding of what ELF speakers do to better understand each other. In this respect it is also pointless to ask questions such as, 'What are typical ELF speakers, and which of them are worth studying? Expert users only? Non-native speakers amongst themselves only?' Such questions have no point because ELF situations are by their nature self-regulating: interlocutors decide to use ELF when it is the best option for the purpose at hand. How ELF is used varies and takes care of itself. But it is worth trying to understand as far as possible *emically*, from the participants' perspectives, what they do when they negotiate meanings in these encounters. Such understanding will also call into question traditional ideas as to what constitutes a competent, or expert, language user. In the words of Claire Kramsch,

> That, one could argue, is the characteristic of a 'competent language user': not the ability to speak and write according to the rules of the academy and the social etiquette of one social group, but the adaptability to select those forms of accuracy and those forms of appropriateness that are called for in a given social context of use. This form of competence is precisely the competence of the 'intercultural' speaker, operating at the border between several languages or language varieties, manoeuvring his/her way through the troubled waters of cross-cultural misunderstandings. (Kramsch 1998, 27)

Another particularly promising point of conceptual reference in this respect is social psychology, notably accommodation theory. Again, it was Jenkins (e.g. 2000, 2002) who demonstrated the significance of accommodation among ELF users towards one another in what often amounts to a remarkable display of 'tolerance for diversity'.

The current descriptive work on ELF is thus likely to contribute to the acknowledgement of diversity and appropriacy in specific sociolinguistic contexts, both in its premises as well as in its findings.

## Misconception 3: ELF description aims at the accurate application of a set of prescribed rules

The only rules that have been prescribed so far have been those of native-speaker language use in native-speaker contexts, made even more exact through recent corpus descriptions and then transferred to non-native teaching contexts. And it is precisely the absolute prescriptive validity of this that research into ELF use is calling into question. Of course, any kind of teaching is based on a kind of prescription, and it would be simply disingenuous, and also rather silly, to deny this: when you teach you need to know what you are trying to teach – and equally importantly, what for, why and to whom. As for users of English who have decided that they will need to use English mainly as a lingua franca in intercultural encounters, such prescription in the pedagogic sense could then consider the findings of research into ELF. Having found, empirically, what is crucial for international intelligibility and what tends to be counterproductive, it would surely be perverse not to make these findings available for ELF users whose communicative goal is just such intelligibility. This is not a matter of imposing a norm, which is essentially what happens at the moment, but of offering an alternative possibility.

I should also like to emphasize that I have never made any general pronouncements as to what should be taught and what shouldn't be – this is a complex pedagogic matter which will have to be decided by teachers for their particular contexts and their particular learners, and for which they will need – and this I *have* argued, see e.g. Seidlhofer 1999 – serious and sound teacher education. When doing empirical research into ELF I am doing this as a descriptive linguist, and it is not my task, and indeed impossible, to pre-empt any local pedagogic decisions. As Widdowson pointed out some time ago in a seminal paper about the relationship between description and prescription,

> The prescription of language for such contexts of instruction can, and should be, informed by the description of language in contexts of use, but not determined by it. ... For prescription has its own conditions of adequacy to meet, and it is the business of language pedagogy, and nobody else's business, to propose what these conditions might be. (Widdowson 1991, 23)

## Misconception 4: ELF researchers are suggesting that there should be one monolithic variety

Whether ELF should be called a variety of English at all is an open question, and one which cannot be answered as long as we do not have any good descriptions of it. It is well known that divisions between languages are arbitrary, and therefore those between varieties of a language have to be as well. Once descriptions are available of how speakers from different linguacultural backgrounds use ELF, this will make it possible to consider whether it would make sense to think of English as it is spoken by its non-native speakers as falling into different varieties, just as is the English spoken by its native speakers. For the time being, this is an open question, and indeed the book proposal wisely talks about 'a kind of international communication'. It is likely that ELF, like any other natural language, will turn out to vary, and to change over time. It does not make much sense, therefore, to talk about a monolithic variety as such: a variety can be treated as if it were a monolith, but this is a convenient fiction, for the process of variation itself never stops.

Jenkins and I do not adhere to such a monolithic view; rather, we have always acknowledged the important work in World Englishes. For instance, in a paper which looks critically at the customary distinction between Outer and Expanding Circles we deplore the fact that the pioneering work on indigenized varieties of English has not so far extended to more general global uses of English:

> In most Outer Circle contexts, of course, the long and vigorous struggle for the acknowledgement of their very own socio-political identities has been largely successful. ... The naïve notion of a monolithic, uniform, unadaptable linguistic medium owned by its original speakers and forever linked to their rule(s) has been recognized as simply contrary to the facts ... Outer Circle linguistic independence has, on the whole, been given the linguistic seal of approval.
>
> In the Expanding Circle, a totally different situation presents itself. (Seidlhofer and Jenkins 2003, 141f.)

As for the descriptive research which VOICE will make possible, it will only partly be a matter of tracing empirical evidence of particular features of the ELF code. What will be equally important will be to refer to a broader conceptual framework in order to provide an explanatory dimension to the enquiry: it is one thing to say that certain features of the code occur as data, but quite another to explain their generalizability. I therefore envisage that it will be more interesting, and more useful, to try and find common underlying processes of how speakers make use of ELF, and what they do to the code when using it. Trudgill (1999) is again relevant in this respect in that he discusses such general processes in a comparison between Standard English and other, non-standard dialects of English. In a section headed 'grammatical idiosyncrasies of Standard English' (p. 125), Trudgill lists eight such idiosyncrasies. What seems particularly interesting to me is that what Trudgill is describing here are complementary processes of regularization and particularization: in some cases many non-standard dialects are more regular than Standard English (e.g. *I be, you be, he be,* etc. vs Standard English *I am, you are, he is,* etc.) and in others they are more 'differentiated', or subtler, in their distinctions (e.g. *you* and *thou* or *you* and *youse* vs Standard English *you* for both singular and plural).

Not surprisingly, the same processes seem to be emerging from the ELF data: ELF speakers, like speakers of many non-standard dialects of English, tend to avoid many of Trudgill's 'grammatical idiosyncrasies of Standard English' and instead exploit regularities that are in principle possible in the system, but not codified in Standard English. An obvious example is the regularization of Standard English present tense verb morphology by not having the third-person singular -*s* marking, which also Trudgill points out as 'unusual and irregular', but using zero for all persons. While such processes are, then, essentially processes of regularization, there are also processes of particularization that even a cursory look at the interactions captured in VOICE reveals. A case in point is that ELF speakers will often introduce elements or distinctions that are important to them but not encoded in Standard English: the most striking example here are translations, often accompanied by explanations, of particularly apt and expressive phrases or idioms in a speaker's first language, such as wishing 'good appetite' to others at the table at the beginning of a meal. Again, this process of 'transdialectal enrichment' (my term) is something that has been observed on a large scale in traditional dialects of English: for example, speakers of Welsh English talk about 'killing the hay' where Standard English speakers say 'cutting the hay'.

The point I am trying to make is that for the analysis and description of ELF, it is possible to draw on a great deal of relevant existing work in sociolinguistics and related areas. It would be a mistake to assume that the salient features of ELF emerging from empirical work will be unique to ELF – on the contrary, we should expect to find commonalities with processes that have been observed in work on language variation and change, and in particular in language contact situations. There is, then, nothing 'monolithic' emerging out of ELF research, but what is to be hoped for is a better understanding of general processes underlying this global use of English, which all participants stand to gain from.

## Misconception 5: ELF researchers suggest that ELF should be taught to all L2 non-native speakers

Precisely because EFL and ELF are so different in their conceptualisations, this would be a ludicrous suggestion to make. It is up to learners and users of English to decide which kind of English they need and want. What would be a sensible suggestion, however, is that some awareness of the global roles of English should be achieved by all English users in the Inner, Outer and Expanding Circles alike. As Bamgbose (1998, 11) reminds us, 'the point is often missed that it is people, not language codes, that understand one another.' It is simply that all concerned need to be prepared to make an effort to make global communication more than just a buzzword.

## Conclusion: Live and let live

This volume is intended as a contribution to an exchange of views and a constructive debate between proponents of World Englishes, or nativized varieties of English, and proponents of EIL, or ELF. It seems to me that each group (although the 'groups' themselves are of course abstractions and constructions) can benefit from learning more about what is happening in the field of 'English in the World' as a whole, and again, I am hopeful that this collection will make this possible. There are certainly important differences between World Englishes and EIL – simply by virtue of the very different sociohistorical and sociocultural settings in which these Englishes have arisen and are being used. But acknowledging and understanding these differences does not have to entail the setting up of what are actually false dichotomies, such as WE vs EIL, pluricentric vs monolithic, tolerance of diversity vs prescribed rules. It is perfectly clear that the functions of language are manifold in all societies, and that any language serves the purposes of identification and communication. Identification with a primary culture on the one hand and communication across cultures on the other are equally worthwhile endeavours, and there is no reason why they should not happily coexist and enrich each other.

# References

Bamgbose, A. 1998. 'Torn between the norms: innovations in world Englishes'. *World Englishes* 17/1, 1–14.

Firth, A. 1996. 'The discursive accomplishment of normality. On "lingua franca" English and conversation analysis'. *Journal of Pragmatics* 26/3, 237–59.

Jenkins, J. 2000. *The Phonology of English as an International Language.* Oxford: Oxford University Press.

Jenkins, J. 2002. 'A sociolinguistically based, empirically researched pronunciation syllabus for English as an International Language' *Applied Linguistics* 23, 83–103.

Jenkins, J. and B. Seidlhofer. 2001. 'Teaching English as a lingua franca for Europe'. *Guardian Weekly,* April 2001 (also on *http://www.guardian.co.uk/ GWeekly/Story/0,3939,475315,00.html*).

Jenkins, J. 2003. *World Englishes.* London: Routledge.

Kachru, B. (ed.) 1992. *The Other Tongue* (2nd edition). Urbana and Chicago: University of Illinois Press.

Knapp, K. 1987. 'English as an international *lingua franca* and the teaching of intercultural communication'. In W. Lörscher and R. Schulze (eds), *Perspectives of Language in Performance. Tübinger Beiträge zur Linguistik* 317(2). Tübingen: Narr. 1022–39.

Kramsch, C. 1998. 'The privilege of the intercultural speaker'. In M. Byram and M. Fleming (eds), *Language Learning in Intercultural Perspective.* Cambridge: Cambridge University Press.

Seidlhofer, B. 1999. 'Double standards: teacher education in the Expanding Circle'. *World Englishes* 18/2, 233–45.

Seidlhofer, B. 2001a. 'Closing a conceptual gap: the case for a description of English as a lingua franca'. *International Journal of Applied Linguistics* 11, 133–58.

Seidlhofer, B. 2001b. '*Habeas corpus* and *divide et impera*: "Global English" and Applied Linguistics'. In K. Spelman Miller and P. Thompson (eds), *Unity and Diversity in Language Use.* London: Continuum (2002). 198–217.

Seidlhofer, B. 2002a. 'The shape of things to come? Some Basic questions'. In K. Knapp and C. Meierkord (eds), *Lingua Franca Communication.* Frankfurt/Main: Lang. 269–302.

Seidlhofer, B. 2002b. 'A concept of "international English" and related issues: From "real English" to "realistic English"? Autour du concept d'anglais international: de l'anglais authentique' à l'anglais réaliste'?' Strasbourg: Council of Europe. 2002 (see also http://www.coe.int/T/E/Cultural_ Co-operation/education/Languages/Language_Policy/Policy_development_ activities/Studies/SeidlhoferEn.pdf).

Seidlhofer, B. and J. Jenkins. 2003. 'English as a Lingua Franca and the Politics of Property'. In Mair, C. (ed.), *The Politics of English as a World Language. New Horizons in Postcolonial Cultural Studies.* Amsterdam: Rodopi. 139–54.

Trudgill, P. 1999. 'Standard English: What it isn't'. In T. Bex and R. J. Watts

(eds), *Standard English: The Widening Debate*. London: Routledge. 117–28.
Widdowson, H. G. 1991. 'The description and prescription of language'. In Alatis, J. (ed.), *Georgetown University Round Table in Language and Linguistics. Linguistics and Language Pedagogy: The State of the Art.* Washington DC: Georgetown University.

## Endnotes

1 I am using 'EIL' and 'ELF' interchangeably. It is worth emphasizing, however, that, as I indicate in my title, I am focusing on ELF in the Expanding Circle, i.e. on English used in areas where it is learned as a foreign language and not usually employed for intranational communication, as it typically is in Outer Circle countries.
2 See the Seidlhofer 2001 and 2002 references for more information on VOICE, as well as Seidlhofer and Jenkins 2003. Homepage: http://www.univie.ac.at/Anglistik/VOICE/

# Defining the 'Successful Bilingual Speaker' of English

*Luke Prodromou*

Globalization is pulling English in two very different directions: the language has splintered into countless regional varieties, some with a high degree of self-regulation and divergence from English as a Native Language (ENL). At the same time, there is a need for an international lingua franca which will be comprehensible in a wide variety of settings, involving linguistically, ethnically and culturally hetero- geneous speakers. In this article, I shall examine recent proposals for a Lingua Franca common core and identify certain potential difficulties with the proposal. I shall conclude with a possible solution based on my own corpus-based research into proficient non-native speakers.

## In search of the successful bilingual

Two articles published recently address the issue of English as an International Language (EIL) but seem to arrive at conflicting conclusions. Both articles (Alptekin 2002 and Timmis 2002) tackle the highly controversial question of native vs non-native models of English in the context of English as an International Language (EIL) or English as an international Lingua Franca (ELF – I shall use the terms interchangeably in this paper). Alptekin challenges native-speaker norms in the description of English as an International Language and, by extension, methodologies that are dominated by an Anglo- American cultural perspective:

> ...the conventional model of communicative competence, with its strict adherence to native speaker norms within the target language culture, would appear to be invalid in accounting for learning and using an international language in cross-cultural settings (Alptekin 2002, 63).

Timmis, on the other hand, investigates the attitudes of teachers and students towards native-speaker norms and argues that students' views may contradict the assumptions of applied linguists who argue against the predominance of native-speaker models of language and culture in ELT: 'how far is it our right or responsibility to politically re-educate

our students? When does awareness raising become proselytizing?'
(Timmis 2002, 249).

Alptekin reflects the increasingly centrifugal tendencies of
English as an international language; his proposals reflect the diverse
strands of the 'world Englishes' movement, spearheaded by Kachru
(1992) and Canagarajah (1999). Proposals for replacing the supremacy
of the native-speaker teacher as a model with the 'intercultural
speaker' have also been made by, amongst others, Kramsch (1998),
Rampton (1990), Prodromou (1992) and Modiano (2001).

Timmis' paper, in contrast to Alptekin, expresses some of the
arguments for a centripetal position on English in the world today;
Timmis echoes the frequently voiced concern that, amidst the
diversity, there should be a workable model of comfortable intelligibility for international purposes (cf. Quirk 1985, Preisler 1999) and
that, given students' apparent preferences, native varieties of English
are probably the best starting point for such a model.

In this article, I shall review these two opposing views on EIL and
suggest a possible solution to some of the apparently irreconcilable
tensions in the two positions, drawing on the insights beginning to
emerge from non-native corpora of spoken English, that of Seidlhofer
(2001a, 2001b) and my own work, which is based on a 200,000 corpus
of spontaneous non-native spoken English (Prodromou 2003).

## Critique of native models

Alptekin argues that it is unrealistic and inappropriate to impose a
uniform native model (itself diverse in practice) on the heterogeneous
contexts in which Englishes are now being used around the world. The
imposition of native models on non-native contexts, based on the
argument of authenticity, actually entails a restriction in the autonomy
of the learner, whose own cultural authenticity will tend to be
peripheralized by the 'authority' of the native-speaker (Widdowson
1996, 1998). The non-native teacher's authority also suffers in the
native-dominated scheme of things because it is precisely in the area of
the learners' culture that non-native teachers are at their best. While,
on the one hand, the non-native teacher is expected to apply the
linguistic, pragmatic and cultural features of the native speaker, their
own strengths – their knowledge of English grammar, the students'
language and culture – are peripheralized (cf. Basanta 1996, 263).

Alptekin's proposals for developing a realistic model for EIL are
based on the concept of 'global appropriacy' and 'local appropriation'.
Within this dual framework, users of English will be comfortably
intelligible in both international and national cultures. Taking this

ability to survive successfully in 'international' and 'national' cultures as our starting point, the question is: What model of English do we take as the basis for syllabuses, textbooks and examinations? Alptekin's response seems to be: 'Successful bilinguals with intercultural insights'.

Alptekin, however, says nothing specific about what 'successful bilinguals' do with the language. A major area for debate, therefore, will be exactly how we define Alptekin's 'successful' (non-native) user of the language. One advantage of Standard English varieties, the argument goes, is that while they may not be everyone's cup of English tea, they are, nevertheless, varieties which exist and have been codified and can thus serve as the basis for an acceptable and accessible international lingua franca (Preisler 1999, 264). Indeed, in the written medium, native-like norms seem to provide common linguistic ground for a wide range of non-native varieties (in journalism, scientific writing, and so on) and even in more formal spoken registers the tendency will be to conform to patterns which are considered grammatical, at least by existing native-speaker practices.

Thus, the challenge facing those who hold Alptekin's position is to come up with an empirically based and coherently codified alternative to native norms, based on a valid description of the 'successful bilingual'.

## What is a successful bilingual?

What type of 'bilinguals' is Alptekin referring to? Is it

- Those who have two mother tongues?
- Those who are considered native-like in two languages?
- Those who are considered near-native speakers?
- Those who are clearly not native speakers of English but use the language successfully in their own terms?

If Alptekin is referring to either of the first two then the argument risks becoming circular – these 'successful bilinguals' are judged native-like by the written, codified norms of ENL, so, the riposte might be, why not just use the native speaker as we do today? If, on the other hand, Alptekin is referring to the near-native speaker, then one will want to know how 'near' near-native is: in what way does the near-native differ from the native speaker, and how good does one have to be to count as a 'near'-native speaker? Which of the following are necessary to earn the badge of the successful bilingual?

- Correct grammar
- Correct grammar and a large vocabulary
- Native-like fluency on the level of idiomaticity: the use of collocations and lexical phrases (Pawley and Syder 1983, Nattinger and DeCarrico 1992)
- Command of culturally-loaded idioms (proverbs, sayings, catchphrases)
- Socio-pragmatic competence
- Socio-cultural competence
- Native-like pronunciation

Where we draw the bar for inclusion in the category of 'successful bilingual' will exclude as well as include large numbers of users of English as an International Language, who may be perfectly efficient users of the language, though not in a position to fulfil the criteria for entry into the elite corps of 'bilingual users'. All this will affect the language we put into textbooks, the language we assess, what we correct, what we accept, and so on.

The questions, then, are: What exactly do 'successful bilinguals' do when they use ELF? Where does one look for such models of ELF? Do we need models at all?

## The Lingua Franca Common Core

One project now underway which aims to capture ELF in at least some of its lexico-grammatical and discoursal variety is the University of Vienna ELF Corpus (Seidlhofer 2001a, 2001b). The subjects chosen to form part of this corpus are all non-native speakers, in face-to-face communication with other non-native speakers. In contrast to Alptekin's view that the 'successful bilingual' should be able to communicate in both non-native to non-native and non-native to native contexts, the Vienna team, at this stage at least, stipulate that the ELF they wish to describe will not involve native speakers or predominantly native-speaker contexts (Seidlhofer 2001a, 44).

Moreover, Alptekin's 'successful bilinguals, with intercultural insights and knowledge' (2002, 57) seem to be at a different level of proficiency to Seidlhofer's users of ELF, whose success in the language will be variable but who share 'common features of ELF use, irrespective of ... levels of proficiency' (2001a, 44). There may even be aspects of the Vienna definition of ELF which include 'deviant' but 'unproblematic' utterances (Seidlhofer 2001b, 15). 'Deviant' is in inverted commas because it is defined with reference to native norms, the legitimacy of which is precisely what Seidlhofer's research –

rightly, in my view – seeks to question. 'Unproblematic' refers to the fact that such items will not tend to cause misunderstanding in ELF.

It can be seen why the definition of the 'successful bilingual' or 'user of ELF' implicit in Seidlhofer's work is likely to put the proverbial cat amongst the pigeons. Seidlhofer and her team are embarking on a project to build and analyse a non-native speaker corpus in order to document and codify exactly what happens in non-native to non-native interaction, and to use the results as the basis for an appropriate model for ELF. This is a welcome step in furthering our understanding of non-native varieties of English and in providing a corrective to the native-speaker-dominated corpora already in existence. There are, however, several potential difficulties with the Vienna proposal as the basis for an ELF core.

## The Vienna corpus: grammar

One area of possible controversy is the role and status of grammar in ELF. Should there be a grammatical common core for ELF, similar to Jenkins' phonological core? Seidlhofer (2001b) presents a preliminary list of grammatical items which are 'deviant', compared to native speaker models, but which she suggests are 'usually unproblematic':

1. Simple present 3rd person *–s* omitted: *he look very sad*
2. Omission of article: *our countries have signed agreement*
3. Treating *who* and *which* as interchangeable
4. Substituting bare infinitive for *–ing*: *I look forward to see you*
5. Using *isn't it?* as a universal tag

One problem relates to whether the aspirations of students who want to become 'successful bilinguals with intercultural communicative competence' will be met by setting the level of acceptability of 'ungrammatical items' at the level implied by Seidlhofer's (albeit brief and provisional) list. Although the criterion of intelligibility may be met by accepting sentences like 'they have three children, isn't it?', one wonders whether the subjects chosen by Seidlhofer to form part of the Vienna non-native speaker corpus are the kind of 'successful bilingual' that Alptekin has in mind and whether they meet the *aspirations* of the students in Timmis's survey. There seems to be a fallacious comparison between the difficulty learners have in acquiring the phonological features of native-like speech (Jenkins 1998, 2000) and their ability to acquire canonical grammar patterns. Few teachers can point to students who have become indistinguishable from native speakers on the phonological level, but we have countless examples of learners who have reached a high level of proficiency both in grammar and vocabulary.

From the point of view of the non-native-speaker teacher of English, setting the bar of grammatical acceptability low seems unnecessarily cautious. If there is one strength non-native teachers are acknowledged to possess, often in greater abundance than their native-speaker counterparts, it is command and knowledge of the grammatical system of English as it is codified in the traditional grammar books. I am not referring to the 'spoken grammar' investigated by Timmis (2002), which is another kettle of fish, from a pragmatic perspective, but the variety of grammar which 'looks as good on paper as it sounds in speech' (Quirk 1985, 6). To ask non-native teachers of EFL to be models of native pronunciation is, in most cases, both unrealistic and unnecessary; but to ask them to teach correct English grammar is something they excel in and seem to enjoy. In my experience, pronunciation practice tends to raise teachers' affective filter, while grammar tends to lower it. For better or worse, the myth of grammar has a powerful hold on non-native teachers' affection and imagination. Acquisition of grammar, unlike phonology and idiomaticity, is not mysteriously elusive. I feel, therefore, that in terms of student aspirations and teacher competence, motivation and self-esteem, the bar for the common grammatical core can be set much higher than is suggested by the examples of acceptable items listed by Seidlhofer.

## European variety

The second doubt I have concerning Seidlhofer's corpus is that it will be based on 'the lexico-grammar of this emerging Euro-English' (2001, 16). Can this Euro-English form the basis for 'successful bilinguals in national and international contexts' (Alptekin 2002)? First of all, there is the unlikely possibility that learners from diverse European backgrounds will display the same common core features – Hungarians and Italians, Basques and Turks will not make the same kind of 'errors' (or 'simplifications' as Seidlhofer calls them), and given their differing levels of proficiency, learners or real-world users will not display the same degree of error or simplification when communicating in ELF. Put simply, some users will be of the kind of level indicated in Seidlhofer's samples, others will be lower but, more importantly, others will be of a higher level of proficiency. How much convergence is there likely to be, given this heterogeneity of levels within the European context?

There are, moreover, cultural implications of 'Euro-English'. If a homogenous lexico-grammatical model of Euro-English were to emerge, whose culture would it reflect, that of Alptekins' Turks or Seidlhofer's Viennese? Or would it be culturally neutral, unmarked by the traces of national cultures and perhaps 'without love, without sighs, without tears' (Fishman 1992, 24)?

Europe is part of a global community in which language users travel from Europe to other parts of the world and non-Europeans travel from all corners of the globe to Europe for a range of personal, social or economic reasons. In other words, users of ELF, as Alptekin says, need to be successful in national and *international* settings. If one accepts the disappearance by a process of simplification of, say, the simple present 3rd person –s, will this meet the potential proficiency expectations of Dutch, Chinese and Mexican speakers of ELF? The Lingua Franca core needs to set its sights higher rather than lower, wider rather than narrower, to include the maximum number of participants in its framework of comfortable international intelligibility. The world is ELF's oyster.

## ELF: an indigenized variety?

A further factor which complicates the picture of ELF put forward by Seidlhofer is the failure to distinguish between ELF and indigenized varieties. The new Englishes of Africa or Asia are varieties within a particular region or speech community which have evolved their own norms. How plausible is it to talk of endonormative standards in ELF, as one does in the case of Singaporean English or the English of West Africa? The speech community of ELF is by definition diverse and hetereogeneous – where is the linguistic common ground to come from? Austria? Spain? Russia? Speakers of Euro-English will want to use this variety as an international lingua franca with non-Europeans; this international function is not one that the indigenized varieties of Asia or Africa are called upon to play. The Lingua Franca core needs to open its net wider, in order to capture the maximum range of intercultural encounters involved in the use of English worldwide and to identify linguistic norms which will be acceptable across regions and cultures. Cellphones, email, websites, chatrooms and global mobility mean diversity is ever-present and inescapable.

## ELF and ENL

I have one final objection to the model for ELF put forward by Seidlhofer, who quotes Widdowson on the irrelevance of native speakers to how English develops in the world:

> (native speakers) have no say in the matter ... they are irrelevant.
> The very fact that English is an international language means that
> no nation can have custody over it (Widdowson 1994, 385).

One agrees that native speakers have no right to dictate rules to non-native speakers of English. But what is odd about Widdowson's argument here is that it implies that 'native speakers' are not a part of the rich tapestry that is English as an International Language – and yet clearly they are, both as users of EIL and therefore potential interlocutors of non-native speakers, and as speakers of the most codified and widely accepted variety of English we have, especially its written forms. This native variety hitherto seems to have facilitated 'comfortable intelligibility' across a wide variety of Englishes. Native speakers from the BANA countries (Britain, Australia, New Zealand, Ireland, Canada and the United States) are also players in the game of EIL – and, in terms of sheer numbers, important players. One is not necessarily arguing in favour of native-speaker domination of the rest of the English-speaking world if one recognizes native varieties of English, especially their written grammar and their basic referential lexical store, as important strands in the pattern of EIL. (I am again distinguishing these levels of language from corpus-based spoken grammar and idiomaticity, which are for me in a different category as far as EIL is concerned). ELF users who are not native speakers of English will, nevertheless, be meeting and interacting with native speakers as well as non-native speakers who will also have been exposed to canonical grammar and lexis. ELF includes, but is not defined by, native varieties, and these native varieties have to a large extent shaped non-native varieties. Conversely, ELF includes, but is not defined exclusively by, non-native varieties. To go into class and teach or legitimate the simplified utterances quoted by Seidlhofer, though ideologically appealing, feels intuitively to fly in the face of linguistic realities. The model most students will be exposed to, if Alpterkin's proposal is taken up, will be that of a successful non-native bilingual, who will be a constant reminder that there is a level beyond ELF which is more proficient and prestigious than the simplifications many perfectly effective users produce. Indeed, in the multicultural Internet world in which communication takes place across borders, it will be impossible to insulate ELF from some contact with native-speaker norms. To do justice to our students' needs and aspirations we should try to empower them to cope with the variety of Englishes, both non-native and native, which they will encounter in the world outside their classroom walls or invisible European walls. Is there a way of reconciling these tensions in Seidlhofer's proposals?

## On the trail of the 'successful bilingual'

Most corpora have so far been based on the naturally-occurring speech or writing of native speakers of English; apart from the non-native national varieties of English which are part of the International Corpus of English (Greenbaum 1996) there is now an International Learners' Corpus of English based on students' written work (Granger 1998). There are relatively few studies of English as an international lingua franca in a European context (see Firth 1996 and Seidlhofer 2001). My own corpus differs from previous work on non-native speech in focusing exclusively on natural, spontaneous speech produced by *proficient* non-native users of English as a foreign language.

## Corpus Design

The general aim of my corpus was

- to describe varieties of English as an international language which might form the basis of a model for teachers, learners, syllabus designers and materials writers.

The specific aim was

- to explore the role of idiomaticity, in the broad sense, in non-native speaker discourse.

The basic design of my non-native corpus is as follows:

**Date of recordings**: 2000–2003
**Type**: Spoken, spontaneous, unscripted
**Length of complete corpus** (including native-speaker interlocutors): 200,000 words
**Length of non-native speaker sub-corpus**: 150,000 words
**Number of informants/successful users**: 45
**Gender:** 50% male, 50% female
**Nationality**: European (19 countries) and Latin American (6 countries)
**Age:** Adult
**Education:** University graduates and postgraduates
**Profession:** Teachers, trainers and lecturers but also business people, publishers and administrators
**Level of English**: Advanced
**Register**: Informal or non-formal conversation

> **Roles**: Family (married couples), friends, colleagues, acquaintances
> **Setting:** Home, office, car, train, restaurant, cafe, hotel
> **Topics**: Social chat, gossip, conversation about work, friends, politics, some discussion

It was important that a fair proportion of my non-native speakers should be acknowledged experts in the teaching or description of English, or should be recognized by people who know them as – above average – successful users of English. Secondly, they had to be people who would have occasion to use English with people from ethnic backgrounds other than their own, and to code-switch effectively depending on their interlocutor. These criteria of 'expertise' (see Rampton 1990) have to do with the requirement referred to by Alptekin (2002) that teachers in EIL contexts should be 'successful bilinguals with intercultural insights'.

## Criteria for inclusion

A complex issue in identifying 'successful users' is deciding criteria for inclusion in the category which do not end up being circular. The point was to build a corpus of speakers who seemed, on the basis, initially, of my subjective impressions, to have a high level of English. I would then investigate what these successful users had in common, how they differed amongst themselves, what they had in common with native speakers, and how they differed from native speakers.

The procedure was as follows:

1. On my travels in Europe and Latin America, whenever I met a non-native speaker in a social or professional context who sounded fluent in English, grammatically accurate and pragmatically successful, I arranged to record them in informal, spontaneous contexts.
2. On several occasions, a third party who knew what my research was about would recommend I record someone whom they considered an outstanding user of English.
3. For some of the informants, I was able to contact people who knew them and ask these 'objective observers' to express an opinion on the informant's English. This intuitive assessment, based on extensive contact with the informant, was invariably positive.

4. Many of my informants are recognized international or local experts in the teaching of English.
5. All of the informants use English regularly in personal, social or professional contexts with native and non-native speakers.
6. I asked each participant to complete a questionnaire designed to elicit relevant bio-data; from this data, it emerged that nearly all of my informants had a high-level English language qualification. The participants in my corpus confirmed that they were not 'learners' but regular users of English.
7. I transcribed the recordings and was able to confirm that the level of English was grammatically and lexically accurate. I left open the question of the role played by collocation and idiomaticity, as this was one of the objects of the investigation.
8. I compared my impressions and data of successful users with definitions widely used by international examining bodies (Cambridge Proficiency, Michigan Proficiency, IELTS). For example, Level 5 of the ALTE framework, to which the Cambridge Proficiency corresponds, defines the Good User in terms of cultural flexibility and linguistic competence beyond the grammatical system:

> at this level the learner is approaching the linguistic level of an educated native speaker and is able to use the language in a range of culturally appropriate ways. Users at this level are able to improve their use of the language by extending their vocabulary and refining their usage and command of style and register (rather) than by learning about new areas of grammar. (UCLES, 2002, 6)

9. I circulated anonymous samples of the transcriptions to native speakers or non-native professional ELT people and asked them to give each sample a score to indicate the level of English suggested by the sample. The assessment was invariably very positive (i.e. 'excellent').

I appreciate that some of the criteria above are open to criticism on the basis of measuring non-native speaker competence by the yardstick of native-speaker norms (e.g. 8). There are several reasons why I used the criteria of Anglo-American examining bodies as a means of triangulating my definition of the successful user. The first relates to Timmis' research on learners' needs and wants, and the conclusion he draws that the native-speaker model is still one that many learners aspire to, even if it is unattainable for most of them (cf. my own earlier survey which confirmed, contrary to my expectations and personal convictions, that 60 per cent of my 300 respondents aspired to native models of fluency: Prodromou, 1992). Taking students' aspirations into account, even if applied linguists disagree with the outcome, is at the heart of a genuinely learner-centred approach to pedagogy. Secondly, the examinations run by the Universities of Cambridge, Michigan, IELTS and TOEFL, enjoy widespread recognition, and thus their definition of Good Users reflects or has shaped the perceptions of the ELT profession and the public at large. Both students' aspirations and public perceptions affect the kind of English that will be acceptable and attractive in the classroom. Given current orthodoxies, it seems implausible that most learners and teachers will be enthusiastic about a model of English that legitimizes non-canonical grammatical forms and does not potentially lead to recognized levels of certification, whether national or international.

## The status of idiomaticity

Another reason why I included native-speaker-driven criteria is that one aim of my research was to explore and deconstruct the validity of certain aspects of these criteria, by measuring them against the data I had collected and the actual linguistic and pragmatic strategies of my Successful Users. I was particularly interested in examining the assumption that a successful non-native user necessarily commands a repertoire of native-like styles and idiomatic expressions. References to understanding of 'idiomatic' and 'colloquial' language and 'cultural allusions' are common in the definitions of the successful user in these examinations, as they are in the literature of second language acquisition.

My working hypothesis in initiating this research was that idiomaticity has cultural implications which affect its status in second language acquisition, and that as such it is resistant to acquisition by non-native speakers, however successful they are. The hypothesis is put forward by Medgyes (1994) and substantiated by research (cf. Wray 2002, for a survey of this research). While I have come across no reason in the research or in perceived performance of successful users that makes me doubt the validity of codified grammar as a basis for a lingua franca common core, the evidence concerning the role of idiomaticity in non-native discourse raises a lot of questions, which my research seeks to address.

The hypotheses I aimed to explore are as follows:

1. Successful non-native users of English have complete command of the grammatical system of English.
2. Successful non-native users have a vocabulary completely appropriate to their needs.

3. Successful users of English avoid using (native-like) 'colourful' idiomatic expressions.
4. Successful users of English use fewer lexical phrases and collocations than native speakers.
5. Any 'idiosyncracy' non-native users display compared to native speakers will be in the domain of idiomaticity.
6. Any 'errors' successful users make will tend to occur in the area of idiomaticity.
7. The kind of English resulting from points 1–6 is a legitimate appropriation of the language for local and global purposes.

## Some preliminary insights

Once I had assembled the non-native speaker corpus, I began to test the hypothesis that the successful non-native-speaker user of English differs essentially from the native speaker in the number and kind of idiomatic expressions used. Space does not allow me to go into detail, but one can note here some initial findings.

Successful non-native speakers:

1. have a well-nigh flawless command of grammar.
2. are rarely 'lost for words' insofar as this refers to individual lexical items, used in a more or less referential manner.
3. hardly use any 'pure' idioms of the 'raining cats and dogs' variety and very few catchphrases, metaphors and cultural allusions. Some examples of those that do occur in my corpus are: *pass the buck; the cut-off point; it boils down to; making mincemeat of; in the belly of the beast; if it ain't broke, don't fix it.* ('Pure' idioms are also infrequent in native-speaker discourse – see Moon 1998a and 1998b.)
4. are rarely creative with idioms. In native-speaker discourse, though pure idioms are infrequent, when they do occur they are often exploited for creative effects (Moon 1998a and 1998b). This creativity with idiomatic expressions is virtually non-existent in non-native-speaker discourse. One example I came across was: *to bring the conference down*, which may have been a conscious variation on *to bring the house down*; another is *dressed down as* (for *dressed up as*). Carter (1999, 2002) also points out the way native speakers regularly 'play' with non-idiomatic language, too, in everyday conversation (punning, repetition, varying the form of words, etc.). This 'creativity' of everyday speech is found very rarely in my data.

5. tend to make errors, if at all, in the context of idiom use and collocation, e.g.: * *making heads or tails;* * *making a mincemeat of;* * *make your own mind;* * *from my heart* (for *by heart*); * *waylay problems.*

6. employ a wide variety of (generally transparent, non-metaphorical) collocations and lexical phrases: *this and that; commit suicide; deeply religious; have a good trip;* and so on.

## Hedging devices

A comparison of two-word lexical phrases in native and non-native spoken corpora reveals a great deal of similarity between ENL and EIL but also some intriguing differences. For example, in native speaker discourse hedging devices are very frequent (*you know, I mean, I think, sort of, a bit, you see*); this is true of non-native speaker discourse, but to a lesser degree (see Figure 1).

**Figure 1: Top twelve two-word lexical phrases in NS and NNSC**

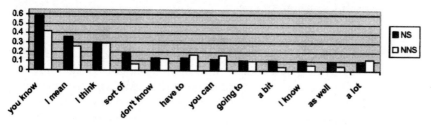

The pattern of similarity in frequency is, however, broken by *sort of*, which is also a hedge (I filtered out the non-hedge uses of *sort of* from both corpora). The next item to break the pattern of similarity is *a bit*, which is also widely used as a hedging device. The pattern revealed in this comparison of two-word lexical phrases suggests the possibility that there is an Idiomatic Common Core operating in native and non-native spoken discourse. The basis for this Idiomatic Common Core, as well as the areas which seem to lie outside it, needs to be explored with reference to the way lexical phrases are deployed in face-to-face interaction for the achievement of particular pragmatic intentions.

Clearly, the role of hedging devices in non-native spoken discourse is an area requiring further investigation, which goes beyond the scope of this paper.

## Phrasal verbs

Successful non-native speakers seem to use fewer phrasal verbs than native-speakers. This confirms research by previous scholars (e.g. Irujo 1993, Dagut and Laufer 1985). Figure 2 summarizes the frequency of particular phrasal verbs in the non-native corpus and Table 1 shows the most frequent phrasal verbs in native spoken corpora, as listed by Biber et al. 1999, compared to the most frequent phrasal verbs in the present corpus of non-native spoken English.

**Figure 2: Most frequent phrasal and prepositional verbs in NNSC**

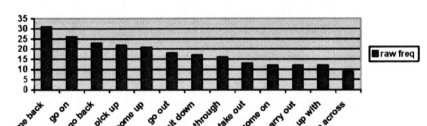

**Table 1:** Phrasal verbs in native- and non-native-speaker spoken corpora (in order of frequency)

| NS | NNSC |
|---|---|
| *Come on* | *Come back* |
| *Go on* | *Go on* |
| *Get up* | *Go back* |
| *Get in* | *Pick up* |
| *Find out* | *Come up* |
| *Sit down* | *Go out* |
| *Get out* | *Sit down* |
| *Come over* | *Go through* |
| *Go off* | *Take out* |
| *Shut up* | *Come on* |
| *Sit up* | *Carry out* |
| *Pick up* | *Come up with* |

| NS | NNSC |
|---|---|
| Put on | Come across |
| Get back | Go (a)round |
| Get off | Put on |
| Come off | Get away |
| Run out | Come over |
| Stand up | Go into |
| Come along | Put in |
| Give up | Get up |
| Make up | Make up |

This comparison again, as in the case of two-word lexical phrases, reveals a great deal of overlap in the two corpora but also some puzzling divergences, and indicates the possibility of an Idiomatic Common Core in ENL and ELF. Why non-native speakers reveal a liking for *come back* and *go back*, which do not appear at all in the top twenty native-speaker phrasal verbs (Biber et al., 410), is worthy of further investigation. Research into the possible reasons for these differences will entail, like all the phraseological patterns in the non-native speaker corpus, an examination of language in context, as a pragmatic tool of face-to-face interaction.

It may be of interest to the reader to see the other, less frequent phrasal verbs used by my non-native informants:

| | | | |
|---|---|---|---|
| come through | come up | get across | get back |
| go down | go off | make off | look after |
| look forward | look into | look up | look through |
| put down | set up | give up | point out |
| shut up | take off | take up | turn out |
| turn into | | | |

## ELF: product or process?

In this paper, I have argued the importance of defining the successful 'bilingual' and 'intercultural' teacher in terms which will make the model acceptable, accessible and attractive to the learner and teacher in international ELF contexts (the issues surrounding ESL involve a distinct set of contextual and pedagogic factors). I have outlined some of the possible problems which a model of ELF incorporating user errors may present, in terms of student aspirations and syllabus design ('error', that is, as defined by current codified forms of English). I should stress that I do not see either model as a template to be imposed on the diverse contexts in which English is taught worldwide. What we are describing, I hope, is not a 'product' but a 'process'. It would be a mistake to attempt to replace one product, based on ENL, with another, based on ELF. In language use, a hundred flowers (or more) should bloom.

What I have described, the building of a non-native speaker corpus, is rather a convenient device for beginning to investigate the differences between native and non-native uses of spoken English. The attempt to identify what successful non-native users do with the language involves a *quantitative* element (speakers often do this, they rarely do that) but the pedagogic implications become apparent at the *qualitative* stage, when the researcher asks why particular patterns of frequency occur. This question can only be answered by considering the impact of context on language choice; context, in turn, involves an examination of real-time social interaction between speakers who share common linguistic and cultural schema in the case of the native speaker, while in the case of non-native speakers using English in international lingua franca contexts, linguistic and cultural schema will invariably be very different.

In other words, the definition of the successful non-native user of English will uncover the importance of the *process* of face-to-face interaction in pragmatic terms, rather than a static linguistic *product*. The pragmatic role of hedging devices, for example, such as *you know, sort of, like, just* and so on, which occur in varying degrees in the two corpora, will be understood in relation to the way they invoke shared knowledge and create convergence between speakers (see, for example, Poos and Simpson 2002, Loewenberg 1982, Ostman 1981).

## Conclusion

Hitherto, descriptions of context have been native-speaker-driven and have given rise to concepts of authenticity which are defined in terms of texts produced by native speakers for native speakers. The implications of analysing non-native speaker discourse in its own right, rather than as a deficit model of native-speaker varieties, are that discourse is seen as a dynamic process of negotiation of meanings; authenticity, as Widdowson (1996) says, is not *given* but *created* by the speakers. What I see emerging from the analysis of non-native speaker corpora is an awareness of the importance of context and the degree of 'commonality' binding the speakers. This 'commonality', which is 'deep' when we use our mother-tongue and generally 'shallow' when we use a foreign language with people we do not know very well, will constrain our linguistic choices and shape our discourse.

The interface between context and language choice in the discourse of successful users of English as an international lingua franca is where I think future research into non-native corpora should focus its attention. The first signs are that the role of idiomaticity and phraseology in general, which have played such a prominent role in definitions of *native*-like fluency in recent years (cf. Pawley and Syder 1983, Nattinger and DeCarrico 1992, Sinclair 1991) may have to be reassessed with reference to *non-native* fluency.

## References

Alptekin, C. 2002. 'Towards intercultural communicative competence in ELT'. *ELT Journal* 56/1, 57–64.

Basanta, C. 1996. 'Comment: in the name of the teacher'. *ELT Journal* 50/3, 263–4.

Bex, T. and R. Watts (eds). 1999. *Standard English: the Widening Debate*. London: Routledge.

Biber, D., S. Johansson, G. Leech, S. Conrad and E. Finegan. 1999. *Longman Grammar of Spoken and Written English*. Harlow: Longman.

Canagarajah, A. 1999. 'Interrogating the "Native Speaker Fallacy": non-linguistic roots, non-pedagogical results'. In G. Braine (ed.), *Non-Native Educators in English Language Teaching*. New Jersey: Lawrence Erlbaum. 77–92.

Carter, R. 1999. 'Common language, corpus, creativity and cognition'. In *Language and Literature*, 8/3, 195–216.

Carter, R. 2002. 'Language, Creativity and Creating Relationships'. *Humanising Language Teaching*. Year 4, Issue 6, November 2002. *http://www.hltmag. co.uk*

Dagut, M. and B. Laufer. 1985. 'Avoidance of phrasal verbs: a case of contrastive analysis'. *Studies in Second Language Acquisition* 7, 73–9.

Firth, A. 1996. 'The discursive accomplishment of normality. On "lingua franca" English and conversation analysis'. *Journal of Pragmatics* 26/3, 237–59.

Fishman, J. 1992. 'A sociology of English as an additional language.' In Kachru, 1992, 19–25.

Granger, S. (ed.). 1998. *Learner English on Computer*. London: Longman.

Greenbaum, S. (ed.). 1996. *Comparing English Worldwide. The international corpus of English*. Oxford: Clarendon Press.

House, J. 1999. 'Misunderstanding in intercultural communication: interactions in English as a lingua franca and the myth of mutual intelligibility'. In C. Gnutzmann, *Teaching and Learning English as a Global Language*. Tubingen: Stauffenburg. 73–89.

Irujo, S. 1993. 'Steering clear: avoidance in the production of idioms'. *IRAL*. XXXI/3, 205–19.

Jenkins, J. 1998. 'Pronunciation norms and models'. *ELT Journal*, 52/2, 119–26.

Jenkins, J. 2000. *The Phonology of English as an International Language*. Oxford: Oxford University Press.

Kachru, B. (ed.). 1992. *The Other Tongue* (2nd edition). Urbana: University of Illinois Press.

Kramsch, C. 'The privilege of the intercultural speaker'. In M. Byram and M. Fleming (eds), *Language Learning in Intercultural Perspective*. Cambridge: Cambridge University Press. 23–37.

Loewenberg, I. 1982. 'Labels and hedges: the metalinguistic turn'. *Language and Style* XV/3, 193–207.

McCarthy, M. and R. Carter. 1995. 'Spoken grammar: what is it and how can we teach it?' *ELT Journal*, 49/3, 207–18.

Medgyes, P. 1994. *The Non-Native Teacher*. Basingstoke: Macmillan.

Modiano, M. 2001. 'Linguistic Imperialism Revisited'. *ELT Journal*, 55/4, 339–46.

Moon, R. 1998a. 'Frequencies and forms of phrasal lexemes in English'. In A. Cowie (ed.), *Phraseology*. Oxford: Oxford University Press. 79–100.

Moon, R. 1998b. *Fixed Expressions and Idioms in English*. Oxford: Clarendon Press.

Munby, J. 1978. *Communicative Syllabus Design*. Cambridge: Cambridge University Press.

Nattinger, J. and J. DeCarrico. 1992. *Lexical Phrases and Language Learning*. Oxford: Oxford University Press.

Ostman, J. 1981. *You Know: a Discourse Functional Approach*. Amsterdam: John Benjamins.

Pawley, A. and F. Syder. 1983. 'Two puzzles for linguistic theory: native-like selection and native-like fluency'. In J. C. Richards and R. W. Schmidt (eds), *Language and Communication*. London: Longman.

Pennycook, A. 2002. 'Turning English inside out'. *Indian Journal of Applied Linguistics*, 28/2, 25–43.

Poos, D. and R. Simpson. 2002. 'Cross-disciplinary comparisons of hedging'. In R. Reppen, S. Fitzmaurice and D. Biber (eds), *Using Corpora to Explore Linguistic Variation*. Amsterdam: John Benjamins. 2–23.

Preisler, B. 1999. 'Functions and forms of English in a European EFL country'. In T. Bex and R. Watts (eds), 239–267.

Prodromou, L. 1992. 'What culture, which culture?' *ELT Journal*, 46/1, 39–50.

Prodromou, L. 2003. 'In search of SUE: the successful user of English'. *Modern English Teacher*, 12/2.

Quirk, R. 1985. 'The English language in a global context'. In Quirk and Widdowson (eds) 1985.

Quirk, R. and H. G. Widdowson (eds). 1985. *English in the World*. Cambridge: Cambridge University Press and the British Council.

Rampton, B. 1990. 'Displacing the native-speaker'. *ELT Journal*, 44/2, 97–101.

Seidlhofer, B. 2001a. 'Brave New English?' *The European English Messenger*, X/1, 2001.

Seidlhofer, B. 2001b. 'Towards making "Euro-English" a linguistic reality.' *English Today* 68, 14–16.

Sinclair, J. 1991. 'Shared knowledge'. In *Proceedings of the Georgetown University Roundtable in Linguistics and Pedagogy – the State of the Art.* Georgetown: Georgetown University Press. 496–9.

Stubbs, M. 2001. *Words and Phrases.* Oxford: Blackwell.

Timmis, I. 2002. 'Native-speaker norms and International English: a classroom view'. *ELT Journal,* 56/3, 240–49.

University of Cambridge Local Examinations Syndicate. 2002. *Certificate of Proficiency Handbook.* Cambridge: UCLES.

Widdowson, H. 1994. 'The Ownership of English'. *TESOL Quarterly,* 28/2, 377–89.

Widdowson, H. 1996. 'Comment, authenticity and autonomy in ELT'. *ELT Journal,* 50/1, 67–8.

Widdowson, H. 1998. 'Context, Community and Authentic Language'. *TESOL Quarterly,* 32/4, 705–16.

Wilkins, D. 1976. *Notional Syllabuses.* Oxford: Oxford University Press.

Wray, A. 2002. *Formulaic Language and the Lexicon.* Cambridge: Cambridge University Press.

# Which Model of English: Native-speaker, Nativized or Lingua Franca?

*Andy Kirkpatrick*
*Curtin University of Technology, Perth, Australia*

## Introduction

The model of English that should be used in classrooms in Outer and Expanding Circle countries (Kachru 1992a) has been a subject of debate for some time (Kachru 1992b, 1995, Conrad 1996, Widdowson 1997). The choice is often made on political and ideological grounds rather than educational ones. It is a choice fraught with conflicts of ideologies and interests. Ideologically speaking, there are those who argue that linguistic imperialism ensures that the spread of English is necessarily equivalent to the spread of native-speaker norms of language and the spread of Anglo-American interests (cf. Phillipson 1992, 2002). Thus the choice of an exonormative native speaker model is seen as a consequence of linguistic imperialism rather than a genuinely 'free' choice. Others take a different view, arguing that consumers or learners of English have the power to make pragmatic choices about the type of English they want to learn (Conrad 1996, Davies 1999, Li 2002a). Thus the choice of an exonormative native-speaker model is seen as the rational consequence of a pragmatic decision.

In terms of conflicts of interests, publishers and international English language teaching institutions may have strong commercial reasons for promoting an exonormative native-speaker variety of English, and will lobby for its adoption. Generally speaking, publishers prefer the native-speaker model, as this means they can publish their ELT textbooks for a global market. International English language teaching institutions will push for a native-speaker model, as their materials and testing paraphernalia are based on native-speaker models, and they have ready access to native-speaker teachers. They will suggest that native-speaker teachers are somehow innately superior as language teachers, despite the many well-argued cases that show this to be a fallacy (cf. Rajagoplan 1997, Braine 1999, Canagarajah 1999).

Unfortunately the real consumers, the learners and the teachers, are seldom consulted about which model of English to learn and teach. In this chapter I want to describe the possible models of English that could be used in language teaching in Outer and Expanding Circle countries from the point of view of various stakeholders, and to consider the advantages and disadvantages of each. In my mind, there are three potential models. The first is an external native speaker variety; the second is a local nativized variety; and the third is a lingua franca model. I shall discuss each in turn.

## A native-speaker model

From the point of view of the ELT industry, the ELT publishing industry, educational bureaucrats and also politicians, this remains the most popular and sought-after model.

In addition to the reasons identified above, there are several other reasons for this. The first is that native-speaker models have been codified. There are grammars and dictionaries to which teachers and students alike can refer. There are norms against which the English of the learners can be evaluated and tested. There is a prestigious corpus of literature written in these varieties.

The second is that, through their codification, they are seen as standard varieties of English. This reassures politicians and bureaucrats who fear that, unless their people learn a standard English based on native-speaker norms, they will not be intelligible in the international community.

A third reason is that they represent power. This power works in more than one way, as those who argue for their adoption themselves represent extremely powerful interests, whether these be media, publishing and/or language teaching interests. The models that represent power are, by definition, those most powerfully represented in this debate.

The fourth reason is that, to a greater or lesser degree, they have historical authority. This, coupled with their codification, allows people to argue for their inherent superiority as models over more recently developed nativized varieties. These reasons all lead to a final reason, which is that the people who have to make decisions about which model to choose do not really have to think too hard about it. Choosing a native-speaker model is the easy or safe option.

If there are several powerful reasons for choosing a native-speaker model, does it then follow that there are advantages for the people on whose behalf the decision has been made, the learners and teachers? Well, it is obviously advantageous for those teachers who are themselves native speakers. They will be seen as providing the correct model, the source of the standard. It must be pointed out here, however, that these teachers represent a tiny minority of the total number of English teachers in Outer and Expanding Circle countries. The choice of a native-speaker model advantages a tiny fraction of the total number of teachers.

The adoption of a native-speaker standard will also be advantageous for those learners whose motivation for learning the language is to understand the mindset of native speakers of the language, and who wish to become familiar with the literary and cultural traditions associated with the particular standard. In other words, it is an advantageous model for those learners whose major aim is to converse with native speakers and to understand whichever native-speaking culture it is that they are interested in. Of course, there is nothing wrong with this. But again, it must be pointed out that these learners represent a small minority of the number of people learning English in Outer and Expanding Circle countries, the vast majority of whom are learning English in order to be able to communicate with fellow non-native speakers.

The adoption of a codified native-speaker standard, it is argued, also ensures international comprehensibility. Some have argued that the adoption of a nativized variety would result in the development not of different dialects of English, but of different mutually unintelligible languages of English (cf. Davies 1999). For example, Widdowson (1997) argues that Nigerian English is a different species of English rather than a different variety. I will dispute this view later, but the adoption of a native-speaker variety has obvious advantages for those who already speak a codified native-speaker standard. Its advantages for the great majority of learners and teachers in Outer and Expanding Circle countries are, however, not quite so obvious. First, it suggests that nativized varieties of English are likely to be less intelligible internationally than native-speaker varieties, and are thus inferior to native-speaker varieties as models. Yet this suggestion is based on a false premise. Nativized varieties have been shown to be more, not less, intelligible in international settings than native-speaker varieties (Smith and Rafiqzad 1983). Smith and Rafiqzad conclude, 'There seems to be no reason to insist that the performance target in the English classroom be a native speaker' (1983, 380). Further, learners whose first language is syllable-timed, such as Chinese, Malay and French, are likely to find speakers of stress-timed languages, such as British English, less intelligible than speakers of syllable-timed varieties 'on account of the massive reduction and neutralisation of unstressed syllables' (Hung 2002, 8). This suggests that teachers who are speakers of syllable-timed varieties will be more intelligible to learners whose first languages are also syllable-timed, than native-speaker teachers will be.

The third reason listed above for the adoption of a native-speaker standard is that these represent power. But what advantages does the imposing of this model as a standard for teachers and learners of English in Outer and Expanding Circle countries have, and for whom? Again, the advantages attach to those who already speak the variety in question. As a model for the great majority of learners and teachers, however, I would argue that it is actually disempowering. First, it is impossible for learners to sound as though they were native speakers of, say, American English, unless they actually go and live somewhere where that model is in constant use. For those who are learning English in their home countries, and this is the great majority, the native-speaker model on offer is one that is impossible to achieve. This is true even for people who have spent a significant part of their education in a native-speaking country. As one who advocates the learning of 'good' English, by which is meant a native-speaker variety, it may pain Lee Kuan Yew to know that he is instantly recognizable as a Singaporean as soon as he begins to speak English, despite several years reading Law in England.

While a native-speaker model is one that is impossible for learners who are learning outside native-speaker domains to attain, the problem is even worse for teachers of English. They are being required to teach a model that they themselves do not control. They will inevitably feel that their own variety is inferior to the superimposed model. To imagine how insecure all English teachers must feel who are told that a model of English which is not their own is to be the model, let's consider a group of native speakers who arrive in another native-speaking country and are told to teach the local endonormative variety. Imagine that a group of American English language teachers arrive at a university in Australia to teach on an intensive English programme for international students. They are told that they must teach Australian English. They are also told that any varietal differences from Australian Standard English in terms of phonology, lexis, syntax, discourse and pragmatics will be treated as errors. That is to say, when the students are assessed, any accent or usage they use that does not conform to Australian Standard English will be classified as incorrect. These American teachers would probably suddenly feel insecure in their own model. But this is precisely the position that those who insist on a native-speaker norm in Outer and Expanding Circle countries take. The insistence on a native-speaker norm diminishes local teachers of English and undermines their self-confidence and self-respect. At the same time, the very advantages that they can bring as teachers are disregarded. For example, their fluency in a local variety of English, far from being seen as a model worth emulating by the students, is presented as a questionable ability in an inferior version of a native-speaker model. And, as I shall argue below, the choice of one of the alternative models allows the local English teacher to become highly valued for many further reasons, rather than diminished.

The fourth reason that was identified above for the choice of a native-speaker model was that it provided historical authority. This reason is inextricably linked to codification, standard and power. Native-speaker varieties of English have been codified precisely because they have a history. But history does not lead to one standard. It brings with it variety. As Gorlach has pointed out, 'Old mother countries exhibit much greater regional diversity of speech than the colonial societies that developed from them' (1991, 15). And while it is true that varieties need a history before they are likely to be codified, it needs to be stressed that a language or variety does not need codification in order to establish its existence. This is a bit like demanding that people have a birth certificate before allowing that they are alive.

It is also important to acknowledge that if the history of a language tells us anything, it is that languages are subject to constant change, both diachronic and synchronic. Codification of a living language does not set a standard in stone. The only languages that can be effectively codified and standardized are those languages that no-one speaks any more. The argument that codification provides an everlasting set of linguistic criteria against which to judge the correctness or otherwise of language in use is, quite simply, simplistic.

The final reason for choosing a native-speaker variety is that it presents the choice of least thought for politicians and bureaucrats. Without wishing to appear overly cynical, the choice of least thought is always likely to be the choice of choice for the majority of such people. As applied linguists, we need to present arguments that make that choice more difficult. This chapter is one such attempt.

## A nativized model

The reasons for choosing a nativized model would be more readily articulated by the teachers and learners themselves than by the global ELT institutions, politicians and bureaucrats. As we have argued above, global ELT institutions or publishers would be likely to advise against the choice of a local nativized model of English for the classroom. A government that chose a more vernacular form of English would indeed create far-reaching consequences (Gorlach 1991). For a start, such a choice would be prejudicial against native-speaker models and all that they entail. Native speakers would no longer be the unquestioned authority: local teachers would be. Native-speaker norms would be treated as alternative varieties rather than standard norms. The local nativized variety would provide the standard norms. Texts based on a 'global' Standard English would no longer be the key texts: texts based on local cultures would be.

However, the fact remains that even governments that profess to a fear that the learning of English will, necessarily, lead to an adoption of Anglo-American values, remain convinced that it is a native-speaker model that should be taught in the classroom. Hence, countries such as Korea and the People's Republic of China routinely advertise for speakers of English who are 'native speakers'. Such teachers need no specialist training and need no knowledge of the local cultures or languages. As long as they speak 'native-speaker' English, it is enough.

We need them to provide compelling reasons if we are to persuade governments to choose a nativized model over a native-speaker model. In the context of an Outer Circle country, the reasons and the advantages are many. First, such a choice provides learners and teachers alike with a relevant and appropriate model. Instead of being considered speakers of sub-standard varieties, the teachers now become speakers of the target standard. The acceptance and promotion of a local nativized model also legitimizes other nativized models.

The choice of the local model empowers teachers in a variety of other ways. First, they become role models for the learners. Second, the linguistic background and resources that the local English teachers possess now become highly valued, rather than ignored or even decried. The process of learning the language that they are now teaching gives these teachers the important ability to empathize with the learners (Medgyes 1994). Being also able to speak the languages of their students, these teachers are able to use the linguistic resources of the classroom. Far from feeling guilty about this, they should feel proud of their multilingual prowess. It is really hard to see how a monolingual native speaker can, necessarily, provide a better model and be a better language teacher than a multilingual teacher who understands local cultural and educational norms. In a very real way, the choice of a nativized model over a native-speaker model is the choice of democracy over imperialism.

In contrast, for a country in the Expanding Circle, the advantages of choosing a nativized model are not so apparent. In such a case, the context and the purposes for which the learners need English are vital. Let us take the case of Indonesia as an example. Here I think it would be possible to argue that the model of choice could well be Singaporean or Malaysian rather than the obvious native-speaker model, given its geographical proximity, Australian. Why? First, Malay and Indonesian are virtually the same language so the linguistic characteristics of Malaysian English are likely to be replicated in Indonesian English. Second, there are many cultural similarities. Both are Muslim countries but with significant numbers of people from different ethnic backgrounds, religions and cultures. Despite the cultural diversity in both countries, the cultures share a number of norms that are linguistically realized, including terms of address, topic placement and request schemata. A third reason and advantage for Indonesia to adopt a regional nativized variety of English is a very practical one. Both Indonesia and Malaysia are members of the regional grouping ASEAN, so collaboration in ELT and teacher training would be easy to establish and relatively cheap to provide. Finally, and most importantly, the great majority of Indonesia's learners of English are learning English in order to communicate with fellow non-native speakers within ASEAN and the region, rather than with native speakers of English. In this context, a regional nativized variety of English that reflects and respects the cultures of the region would seem to be an appropriate choice (Kirkpatrick 2002a).

But the choice of a nativized model might not be welcome in all Expanding Circle countries. For a country like China, for example, the choice might be different. I suspect there would be great reluctance on the part of politicians and educational bureaucrats to choose a regional nativized variety of English. China's traditional and strongly held attachment to standards and correctness (Kirkpatrick and Xu 2002) would also suggest that, if it is to use an exonormative model, it will be a native-speaker model. Certainly, there is little doubt that the politicians and bureaucrats consider native-speaker models to be superior and that they are looking to native-speaker models, as China is constantly advertising for native speakers of English to act as teachers. Again, relevant training and multilingual and multicultural prowess is considered less important than being a native speaker.

A survey into attitudes of students towards varieties of English conducted at a university in Beijing (Kirkpatrick and Xu 2002) indicated that a slight majority of the students surveyed were keen to learn a native-speaker variety of English, and their clear preference was for American English over British English. However, the students also strongly rejected the assertion that 'only native speakers can speak standard English'. As China English develops, itself the subject of great topical debate, it may be that it will, in the future, offer an acceptable choice for Chinese students. For the time being, however, it would appear that American English is the variety of choice for the majority of all stakeholders in China.

What this discussion shows is that the choice of which variety to adopt as a model is dependent upon the context. The context must include the reasons why people are learning English, and the relative availability of an appropriate nativized model. Different contexts will suggest different models. But one problem common to both native and nativized models is that they come, to greatly varying degrees, with cultural baggage.

## A Lingua Franca model

The great majority of learners of English are learning English so that they can communicate with other non-native speakers of English. If this is in doubt, recent estimates of the numbers of people learning English in China alone vary from between 200 and 350 million (Bolton 2002, Kirkpatrick and Xu 2002). While native speakers will naturally be part of the group with whom these learners may need to communicate in the future, the majority will be fellow non-native speakers, whether they be Europeans, people from the Middle East, or Asians. We can state the same fact in a slightly different way. We can say that the major role of English today is as a lingua franca. This use is worldwide. English is used as a lingua franca in Europe. It is used as a lingua franca throughout India, Africa and Asia. Yet despite its essential role as a lingua franca, there have been surprisingly few attempts to try and describe, let alone codify, lingua franca English. This represents a great gap in current applied linguistic research (Seidlhofer 2001). For if we had detailed knowledge about the linguistic features of lingua franca English, this would be the sensible classroom model for those who are learning English to use it as a lingua franca. Until we have a description of lingua franca English, however, few stakeholders will have any reason to support it. The ELT institutions and publishing houses will argue, rightly, that it is difficult to teach and develop texts around a model that is virtually undescribed. Not surprisingly, politicians and educational bureaucrats will take the same view. Teachers and learners, while they may acknowledge the role of lingua franca English, will be hesitant about teaching and learning it until they know what 'it' is.

However, while research into lingua franca English is rare, it is not unknown. Jenkins has undertaken a study into the phonology of international English (2000). This is of particular pedagogic value, as it shows which sounds and aspects of pronunciation hinder mutual intelligibility, and which do not. This should be an enormous boon to learners and teachers alike. Now that Jenkins has shown that an inability to produce certain sounds, or to distinguish between others, is unlikely to hinder mutual intelligibility, classroom teachers can ignore them with a clear conscience and spend classroom time on more useful issues. Other current lingua franca English research includes James's (2000) study into the English lingua franca used in the Alpine-Adriatic region. Seidlhofer (2001) is compiling a corpus of English as a Lingua Franca at the University of Vienna. We need to complement these studies by starting to compile a corpus of lingua franca English in the Asian region, perhaps beginning with an investigation of the English used at ASEAN meetings, as English is the de facto lingua franca of ASEAN (Krasnick 1995).

The adoption of a lingua franca model for those who are learning English in order to use it as a lingua franca should be liberating for teachers and learners, in much the same way that the adoption of a nativized model is liberating, for several reasons. First, teachers are no longer faced with a native-speaker model that they themselves do not speak and which may, in any event, be culturally inappropriate. They will be freed from the self-conscious feeling that their own variety is being constantly and negatively evaluated against the externally imposed standard. Instead, with the adoption of a lingua franca model, the focus of the classroom becomes one of communication, rather than the acquisition of some idealized norm.

Second, the cultural content of the classes becomes significantly broadened. Instead of concentrating on the cultures associated with native-speaker models, students who are learning lingua franca English will be learning about the cultures of the people with whom they are most likely to use their English. For example, in the context of Indonesian learners, the curriculum can provide information about Australasian cultures, with a primary focus on the cultures of ASEAN (Kirkpatrick 2002). The language materials will be designed to allow learners to be able to learn about, compare and discuss each other's cultures.

A third reason why the adoption of a lingua franca model can be liberating for both teachers and learners is that it comes without any suggestion that it is somehow owned by someone else. Lingua franca English becomes the property of all, and it will be flexible enough to reflect the cultural norms of those who use it. In this it differs markedly from both native and nativized varieties of English, as native and nativized varieties must by definition reflect the cultural norms of their speakers. These can, of course, be markedly different. An excellent example of how these differences can interfere with their roles as lingua franca English is provided by Australian Aboriginal English. This has become an extremely successful marker of Aboriginal identity and is now the first language of most Australian Aboriginals (Harkins 2000). Its very success as a marker of Aboriginal identity, however, militates against its success as a vehicle of intercultural communication with non-Aboriginal Australians, as the cultural and pragmatic norms encoded in Australian Aboriginal English cause frequent misunderstandings in cross-cultural communication (Kirkpatrick 2002b). Thus a nativized variety that acts as a marker of identity and as a lingua franca among Aboriginal people does not work well as a lingua franca between Aboriginal people and other Australians.

It is important to stress, however, that I do not see a lingua franca model as being a single standard, devoid of cultural influences. In this respect, this concept of lingua franca English is quite different from the concepts of English as an International Language proposed by others, whether these be a simplified form of English (Quirk 1982) or a specific academic register (Widdowson 1997). I think it is inevitable and desirable that speakers will transfer some of the pragmatic norms of their L1 to lingua franca English. These might be reflected in address forms, for example where a speaker feels the need to provide some form of honorific if speaking to someone who, in their culture, would require such an honorific. Thus David Li's notion of 'pragmatic dissonance' (2002b) can be overcome in lingua franca English. He reported the discomfort he felt in addressing senior colleagues by their first names, when obeying the pragmatic rules of native-speaker English. In lingua franca English, Li would be quite able to address a senior colleague in a culturally appropriate way. By the same token, lingua franca English can free speakers from what they might feel to be the cultural straitjackets of their L1s. So Korean speakers can happily drop honorifics and respect conventions when conversing in lingua franca English, if they so desire. That is the point. When communication becomes the primary focus, users of lingua franca English become free from standard monolithic norms. And, as communication is the goal, the danger of mutually unintelligible lingua franca Englishes developing disappears. Lingua franca English is much more than an ESP and it is much more than a register. We can rephrase Bamgbose's call, 'Communication across world Englishes has to be seen in terms of accommodation between codes and in a multilingual context' (Bamgbose 2001, 359) as 'communication in lingua franca English has to be seen in terms of accommodation between codes and in a multilingual context'. Native-speaker and nativized models are not internationally applicable in a world increasingly characterized by migration, racial mixing and diversity.

## Conclusion

I argue, then, that a lingua franca model is the most sensible model in those common and varied contexts where the learners' major reason for English is to communicate with other non-native speakers. It also closely approximates, I believe, with Kachru's idea of a 'polymodel' approach to the teaching of English (1992b, 66), as it imposes neither rigid 'correct' norms, nor adherence to a single model. Nevertheless, until we are able to provide teachers and learners with adequate descriptions of lingua franca models, teachers and learners will have to continue to rely on either native-speaker or nativized models. We have seen how a native-speaker model, while appropriate for a minority of teachers and learners, is inappropriate for the majority for a range of linguistic, cultural and political reasons. A nativized model may be appropriate in Outer and in certain Expanding Circle countries, but this model also carries the disadvantage of cultural inappropriacy when learners require English as a lingua franca to communicate with other non-native speakers. It is time, then, for applied linguists to provide a description of lingua franca English, for by so doing they can liberate the millions upon millions of people currently teaching and learning English from inappropriate linguistic and cultural models.

## References

Bamgbose, A. 1997. 'Torn between the norms: innovations in World Englishes'. *World Englishes* 17/1, 1–14.

Bamgbose, A. 1998. 'World Englishes and globalization'. *World Englishes* 20/3, 357–64.

Bolton, K. 2000. 'The sociolinguistics of English in Hong Kong'. *World Englishes* 19/3, 265–85.

Bolton K. 2002. 'Chinese Englishes: from Canton jargon to global English'. *World Englishes* 21/2, 181–200.

Braine, G. (ed.) 1999. *Non-native Educators in English Language Teaching*. Mahwah, New Jersey: Lawrence Erlbaum.

Canagarajah, A. 1999. 'Interrogating the "Native Speaker Fallacy": non-linguistic roots, non-pedagogical results'. In Braine, G. (ed.), 77–92.

Conrad, A. 1996. 'The international role of English: the state of the discussion'. In Fishman, Conrad, and Rubal-Lopez (eds), 13–36.

Davies, A. 1999. 'Standard English: discordant voices'. *World Englishes* 18/2, 171–86.

Fishman, J., Conrad and Rubal-Lopez (eds). 1996. *Post-imperial English*. Berlin: Mouton de Gruyter.

Fishman, J. 1996. 'Introduction: some empirical and theoretical issues'. In Fishman, Conrad and Rubal Lopez (eds), 3–12.

Gorlach, M. 1991. 'English as a world language – state of the art'. In M. Gorlach (ed.), *Varieties of English Around the World*. Amsterdam: John Benjamins. 10–34.

Gorlach, M. 1997. 'Language and nation: the concept of linguistic identity in the history of English'. *English Worldwide* 18/1, 1–34.

Harkins, J. 2000. 'Structure and meaning in Australian Aboriginal English'. *Asian Englishes* 3/2, 60–81.

Hung, T. 2002. 'English as a global language: implications for teaching'. *The ACELT Journal* 6/2, 3–10.

Jenkins, J. 2000. *The Phonology of English as an International Language*. Oxford: Oxford University Press.

Kachru, B. 1992a. 'Teaching World Englishes'. In B. Kachru (ed.), *The Other Tongue: English Across Cultures*. Chicago: University of Illinois Press. 355–66.

Kachru, B. 1992b. 'Models for non-native Englishes'. In B. Kachru (ed.), *The Other Tongue: English Across Cultures*. Chicago: University of Illinois Press. 48–74.

Kachru, B. 1995. 'The speaking tree: a medium of plural canons'. In M. Tickoo, (ed.), *Language and Culture in Multilingual Societies*. Singapore: SEAMEO Regional Language Centre. 1–20.

Kirkpatrick, A. (ed.). 2002. *Englishes in Asia: Communication, Identity, Power and Education*. Melbourne: Language Australia.

Kirkpatrick, A. 2002a. 'ASEAN and Asian cultures and models: implications for the ELT curriculum and teacher selection'. In: A. Kirkpatrick (ed), 213–24.

Kirkpatrick, A. 2002b. 'Australian Aboriginal English as a lingua franca. Ateneo de Manila University, *The ACELT Journal* 6/1, 28–34.

Kirkpatrick, A. and Xu Zhichang. 2002. 'Chinese pragmatic norms and China English'. *World Englishes* 21/2, 268–80.

Krasnick, H. 1995. 'The role of linguaculture and intercultural communication in ASEAN in the year 2020: prospects and predictions'. In M. Tickoo (ed.), *Language and Culture in Multilingual Societies*. Singapore: SEAMEO Regional Language Centre. 81–93.

Li, C. S. 2002a. 'Hong Kong parents' preference for English-medium education: passive victim of imperialism or active agents of pragmatism?' In A. Kirkpatrick (ed.), 28–62.

Li C. S. 2002b. 'Pragmatic dissonance: the ecstasy and agony of speaking like a native speaker of English.' In David C. S. Li (ed.), *Discourses in Search of Members. In Honor of Ron Scollon*. Lanham, Maryland: University Press of America. 559–94.

Medgyes, P. 1994. *The Non-Native Teacher*. London: Macmillan.

Phillipson, R. 1992. *Linguistic Imperialism*. Oxford: Oxford University Press.

Phillipson, R. 2002. 'Global English and local language policies'. In A. Kirkpatrick (ed), 7–28.

Quirk, R. 1981. 'International communication and the concept of Nuclear English'. In L. Smith (ed.), 151–65.

Rajagopalan, K. 1997. 'Linguistics and the myth of nativity: comments on the controversy over "new/non-native Englishes".' *Journal of Pragmatics* 27, 225–31.

Seidlhofer, B. 1999. 'Double standards: teacher education in the Expanding Circle'. *World Englishes* 18/2, 233–45.

Seidlhofer, B. 2001. 'Closing a conceptual gap: the case for a description of English as a lingua franca'. *International Journal of Applied Linguistics* 11/2, 133–57.

Smith, L. (ed.). 1981. *English for Cross-cultural Communication*. London: MacMillan.

Smith, L. and K. Rafiqzad. 1983. 'English for cross-cultural communication – intelligibility'. *TESOL Quarterly* 13/3, 371–80.

Starks, D. and B. Paltridge. 1996. 'A note on using sociolinguistic methods to study non-native attitudes towards English'. *World Englishes* 15/2, 217–24.

Widdowson, H. 1997. 'EIL, ESL, EFL. Global issues and local interests'. *World Englishes* 16/1, 135–46.

# World Englishes or English as a Lingua Franca? A view from the Perspective of Non-Anglo Englishes

*Peter K. W. Tan, Vincent B. Y. Ooi and Andy K. L. Chiang*
National University of Singapore

## Introduction

Much of the discussion about English as a Lingua Franca (ELF) has focused on the situation in the Expanding Circle (in Kachruvian terms, such as in Kachru and Nelson (1996)). In this paper, we wish to explore the issue of the choice between World Englishes (WE) and ELF from the point of view of what we will call the non-Anglo Englishes, using Singaporean English as the main exemplar of this perspective. We have been using the label *non-Anglo Englishes* (as opposed to alternatives like Outer Circle varieties, New Englishes, ESL varieties) because our own approach has been to emphasize them as cultural items (see, for example, Wong (2003) who uses the same label). We do not, of course, wish to set up a false dichotomy: proponents of ELF (for example, Seidlhofer and Kirkpatrick in this volume) stress that ELF should not be seen as a single, homogeneous entity that is totally devoid of cultural underpinnings. However, given the functions that ELF that is supposed to fulfil – intelligible communication between parties for whom English is not a first language, perhaps in a business context – cultural elements must presumably be played down. The distinction, then, is not between the presence or absence of cultural underpinnings, but whether these need to be taken on board fully or played down.

Ministries of Education have had to contend with the issue of the variety of English that is to serve as the model in schools; the tension inherent in this in postcolonial states has traditionally been seen in the choice between a standard Anglo English (principally Standard British English or Standard American English), or a Standard non-Anglo English (Indian English, Nigerian English etc.). McKay, in a volume over ten years ago entitled *Teaching English Overseas*, focused on how the non-Anglo English is useful because this is the variety learners will encounter, the variety that the teachers will feel confident to teach and the variety that learners will identify with (McKay 1992, 92–3). Diagrammatically, this could be represented as in Figure 1.

**Figure 1. Centripetal forces at work**

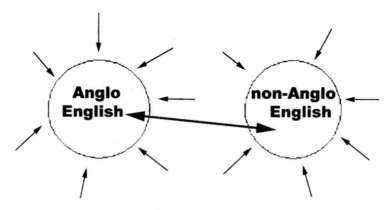

We are not denying that all the Englishes have things in common; we have chosen to represent the circles as non-overlapping, as a kind of strategic simplification. (For the overlapping representation, see Modiano 1999, 10.) The finer arrows indicate the ability of various Englishes to exert centripetal forces: they become focal points or models. Leitner (1992) suggests that there are various 'epicentres', so that English is now a 'pluricentric' language. We have, nonetheless, included a bold arrow to indicate the attraction that Anglo Englishes continue to exert in non-Anglo English contexts, an attraction that linguists like Kachru have tried hard to minimize. The challenge by ELF is relatively new, so that McKay's book ten years later is entitled *Teaching English as an International Language*. The title change itself is noteworthy: English as a language spoken *overseas*, as opposed to English as an *international* language, is symptomatic of the attitude change.

## EFL and the Lingua Franca

We could do worse than take a leaf from McArthur's (2004) article, where he deliberated over the terminology: *world English*, *global English* and *international English*. We find the label *lingua franca* interesting in itself, and some discussion of the original Lingua Franca is salutary and instructive. We do not know many of the details of the original Lingua Franca (see Corré 1992, 2003, Hall 1966, Holm 2000, Kahane et al. 1988), but based on what we do know of language in general we can make intelligent guesses to close up the gaps. What we do know is that Lingua Franca (which is Italian for 'Frankish (i.e. European) tongue') was used in Levant (the southern and eastern Mediterranean) and was a mixed language with vocabulary from Italian and other Romance languages as well as Arabic, but lacked their inflections. It was seen as a common language (or koiné) and, as a pidgin, no-one's language. Our use of the term *lingua franca* (without capitals) is thus an analogical or figurative extension of the sense of the original term (Stockwell and Minkova 2001, 152). In what ways, then, is English, specifically ELF, like the Lingua Franca, and in what ways not?

Firstly, proponents of ELF do not envisage an ELF that is a pidgin with inflections of standard Anglo Englishes reduced, although most treatments of the history of English agree that it underwent inflection levelling and reduction in the transition from Old English (or Anglo-Saxon) to Middle English around the year 1100. In contrast, some informal varieties of non-Anglo Englishes and, it must be stressed, Anglo Englishes have reduced inflections. For example, the traditional variety of English in East Anglia has only one form in the present tense: *I love, you love, she/he/it love, we love, they love* (Cheshire and Milroy 1993, 16).

Secondly, proponents of ELF, in focusing communication in situations where English is a foreign language (e.g. a Japanese speaker communicating in English with a German speaker) emphasize the fact that English is no-one's language, as is true of the Lingua Franca. On the other hand, this is decidedly not true in Anglo and non-Anglo English contexts.

Thirdly, it would be fair to imagine that the Lingua Franca, being no-one's language, not being subject to the forces of standardization, being influenced by a range of native languages, and being spoken over a large area, would exhibit features of variation. Variety and variation are true of most living human languages, including English, although the forces of standardization are much more palpable through, among other things, the agency of education institutions. The proposed ELF also allows for some variation, although there is an attempt to rein in the differences through the proposal of various 'core' features (see Jenkins, this volume).

It seems important for us therefore to stress that the English used for inter-cultural communication, though sharing many features of a naturally developed contact language like the Lingua Franca, will have important differences. These centre around the reasons for standardization and prescriptivism. Part of the reason for the continued preoccupation with these issues is to do with the legacy of eighteenth-century insecurity due to the loss of Latin as the 'common currency', so that European languages had to have this common currency of a prescribed, standard variety.

The whole notion of standardization is bound up with the aim of functional efficiency of the language. Ultimately, the desideratum is that everyone should use and understand the language in the same way with the minimum of misunderstanding and the maximum of efficiency (Milroy and Milroy 1999, 19).

With no nation taking a proprietary interest in the original Lingua Franca, it is doubtful that uniformity (and therefore standardization) would have been an issue of concern. The present interest in ELF probably represents a desire to rein in differences for the reason of mutual intelligibility but also, we suspect, the need to project the correct image. Again, this should not surprise us: the choice of a standard has always been closely associated with a dominant variety which would have the right 'associations' and therefore the right 'image'. In the case of English,

> [t]he origins of a dominant variety ... lie with the merchant class based in London. The dialect they spoke was the East Midland one. ... The lower class spoke another dialect, a south-eastern one, the antecedent of Cockney. ... It is important to stress this linguistic stratification in London, since the subsequent history of standardi-sation has much to do with its relationship to the speech of the Londoner in the street. (Leith 1997, 39)

It seems to us that ELF can also be seen as a manifestation of a change which is socially acceptable in the English-speaking world. Old-world values are pushed aside for newer ones with the right associations. Although the change itself is encouraging, it seems that what we are seeing is a moving of the goalposts, so that there is much that would still be considered not to have the right image.

In the next part of the paper, we want to discuss why the ELF enterprise in the context of non-Anglo Englishes might not solve the difficulties that we have, and might be a move in the wrong direction. We will, through this, give a tacit invitation to reconsider the position of ELF. Perhaps there is merit in making English *more* like the original Lingua Franca, which was unconstrained and unpoliced.

## ELF and the non-Anglo Englishes

When a new centre begins exerting a force, the other forces do not automatically recede. In fact, it is unlikely that so-called native speakers will give up the fight, and we think Wright's view is representative:

> At the moment, there are demands for a standardized international variety precisely so that it can be taught (McArthur 2002, 416). All native speakers in any position to do so should try to oppose such schemes (Wright 2004, 80).

It seems to us, therefore, that with the ELF enterprise, there will be an additional centripetal force thrown into the picture, as in Figure 2.

**Figure 2. Additional centripetal forces at work**

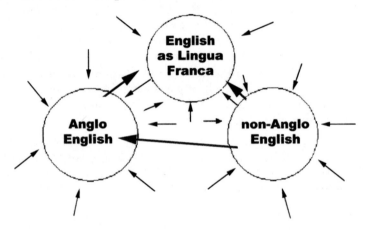

We use the fine and heavy arrows in the same way as in Figure 1. In Modiano's (1999) representation, what he calls EIL (English as an International Language, our ELF) is the central core of the various Englishes; similarly, Jenkins (this volume) talks about the Lingua Franca Core (LFC) in relation to phonology. There are two ways of interpreting the assertion of the core status of ELF. One is to see ELF as a distillation of features of Anglo Englishes. (Modiano discusses mainly British and American English; and the LFC phonological features are those found in the Received Pronunciation (RP) and General American (GA) accents.) If this is the case, ELF simply amounts to slipping in Anglo-English norms under a different label. On the other hand, we can also see how ELF might diverge from some specific Anglo-English norms: for example Jenkins' Lingua Franca Core no. 4 ('Vowel length distinctions') are violated by many Scottish speakers (e.g. no distinction between *cot* and *caught*; *pull* and *pool*). Similarly, Modiano asserts that particular British grammatical structures and items (such as *to sit* for an exam) or American vocabulary items (such as *condominium*) should be replaced within EIL. If this is the case, ELF norms are different from Anglo-English norms, and this is what is represented in Figure 2.

If ELF norms were promoted in schools, pupils in non-Anglo-English contexts would continue to encounter non-Anglo-English norms (for example in the local media) and Anglo-English norms (for example in film, television, literature and the international media). This is certainly true in the Singapore context where there is good exposure to various English varieties. If particular ELF norms were promoted, pupils would need to consciously employ a variety different from all the *real* encounters with English available to them outside the classroom. A Singaporean pupil will encounter Singaporean English in interactions with his or her friends. He or she will also encounter American, British, etc. English in films, on the Internet, in fiction (including literary texts in schools) and on television, but would need to adhere to ELF norms in the English classroom. We cannot see how throwing in another norm, which will complicate the picture, can be a good thing.

The general assumption made is that the promotion of ELF will make for a higher degree of intelligibility between different communities using English. We are going to throw a spanner in the works and suggest that there has been too much focus on the code itself as the element that makes for intelligibility. This is Bamgabose's position as well:

> ... we know that intelligibility is a complex matter, that a native speaker is not necessarily the infallible judge of what is intelligible. ... In a communicative act which involves a speaker and an addressee, both participants contribute to the speech act and its interpretation, and part of this contribution is making an allowance for the accent and peculiarities of the other person's speech.
>
> Preoccupation with intelligibility has often taken an abstract form characterized by decontextualized comparison of varieties. The point is often missed that it is people, not language codes, that understand one another, and people use the varieties they speak for specific functions. (Bamgabose 1998, 11)

In other words, we need to put people into the picture, and it is the desire to converge and to understand that is frequently the more important ingredient in intelligibility. In this light, therefore, I question the need to agree on a standardized ELF norm. If, through teaching ELF norms, learners expect other speakers to speak like them and that they need not make allowances or put effort into cross-cultural communication, we will have done them a great disservice.

Understanding and effort might, at the end of the day, be more important than interlocutors using the same terms or employing the same structures.

In fact there is a lot that indicates that speakers are willing to manipulate the code, to tweak it to fit different contexts and sensibilities; and where these are not developed, it is these skills that need focusing on. In our own research on non-Anglo Englishes in South East Asia, we have noticed features of flexibility, creativity and manoeuvrability in these varieties. Our own corpus on computer-mediated communication[1] included data from personal advertisements and Internet chat, among other things. We can concentrate on just one item to illustrate this point: the pragmatic particle *lah*, described as 'the hallmark of Singapore English' (Besemeres and Wierzbicka 2003). We would therefore expect it to be a significant item in Singaporean English. And indeed, in the sub-corpus of Internet chat on Singaporean channels, the frequency of *lah* (in its various orthographic forms) was 0.17%, and ranked 41 in the list of the most common words (Tan et al. forthcoming). In stark contrast to this, the personal advertisement section of our corpus contained only two occurrences or 0.2 per 10,000 words (Tan et al. 2004). The earlier figure for Internet chat translates to 17 per 10,000 words.

There are several ways of interpreting this discrepancy. Perhaps the authors of the personal advertisements represent a different section of the population from the Internet chat participants. It is generally acknowledged that the average age of chatroom participants is low, perhaps in the late teens, whereas personal advertisement authors could be in their 20s and 30s or even older. Nonetheless, it seems unlikely that age alone is the deciding factor. We examined spoken texts from the spoken section of the International Corpus of English, Singapore (ICE-SIN) and found that *lah* was a high-frequency item at 77.2 per 10,000 words (Tan et al. 2004, 160) – more so than the Internet chat data. What is more likely is that language users were sensitive to the context – the personal advertisements could have a wider audience, whereas chat is usually limited to the participants in the chatroom. Our preferred interpretation is that the users were showing flexibility and sensitivity, signalling different degrees of formality and spokenness (*lah* is associated with informal, spoken language) and Singaporeanness (see the Besemeres and Wierzbicka quotation above).

We also see evidence of willingness to be creative or ludic: the use of *lah* is overwhelmingly associated with the speech acts of statement or request, but we see an instance of the playful, creative use of *lah* (spelt 'la' here) with greetings:

[01:23] <aNt0sAuR> hi la
[01:24] <patchy> & # 03;12choosy& # 03;11?& # 03;10¿& # 03;1200
[01:24] *** rice_bubbles has joined # singapore
[01:24] <aNt0sAuR> choosy?
[01:24] <aNt0sAuR> no la
[01:24] <aNt0sAuR> hi rice la bubbles la
[01:24] *** red has joined # singapore
[01:24] *** Bum-Kiss has joined # singapore
[01:24] <aNt0sAuR> hi red la
(Emphases ours)

The extract seems saturated with *lahs* and the two chatters are consciously over-using it in a playful manner.

Rajadurai (2004), in discussing Malaysian English, also notes the collaboration of variation and accommodation. All this seems to suggest the presence of flexibility, creativity and manoeuvrability in the non-Anglo Englishes as well as the Anglo Englishes (see, for example, Carter 2004). If this is the case, we already see the raw ingredients that make for good cross-cultural communication. The resources are already there, waiting to be tapped. What we need to do is to capitalize on this sensitivity and creativity and develop this further.

The ELF enterprise seems to go against this kind of flexibility and instead to limit choice, and it is our fear that it will discourage the kinds of things we feel should be developed further.

Another issue that we have with the ELF enterprise is the tacit discouragement of any community from identifying with it, whereas we view languages as cultural items, among other things, particularly in non-Anglo-English contexts. Work within Labovian sociolinguistics has established how particular linguistic features, and therefore language varieties, have strong associations. This suggests that it will be difficult to examine language dispassionately and expect the population to fall in line with whatever recommendations have been made. For example, Jenkins' LFC model suggests that rhotic speech should be preferred in English. We know that extensive work has been done on this variable of rhoticity, and that there are strong associations throughout the English-speaking world, the non-Anglo Englishes included. We also know that the issue of accents is resurrected in the local press in Singapore every few years or so, so that a push for an 'ideal' pronunciation style without regard for their associations would run into difficulties. Here, for example, is the beginning of a letter to the press to illustrate the point.

It seems that Singaporeans are obsessed with the way English is spoken on television, for yet another article has been published

> blaming TCS [Television Corporation of Singapore] for its varied use of accents.
>
> Sumiko Tan's article was entertaining but it resurrected an issue which has a long, tiring history of debate. (Chua 1998, 5)

Our contention, then, is that identity issues are relevant for non-Anglo Englishes, and teaching programmes need to take these into account.

Wright (2004) uses the analogy of Latin: whilst a highly standardized classical Latin was being promoted in Medieval Europe, 'native speakers' of Latin (called various things – French, Spanish, Italian and so on) got on with life. The highly standardized variety was an artificial construct, did not belong to anybody and was eventually abandoned by many. Should English choose the Latin model? We could also compare ELF with invented languages like Esperanto, which might have small coteries of dedicated enthusiasts but definitely fall short of the initial aim to be global languages. Imposing ELF norms means that the variety will no longer belong to anybody; and if nobody claims ownership of it, it might be similarly abandoned.

## Conclusion

We acknowledge the position of the English language as a lingua franca, but when we are involved with teaching English as a lingua franca, should we be focusing on *teaching*, or on *English*, or on *lingua franca*? A lot of the discussion suggests that it is the form of English that we should come to grips with. Perhaps there has been too much navel-gazing. In any case, the phenomenon of language change and language manipulation is always with us. We are not in a position to anticipate everything; we cannot stop language from changing so that even if the forms have been agreed upon, they will need constant and regular updating. Perhaps it is not the language forms that we need to be highly concerned about. Perhaps we should focus on the issues of *teaching* and how it is that a *lingua franca* operates. Sensitivity and creativity are necessary skills in the brave new world. Instead of being concerned about teaching the right code, we could then devote attention to coping skills in cross-cultural contexts.

Our own position is that it would not be a bad thing to make English, in some respects, more like the *original* Lingua Franca, where variation existed and where speakers were less concerned about standards. They got on with things, and by all accounts different cultural groups managed to get by and communicate with each other. They didn't worry about standardized varieties. The current proposals give rise to difficulties in throwing in an additional set of norms; in being too confident of the efficacy of a standardized code to solve intelligibility problems; in being too sceptical of the adaptability of speakers; and in being insufficiently sensitive to the associations of particular linguistic norms.

## Endnote

1. We are grateful for the support of the National University of Singapore, research project ref. no. R–103–000–019–112.

## References

Besemeres, M. and A. Wierzbicka. 2003. 'Pragmatics and cognition: the meaning of the particle "lah" in Singapore English'. *Pragmatics and cognition* 11/1, 1–36.

Carter, R. 2004. *Language and Creativity: the Art of Common Talk*. London: Routledge.

Cheshire, J. and J. Milroy. 1993. 'Syntactic variation in non-standard dialects: background issues.' In James Milroy and Lesley Milroy (eds), *Real English: the Grammar of English Dialects in the British Isles*. London: Longman. 3–33.

Chua, C. 1998. 'S'pore accents: why the fuss?'. *The Straits Times* (Singapore), 3 July, 5.

Corré, A. 1992. 'Lecture on the lingua franca'. In A. Harrak (ed.), *Contacts Between Cultures: West Asia and North Africa. Volume 1*. New York: Lewiston. 140–45.

Corré, A. 2003. *A Glossary of Lingua Franca*, 4th edn. Available online: *http://www.uwm.edu/~corre/franca/go.html*

Hall, R. 1966. *Pidgin and Creole Languages*. Ithaca: Cornell University Press.

Holm, J. 2000. *An Introduction to Pidgins and Creoles*. Cambridge: Cambridge University Press.

Kachru, B. and C. Nelson. 1996. 'World Englishes'. In Sandra Lee McKay and Nancy H. Hornberger (eds), *Sociolinguistics and Language Teaching*. Cambridge: Cambridge University Press. 71–102.

Kahane, H. R. and A. Tietze. 1988. *The Lingua Franca in the Levant: Turkish Nautical Terms of Italian and Greek Origin*. Istanbul: ABC Kitabevi A.S. (Originally published by the University of Illinois Press in Urbana, 1958.)

Leith, D. 1997. *A Social History of English*. 2nd edn. London: Routledge.

Leitner, G. 1992. 'English as a pluricentric language.' In Michael Clyne (ed.), *Pluricentric Languages*. Berlin: Mouton-de Gruyter. 178–237.

Low, E. and A. Brown. 2005. *English in Singapore: an Introduction*. Singapore: McGraw Hill.

McArthur, T. 2002. *The Oxford Guide to World English*. Oxford: Oxford University Press.

McArthur, T. 2004. 'Is it *world* or *international* or *global* English, and does it matter?'. *English Today* 79 (20/3), 3–15.

McKay, S. L. 1992. *Teaching English Overseas: an Introduction*. Oxford: Oxford University Press.

McKay, S. L. 2002. *Teaching English as an International Language: Rethinking Goals and Approaches*. Oxford: Oxford University Press.

Milroy, J. and L. Milroy. 1999. *Authority in Language: Investigating Standard English*. 3rd edn. London: Routledge.

Modiano, M. 1999. 'Standard English(es) and educational practices for the world's lingua franca'. *English Today* 60 (15/4), 3–13.

Rajadurai, J. 2004. 'The faces and facets of English in Malaysia', *English Today* 80 (20/4), 54–8.

Stockwell, R. and D. Minkova. 2001. *English Words: History and Structure*. Cambridge: Cambridge University Press.

Tan, P., V. Ooi and A. Chiang. 2004. 'Signalling spokenness in personal ads on the web: The case of ESL countries in South East Asia'. In K. Aijmer and B. Altenberg (eds), *Advances in Corpus Linguistics: Papers from the 23rd International Conference on English Language Research on Computerised Corpora (ICAME 23) Göteborg 22–26 May 2002*. Amsterdam: Rodopi. 151–67.

Tan, P., V. Ooi and A. Chiang. Forthcoming. In Masanori Toyota and Judy Noguchi (eds), *Speech, Writing and Context: Interdisciplinary Perspectives*. Osaka: Intercultural Research Institute, Kansai Gaidai University.

Wright, R. 2004. 'Latin and English as world languages', *English Today* 80 (20/4), 3–13.

Wong, J. 2003. 'The particles of Singapore English: a semantic and cultural interpretation'. *Journal of Pragmatics* 36, 739–93.

# Standard English in the World

*Anthea Fraser Gupta*
*School of English, University of Leeds*

## Models for English

The majority of 'Outer Circle' (Kachru 1985, 1992) speakers of English speak English as a second language: that is, they have not grown up speaking English from infancy, and they use it with people from their own country. In Outer Circle countries, there are also substantial numbers of native speakers of English, people who have learnt English from infancy. The English of the native speakers in these locations is indistinguishable from the English of highly proficient non-native speakers, and the variety of English of both is influenced by the fact of English being, or having been, a non-native language for the over-whelming majority of those who speak it. English is used in a range of domains within these countries, and by substantial numbers of citizens.

In the Inner Circle countries, enough of the population is descended from people of British Isles ancestry to ensure a variety of English that is linked to the unbroken normal transmission of English (Thomason and Kaufman 1988) down the generations, and the majority of the population are native speakers of English. The Inner Circle countries have absorbed substantial numbers of people of non-British Isles ancestry who bring in new words and cultural practices, but whose presence has little effect on the general pattern of English.

Over the course of the 1970s and 1980s it became accepted, first in academic circles, and then in wider society and government, that the Inner and Outer Circle settings are functionally and attitudinally similar. English belongs to its speakers in the Outer Circle, just as much as to its speakers in the Inner Circle, and all of them need to express their own culture through an English adapted to their needs, and expressive of their geographical, national, and cultural identity.

Having spent most of my adult life in Asia, and having been involved in these issues in the Outer Circle, I was surprised to find, on my return to Europe in 1996, that the insights from the Outer Circle had not been fed into the Expanding Circle, despite their having been raised by Kachru (1985) over ten years earlier. In the Expanding Circle

English is predominantly a non-native language, used in very restricted domains (typically with foreigners), and learnt in scholastic settings. The teaching of English in mainland Europe is dominated by a monolithic model, usually based on Standard British English and RP, which may involve favouring 'native speaker' teachers, requiring teachers to adhere to an out-of-date and highly abstracted sense of what is correct, and penalizing students for failing to use the 'correct' accent, typically the Daniel Jones variant of RP which is nowadays little heard. This is my fourth paper making some effort to move the teaching of English as a foreign language into the real world (Gupta 1999, 2001a, 2001b).

The work of those connected with the term 'English as a Lingua Franca' (ELF) (House 1999, Seidlhofer and Jenkins 2003, Jenkins 2000, Seidlhofer and Jenkins 2003) represents a considerable effort to inject a sense of English as a World Language into EFL teaching. The thinking of the ELF group is most developed at the moment in phonology. Jenkins (2000, 2) seems to accept Quirk's notion of a 'common core' as analogous for grammar and lexis. Quirk's common core, as they make clear, (Quirk et al. 1972, 29) did not amount to a full, teachable variety, because sometimes there is no core. For example, there is no single international word for a fast road (*motorway, highway, expressway,* etc.) or for the past participle of *get* (*got* or *gotten*).

A 'core' is a way of imagining variation in English visually, a metaphor that might help us or might mislead. Many of the models of World English are strongly geographical. For example, Peter Strevens's much reproduced diagram (e.g. Crystal 1997, 62) creates a family tree for geographical varieties which is not entirely justifiable historically or linguistically. McArthur's concentric model makes more sense to me (McArthur 1998, 97). Its less localized standard centre works rather better than its more localized non-standard periphery: there seems to be no historical or linguistic reason to explain why Canadian English is between American and Caribbean English. It is on this centre that I would like to concentrate. Something that is being neglected in much of the World Englishes discussion at the moment is the concept of Standard English.

## A fuzzy standard

Standard English is notoriously hard to define (Trudgill 1999). The concept of Standard English is very weak indeed in speech. There are standard pronunciations of words: for example, starting *chaos, chutzpah* and *church* with the same sound would be regarded as incorrect. But there is no standard accent. If speakers ask for the correct pronunciation of an unfamiliar word they map the answer onto their own accent. In all English-using places there are high-prestige and low-prestige accents: accents have high or low prestige because hearers associate their speakers with particular social groups which have high or low prestige. These systems of prestige do not operate at international level. Speakers seldom know the prestige systems of countries other than their own (I have been told by Americans that I speak just like the Queen, something no British person would think!). Even within the Inner Circle, one cannot compare the prestige of accents from one country with those of accents from another: it would be ridiculous, for example, to suggest that Canada is more or less prestigious than New Zealand. Nor are all Inner Circle accents more prestigious than all Outer Circle accents: a high-prestige speaker of (for example) Indian English is likely to have higher prestige all over the world than a speaker of an Inner Circle accent that is associated with low prestige and low levels of education.

All of us find it easier to understand familiar accents than unfamiliar ones. This gives rise to problems of intelligibility or comprehension between people from different places. The more localized the accent, the more likely it is to present problems to hearers from elsewhere. These are problems in Inner Circle varieties as well as in the other two circles. The huge range of accent variation means that there is some tolerance in face-to-face interaction, where interlocutors with goodwill are prepared to exercise patience and work at comprehension. In oral mass media, decisions are made about the kinds of accents that will be intelligible to a sufficiently wide audience. This is reflected in the selection of reporters to fit imagined audiences, and in decisions about the use of dubbing or subtitles.

In writing there is a much stronger sense of Standard English, and much less diversity. I take Standard English as a written performative: it is something writers are supposed to produce in certain contexts, and on which they will accept the possibility of correction, by spell-checks, dictionaries and editors. I will be offended if you correct the way I pronounce the vowel of *dance* (/dans/), but I will be grateful (and possibly embarrassed) if you correct my spelling of *concensus* to *consensus*.

Part of the reason for the difficulty of definition is that Standard English is established not by government bodies or academies, but by a loose consensus of writers. There is no central control of Standard English at either national or international levels. This has long been a part of the linguistic culture of English (Schiffman 1996), and it is something scholars, teachers, and (quite early in the day) learners have to realize.

There is no mechanism for regulated change in English. Change comes about by mechanisms we do not fully understand. New words are not seen as an issue in English: a word can go from dialectal to standard usage in the space of months or even weeks. For example *bling* swept the world in 2002, first appearing as *bling bling*. New ideas for food and drink are especially likely to bring words into English (e.g. *macchiato*). But when it comes to spelling, English is very conservative indeed. We have a spelling system based on fourteenth-century English, which was crystallized in its present form before 1700, and we have no mechanism whatever for reform. It is almost impossible for the spelling of a word to change: the handful of variants we now have (e.g. *colo(u)r, hiccup/ough, dwarfs/ves*) were the variants that survived to the early nineteenth century. We do have some conventional non-standard spellings which we use in informal writing of certain types (e.g. *nite, l8, thru*), but we use these knowing them to be restricted.

So spelling follows a strict standard: there are correct and incorrect spellings, though a few words have more than one correct spelling. On the other hand, lexis is a free-for-all: new words are cheerfully welcomed. Grammar is more difficult to grasp than either orthography or lexis: there is a great deal of choice in grammar, and all too often, there is no way of finding out whether something is standard or not.

## Who writes Standard English?

Overview volumes of World English are prone, like Gramley (2001), to represent Inner Circle varieties by their standard manifestations, while Outer Circle Englishes are represented by some of their more extremely non-standard manifestations. Canagarajah (this volume) says that 'all communities equally despise their local varieties in deference to "native" or "standard" varieties (which attitude shows the power of internalized colonial values)'. In fact, in both Inner and Outer Circles, Standard English (with minor variation) is expected and is used in the same kinds of domains, and in both Inner and Outer Circles there are non-standard varieties in other domains or used by some speakers, against which there are many hard words. Standard English is typically seen as 'correct' and 'grammatical', while non-standard dialects are seen as 'wrong' and 'ungrammatical', regardless of whether the speaker or the speaker's ancestors spoke English as a native language. Disapproval of non-standard varieties is not the prerogative of the formerly colonized. The reason that Singapore has had a *Speak*

*Good English Movement* and India does not is that Singapore has a highly informal contact variety, usually known as Singlish, which has no real parallel in India. Standard English is not the property or prerogative of only the Inner Circle Countries, but of the whole English-using world.

Canagarajah (this volume) wonders how 'we distinguish between speakers with different levels/types of competence (without invoking notions of birth, nationality, or ethnicity and without imposing non-linguistic forms of inequality)'. In practice, skill in Standard English, or lack of it, is the linguistic form of inequality that really matters. And we cannot predict that skill from birth, nationality, ethnicity or native-speakerdom. Users of written English are judged by their skill in Standard English. Skill in Standard English is certainly not linked to native-speakerdom. To put it starkly: without any further information to help your decision, who would you prefer to edit your writing: a non-native speaker of English who is a Professor of English at an Indian (or a Belgian) university, or a monolingual Brit who left school with no qualifications at the age of 15?

There is so much choice within Standard English that the variation from one country to another seems minor. Many years ago, in my first paper on World Englishes (Shields 1977) I discussed the widespread identification of words as local which are in what I then called 'General English'. The practice of comparing real, attested data from an Outer (or Expanded) Circle country with abstracted, theoretical 'native-speaker' English is still all too common. We can only know what Standard English is by careful verification of usage. Luckily this has become much easier since the 1990s when Internet search engines first made it possible to use the web to see what (relatively high-prestige) people all over the world were actually writing.

## Standard English on the Web

The Web carries texts of all types. There is a full range of genres, including genres which allow for playful language, and the incorporation of a range of identity codes, something I explored in another paper (Gupta forthcoming). There are websites that include the representation of non-standard dialects, and there is also 'leet speak', an extreme respelling of English sometimes used in blogs. This kind of insertion of non-standard English is intentional, usually small-scale, and often flagged. For example, a search using Google threw up thousands of sites with the following, clearly non-standard, strings:

*She look good.*

*I done it.*

*I don't have no...*

The contexts of these usages included quotations from songs, and expressions of identity (typically urban, black and cool in these examples). Most were embedded in Standard English texts. There are many non-standard varieties used in this iconic way in a number of different genres. But the English of the Web, like all written English, is predominantly standard in intent.

Because there are texts written by many kinds of people, English which is standard in intent may include features that would be corrected by an editor, and which could be regarded as incorrect in Standard English. But editors don't all agree, and we often cannot say whether an attested example is to be defined as Standard or non-Standard. This is where we need to tease out patterns of usage, to establish whether there is a geographical pattern. What we see is that many areas of fuzziness are international, while some features show complex geographical patterns.

We do not yet have established methods of sampling the Web; I have established methodologies that involve using Google to search for target strings. Searches will generate a crude frequency figure that is of some interest, and the careful choice of string, combined with domain specification, can give more information. But to understand the complex patterns we need to go beyond the number of hits and read the websites. The writer of a website is not necessarily from or even in the country hosting the website, partly because people move around the world, but also because websites can be created in remote locations. Reading the website and tracking its authorship through the hierarchy of the site tells us more about the authorship, and also supplies the linguistic and cultural context of the string. In this paper, I have explored in more detail the first 50 urls generated by every string search, and can therefore give more detailed information about them, which hopefully will be representative of the other sites. It is not always easy, or even possible, to establish the geographical origin of a writer, and the most likely error is that I have placed a writer in the country of residence who, unknown to me, originated in some other country. But I am fairly confident that most identifications are secure (those who come from Elven kingdoms, here, and in all tables, are classed as of unknown origin!). Web searches were made in August 2004, except where otherwise indicated.

In assessing all the figures we need to remember discrepancies in population size and in Internet penetration. For example: the USA has a large population and is over-represented on the Web; Nigeria has a large population but is under-represented on the Web; the UK and Singapore are also over-represented on the Web, but have smaller (in the case of Singapore, very small) populations than the USA and Nigeria.

## Orthography

Spelling in English is strict, but all English users know that it is difficult to be 100 per cent correct, and we even know what errors are likely. A strict standard, a willingness to accept correction, and the expectation that people will make errors, go side by side. The sort of mistakes almost everyone makes (e.g. *adress, comittee, -ant/ent, er/or, seperate*) are certainly seen as mistakes that ought to be corrected, but they do not impede intelligibility and are known to be likely in unedited work from most writers. We use a variety of techniques to eliminate them from edited text, where they would be seen as a sign of lack of care.

Even on the Web, which has a mixture of edited and unedited texts, standard spellings dominate. 'Leet speak' is an extreme and deliberate respelling, similar to that used in SMS messaging, and gets a lot of publicity. But leet speak is actually relatively rare on the Web, compared to standard spellings. For example, Google threw up only approximately 75,500 uses of *l8r*, compared with 57,700,000 uses of *later* (a ratio of 1:764). It is also instructive (and perhaps reassuring) to search for common spelling variants, of a sort that could be made by any user of English, to see what errors occur when Standard English is the target. Again, standard spellings are massively dominant (Table 1).

**Table 1:** Spelling on the web (all numbers are approximate)

|  | No. of hits | Ratio error:correct |
|---|---|---|
| ***committee*** | ***15,000,000*** | |
| commitee | 148,000 | 1:101 |
| comittee | 75,100 | 1:200 |
| comitee | 15,600 | 1:962 |
| ***accommodation*** | ***13,200,000*** | |
| accomodation | 2,300,000 | 1:6 |
| accommodation | 104,000 | 1:127 |
| acomodation | 58,900 | 1:224 |
| ***important*** | ***22,600,000*** | |
| importent | 17,400 | 1:1299 |

| | | |
|---|---|---|
| *pronunciation* | *768,000* | |
| pronounciation | 73,800 | 1:10 |
| *existence* | *7,830,000* | |
| existance | 150,000 | 1:52 |
| *pomegranate* | *166,000* | |
| pomegranite | 10,900 | 1:15 |
| pomigranite | 162 | 1:1025 |
| pomigranate | 19 | 1:8737 |
| pommiegranate | 0 | |
| pommiegranite | 0 | |

There is no noticeable geographical pattern for these spellings (other than the one related to variable Internet penetration). Everyone can make spelling mistakes like this, and everyone is expected to try to eliminate them, but they are forgiven if they make an occasional slip-up. And, of this list, only *accomodation*, *pomegranite* and *pronoun-ciation* are common enough to be suggested as potential alternatives to the current standard spelling. The Web, like all written English, is massively standard.

## Variants and errors

I will now progress to variants that do have a geographical pattern, giving data for one variant where the USA contrasts with the rest of the world, one where it is India that is unusual, and one where it is the UK that stands out.

### Alumin(i)um

Traditionally, there are said to be two norms for spelling and these are usually referred to as 'British' and 'American'. Only a handful of words vary, and usually minutely, most of them being alternatives that persisted on different sides of the Atlantic until the early nineteenth century. More countries follow the 'British' than the 'American' tradition, and most websites from writers based outside the USA use the 'British' spelling tradition. However, many tradition-ally 'American' spellings appear sporadically in regions usually associated with the 'British' tradition (such as *program*, *center*, *tire* and *check*).

The data for *alumin(i)um* illustrate how the American spelling, *aluminum*, dominates numerically, because of the massive representa-tion of the USA on the Web (Table 2). But this is a word that has an official spelling, *aluminium*, sanctioned by the *International Union Of*

*Pure And Applied Chemistry*, and this is the spelling used all over the world except in the US, where only *aluminum* is used, except in explanation of the history of the word and its IUPAC name. This is one of the purest geographical spreads I have found: America is set against the rest of the world. The crude count is slightly affected by the fact that some of those who design sites about aluminium also place the spelling they do not use in the header information, thus ensuring that their site will receive hits whatever spelling is entered.

**Table 2** Alumin(i)um

|  | *Aluminum* | *Aluminium* |
|---|---|---|
| **US** | 33 | 1 |
| **UK** | 1 | 15 |
| **Rest of the world** | 1<br>(Canada) | 19<br>(4 each from Australia and Germany, 2 each from India and Norway, 1 each from Canada, Denmark, Japan, Libya, New Zealand, South Africa, Switzerland) |
| **Unclear source** | 6 | 1 |
| **Target spelling in header only** | 6 | 5 |
| **Faulty link** | 3 | 3 |
| **Not English text** |  | 6 |
| **Total hits (approx.)** | 8,740,000 | 5,880,000 |

**This is the first time I –**

One of the grammatical structures that has often been said to be associated with Outer Circle Countries is the use of the present continuous in contexts such as 'This is the first time I –' rather than the use of the present perfective, said to be associated with Inner Circle countries (discussed in Gupta 1986). As I said 20 years ago, the use of the present continuous seems more logical, given that the perfective is so often associated with reference to past time. And, even 20 years ago, I noticed that it wasn't absent from Inner Circle usage. The pattern of this one is complicated (Table 3). Across the Web as a whole, the perfective is preferred. Both perfective and progressive are well represented in the US: if there is a subtle difference in meaning there, it is hard to understand:

- *This is the first time I have submitted an application for licensure in Maryland.*
- *I live in the New Orleans, Louisiana area. This is the first time I am submitting an ad like this, but, what the heck.*

**Table 3** Aspect after '*This is the first time I*' (first 50 hits for each)

| | This is the first time I have (_en) | This is the first time I am (_ing) |
|---|---|---|
| **US** | 26 | 14 |
| **India** | 0 | 11 |
| **UK** | 8 | 0 |
| **Rest of the world** | 4 (1 each from Bermuda, Canada, Sri Lanka) | 10 (3 from Singapore; 1 each from Australia, Hong Kong, Malta, Pakistan, Tibet, Thailand, Turkey) |
| **Unclear source** | 12 | 13 |
| **Not target structure** | | 2 |
| **Total hits (approx.)** | 63,600 | 6,990 |

The progressive is the most usual variant in India, and the fact that there are so many tokens from India in the first 50 sites shows how much more common this variant is in Indian English than in other Englishes.

However, the absence of progressives from the UK, and the absence of perfectives from India, does not mean that the alternatives are *never* used. An advanced search for 'This is the first time I am' in the domain .uk (websites hosted in the UK) generated over 100 valid examples of the progressive in the UK, including the following, from indubitably local sources (the first, which also has an unexpected form of the indefinite article, is from a national governmental website):

- *This is the first time I am licensing a vehicle with a RPC; what should I do?*

- *This is the first time I am doing this as a teacher and i'm not sure what to expect.*

  *I have long been active in the wider Co-operative Movement, but this is the first time I am offering myself for election into the democratic structures of the Co-operative Group itself.*

A search for 'This is the first time I have' in the domain .in (websites hosted in India) produced only three locatable examples, including one (from the Indian Parliament) in which the reference is to past time:

- *I have heard of the 'seven-year itch' in abortion and matrimony, but this is the first time I have heard about the seven-year itch in a governmental affair.*

On this variable, the world pattern is that there is a choice between the progressive and the perfective, though the perfective is almost never used in India. India is the exception at the moment, though it may turn out that as other Outer Circle countries become better represented on the Web, India will be joined by other places where the perfective is rare. India is not exceptional in its use of the progressive in this structure, but in the absence of the alternative perfective structure.

## I was stood

My final example is of a structure that I predicted (more or less correctly) to be associated with British English. There are some *be +-en* structures in English where the past participle can be interpreted either as part of a passive or as a deverbal adjective (e.g. *be broken*). In a handful of verbs (especially *sit* and *stand*) the use of the -en form where the passive interpretation is not possible results in a *be +-en* structure which is in variation with a *be +-ing* structure. Readers from outside the UK may find this usage very wrong, and in some circles in the UK too it is stigmatized. These expressions do not seem to be currently regional within the UK, and commonly occur in national newspapers and over national radio.

**Table 4** *was stood/standing*

|  | *I was stood in a* | *I was standing in a* |
|---|---|---|
| **US** | 2 | 30 |
| **UK** | 32 | 5 |
| **Rest of the world** | 0 | 9<br>(3 from Canada; 2 from India; 1 each from Australia, Cyprus, Finland, Israel) |
| **Unclear source** | 13 | 6 |
| **Passive** | 3 | n/a |
| **Total hits (approx.)**<br>*Hits on 'I was stood/standing':*<br>all<br>in domain .in<br>in domain .uk | 106<br><br><br>4,830<br>0<br>1,500 | 6,290<br><br><br>220,000<br>92<br>10,100 |

The passives (e.g. '*I was stood in a prominent location in my maker's booth. I was given a very high price tag.*') are easy to exclude. Examples of the target structure include:

- *A mere two weeks later I was stood in a balloon basket for the first time in my life flying out of Roundhay Park in Leeds.*
- *So much history and literature revolves around the Yukon River that I was stood in a speechless awe while I looked out over the ice.*
- *So, May 7th 2004 at 8AM I was standing in a regional rail station in Philadelphia and anticipating the train that would take me to Penn Station.*
- *But here I was standing in a bar in Sydney, dog tired, watching someone who lifted my spirits to a high I couldn't have imagined ...*

Nearly all uses of this structure come from the UK (Table 4). '*I was stood*' does occur in the US (the second example above comes from someone presenting himself as having an unimpeachably US biography) but it is rare. In the world beyond the UK, '*I was stood*' is just not used in this sense. Here it is the UK that stands out from the rest of the world. Only in the UK are there two variants, because one of those variants is used (pretty well) only in the UK.

## Conclusion

In all of these structures there are variants. In many cases, it makes little sense to label variants simply as 'standard' or 'non-standard'. Some (such as '*I was stood*' and *aluminum*) function as part of the standard but only in a particular region. Others (such as the present continuous after '*This is the first time*') exist as variants throughout the world. Lexis is a sponge, and grammar is very leaky indeed.

This type of identification is satisfying and reveals real patterns, showing what variants there are within standard practice, and what the geographical patterns are. Other strings I recommend for examination include:

- *I wrote (to) my mother and*
- *The bacteria/bacterium is/are*
- *There is/are several*
- *I am/have been here since*

## Solutions

I hope I have convinced the readers that:

- Standard English dominates writing;
- Standard English is not predetermined: it follows the behaviour of its users;
- English orthography is strict, but errors occur;
- in grammar, not everyone agrees on correctness in Standard English;
- writers sometimes deliberately write non-standard text;
- the patterns of variation in Standard English are geographically complex;
- being a native speaker does not guarantee ability to write Standard English;
- some structures that learners of English as a Foreign Language are told are wrong are used in Inner Circle Standard English texts.

**107**

How should this inform the teaching of English in Expanding Circle countries? Standard English should certainly be the focus of pedagogy, as it is in Inner and Outer Circle countries. But once learners are able to look at real texts they will encounter error and variation, and it will not be easy for them to know what is best for them to use, and what should be avoided. They will need to know the above from quite an early stage.

Learners should be encouraged to get evidence from usage. They should be encouraged to restrict themselves to Standard English: the deliberate use of non-standard dialects requires great care. But there should not be an emphasis on areas of disputed usage. Teachers should do their best to establish what they should correct firmly, what they should correct tentatively, and what they should accept as correct. It is only by close attention to usage that this can be established.

## References

Crystal, D. 1997. *English as a Global Language*. Cambridge: Cambridge University Press.

*Google*. 2004. <google.com>

Gramley, S. 2001. *The Vocabulary of World English*. London: Arnold.

Gupta, A. F. 1986. 'A standard for written Singapore English?' *English Worldwide* 7/1, 75–99.

Gupta, A. F. 1999. 'Standard Englishes, Contact Varieties and Singapore Englishes'. In C. Gnutzmann (ed.), *Teaching and Learning English as a Global Language: Native and Non-native Perspectives*. Tübingen: Stauffen- burg Verlag. 59–72.

Gupta, A. F. 2001. 'Realism and Imagination in the Teaching of English'. *World Englishes* 20/3, 365–381.

Gupta, A. F. 2001. 'Teaching World English'. *Mextesol Journal* 25/2, 41–55.

Gupta, A. F. Forthcoming. 'Singlish on the Web'. In A. Hashim and N. Hassan (eds), *Varieties of English in SouthEast Asia and Beyond*. Kuala Lumpur: University of Malaya Press.

House, J. 1999. 'Misunderstanding in intercultural communication: interac- tions in English as lingua franca and the myth of mutual intelligibility'. In Claus Gnutzmann (ed.), *Teaching and Learning English as a Global Language: Native and Non-native Perspectives*. Tübingen: Stauffenburg Verlag. 73–89.

Jenkins, J. 2000. *The Phonology of English as an International Language*. Oxford: Oxford University Press.

Kachru, B. 1992. 'World Englishes: approaches, issues and resources'. *Language Teaching* 25, 1–14.

Kachru, B. 1985. 'Standards, Codification and Sociolinguistic Realism: the English Language in the Outer Circle'. In R. Quirk & H. G. Widdowson (eds),

*English in the World: Teaching and Learning the Language and Literatures.* Cambridge: Cambridge University Press. 11–30.

McArthur, T. 1998. *The English Languages.* Cambridge: Cambridge University Press.

Quirk, R. S. Greenbaum, G. Leech and J. Svartvik. 1972. *A Grammar Of Contemporary English.* London: Longman.

Schiffman, H. F. 1996. *Linguistic Culture and Language Policy.* London/New York: Routledge.

Seidlhofer, B. and J. Jenkins. 2003. 'English as a lingua franca and the politics of property'. In Christian Mair (ed.), *The Politics of English as a World Language* (New Horizons in Postcolonial Cultural Studies, ASNEL Papers 7). Amsterdam/New York: Rodopi. 139–54.

Shields, A. F. 1977. 'On the identification of Singapore English vocabulary'. In: W. J. Crewe (ed.), *The English Language in Singapore.* Singapore: Eastern Universities Press. 120–140.

Thomason, S. G. and T. Kaufman. 1988. *Language Contact, Creolization, and Genetic Linguistics.* University of California Press: Berkeley.

Trudgill, P. 1999. 'Standard English: what it isn't'. In T. Bex and R. Watts (eds), *Standard English: the Widening Debate.* London: Routledge. 117–28.

# Part II: Pedagogical Implications of EIL

If the first section in this volume focused on the problems of formulating a conceptual framework for English as an international language (EIL), this section deals with the conceptualizing of pedagogical possibilities for EIL at a more practical level. In particular, its concern is to explore the instructional options that are available to the curriculum developer, course designer, materials writer and language teacher (not to speak of the language learner implicit in all of this) in promoting the teaching and learning of EIL in a manner that is sensitive to the local realities of ESL/EFL learners, and providing access to a globally relevant English language education without violating the multilingual and multicultural sensibilities that characterize their settings.

The five papers in this section present ideas and insights for pedagogical designs that comprise productive alternatives to the way in which the language curriculum has been traditionally conceived in mainstream English Language Teaching (ELT). They represent the thoughtful responses of our contributors to the realities of teaching, learning and using English within richly multilingual and multicultural societies, and an awareness of the special challenges they create. Although the locations and environments focused on and the scope of these contributions are varied, each shares a central concern – an aspiration towards the creation of a wider range of options for pedagogical practice that can effectively address the challenges that teachers face in teaching English in postcolonial, multinational, global settings where (Standard) English is still cultural capital, and the localization of Englishes creates dilemmas that call for a more critically responsive educational practice.

In the first chapter in this section, McKay questions certain assumptions long held in mainstream ELT and argues that current changes in the nature of English and English language learners warrants a re-evaluation of two widely accepted notions of ELT curriculum development: namely, that the goal of English learning is native-speaker competence, and that native-speaker culture should inform instructional materials and teaching methods. Recognizing the current status of English as an International Language (EIL), the author describes central features of an international language and shows how these influence the relationship between language and culture. The paper then proceeds to demonstrate how native-speaker models and culture need to be carefully examined in reference to EIL curriculum development.

The two chapters that follow represent attempts to spell out the specifics of how English as an International Language should be taught to learners needing English for international communication. Tomlinson, recognizing the value of a corpora-based description of the Lingua Franca core as a basic productive model, so long as it is not restrictively viewed as the only goal for learners, emphasizes the need to adopt a multidimensional approach if English is to be taught for effective international communication; and elaborates upon the form this will take in relation to language planning, syllabus design and curriculum development. He goes on to flesh out the methodological implications of such a model in terms of the kind of materials and the classroom procedures that need to be used, and the modes of assessment that become necessary in designing a more flexible, adaptable, and contextually and culturally relevant pedagogy.

Sifakis explores at greater depth the specific nature of what teaching English as an International Language entails if this task is to be conceived in a radically different way, with the aim of setting specific criteria for identifying and teaching EIL learners. Thus in place of the current adherence to an N-bound route, which focuses on accuracy and standards, and threatens to remain norm-orientated with reference to a finite set of descriptive or prescriptive varieties of global English, he proposes English as an Intercultural Language (EIcL), which follows a C-bound route. This route prioritizes as a communicative goal the process of cross-cultural comprehensibility between learners, in which each communicative situation appropriates the use of widely different varieties with elements that are not readily regularized. This would entail the creation of a comprehensive syllabus that not only involves both teachers and learners in developing a more reflective mind-set towards their communication with other non-native speakers, but also takes into consideration all those aspects that characterize C-bound communication. Sifakis helpfully outlines what such a syllabus framework would look like in application, in terms of teacher readiness, learner attitudes, teaching situations and the provision of EIcL tasks.

In the chapter that follows, Ruanni examines how Philippino teachers of English faced conditions of (im)possibility when presented with pedagogical options which encouraged them to depart from a rigid Standard English (SE) model. Ruanni portrays the teachers' dilemma as follows: politically they wish to hang on to the power of SE, but ideologically they wish to move away from it. The teachers deal with their dilemma by envisioning a content-centred language pedagogy that continues to localize English. Ruanni concludes that what is needed are not newer curricular paradigms for teaching and learning English, but newer and more critical ways for teachers to grapple with existing theories.

The final chapter has Joseph and Ramani drawing upon their experiences of teaching English in South Africa, to argue powerfully for the development of a political view of the role of English in challenging its hegemony and redressing the balance between English and indigenous languages. The authors contend that the curricular practices which ensure that it is 'natural' for English to be deployed for CALP (Cognitive Acquisition of Language Proficiency) purposes worldwide force the indigenous languages to remain at BICS (Basic Interpersonal Communication Skills) level. The answer lies in rejecting a deterministic view of the 'multilingualness' of the world and the role of English in it, and replacing it with a theory of professional practice that is sensitive to the multilingual realities of learners. They see the creation of bilingual programmes as a viable alternative to the dominant 'straight for English' or 'English Only' curricula in helping to challenge the hegemony of English in South Africa.

Thus, as we celebrate the spread of English and applaud its success as an international language, it is important to register the fact that the opposing discourses of resistance to English can take different forms. More important, perhaps, is how they may be dealt with by governments, professionals and practitioners, responding to the threat that the dominance of English poses to linguistic and cultural diversity both at the macro and micro levels in the varied contexts around the world, through informed and thoughtful practice to bring about a more just society. This is the major challenge to our current wisdom.

The intellectually stimulating interview with Suresh Canagarajah provides a fitting closure to the volume. Responding to a similar set of questions as put to Tom McArthur in the opening interview, Canagarajah takes up issues nearest to his heart – what he terms the 'micropolitics' of postcolonial resistance. He raises some very interesting questions, such as: What creative alternatives are available in academic and literary writing and research publishing that can serve new communicative practices and ideologies globally, given that English continues to be nativized? How can one ensure that the diverse communities using English in the world today can find textual and linguistic spaces within English to represent their identities, wishes and interests? And how can one develop challenges to its dominance from within?

Many of his ideas call for a paradigm shift in the teaching of English globally and in our concept of learning, not least in our ideology, which needs to view English as context-transforming rather than as context-bound.

# EIL Curriculum Development

*Sandra Lee McKay*
*San Francisco State University*

In this paper the author argues that current changes in the nature of English and English language learners warrants a re-evaluation of two widely accepted notions of ELT curriculum development: namely, that the goal of English learning is native-speaker competence, and that native-speaker culture should inform instructional materials and teaching methods. Recognizing the current status of English as an International Language (EIL), the author describes central features of an international language and how these influence the relationship between language and culture. The paper then proceeds to demonstrate how native-speaker models and culture need to be carefully examined in reference to EIL curriculum development.

As Richards (2001) points out, curriculum development entails a range of planning and implementation processes that form a network of interacting systems so that 'change in one part of the system has effects on other parts of the system' (41). This paper argues that in the current teaching of English two significant aspects of the network have changed, requiring changes in other parts of the system. These changes relate to the nature of English today and the characteristics of its learners.

Most people agree that today English is a global lingua franca. English has achieved this status not because of a growth in the number of native speakers but rather because of an increase in the number of individuals in the world today who are acquiring English as an additional language. This situation has resulted in a tremendous growth in the number of second-language speakers of English. In fact, Graddol (1999) argues that based solely on expected population changes, the number of people using English as their second language will grow from 235 million to around 462 million during the next 50 years. This indicates that the balance between L1 and L2 speakers will critically change, with L2 speakers eventually overtaking L1 speakers (62).

The growing number of people in the world who have some familiarity with English allows English to act as a language of wider communication for a great variety of purposes, contributing to its status as a global lingua franca. In order to develop an appropriate curriculum for English as an International Language (EIL), it is essential to examine how English has achieved its status as an international language and how this role has altered the nature of the language.

## Features of English as an International Language

Brutt-Griffler (2002) argues convincingly that one of the central features of any international language is that it spreads not through speaker migration, but rather by many individuals in an existing speech community acquiring the language, what Brutt-Griffler terms *macroacquisition*. Although the initial spread of English was clearly due to speaker migration, resulting in the development of largely monolingual English-speaking communities (e.g. the United States, Australia and New Zealand), the current spread of English is, as Graddol's projection demonstrates, due to individuals acquiring English as an additional language for international and in some contexts intranational communication. However, unlike speaker migration, this type of language-spread results not in monolingualism but in large-scale bilingualism.

The fact that the spread of English today is primarily due to macroacquisition has several important implications for EIL curriculum development. First, it suggests that many learners of English today will have specific purposes in learning English, which in general are more limited than those of immigrants to English-speaking countries who may eventually use English as their sole or dominant language. Second, many L2 speakers of English will be using English to interact with other L2 speakers rather than with native speakers. Finally, many current learners of English may desire to learn English in order to share with others information about their own countries for such purposes as encouraging economic development, promoting trade and tourism, and exchanging information.

Such purposes for learning and using English undermine the traditional cultural basis of English, in which the teaching of English has often involved learning about the concerns and cultures of what Kachru (1985) terms Inner Circle countries (e.g. Canada, Australia and the United States). Since by its very nature an international language does not belong to any particular country but rather to an international community, as Smith (1976) points out,

a) learners of EIL do not need to internalize the cultural norms of native speakers of English,
b) the ownership of EIL has become 'de-nationalized', and
c) the educational goal of EIL often is to enable learners to communicate their ideas and culture to others.

Throughout this paper I shall argue that since by its very nature an international language is no longer linked to a particular culture, and since one of its primary uses will be for bilingual speakers of English to communicate with other bilingual speakers, it is no longer appropriate to use native-speaker models to inform curriculum development. Hence, it is essential to examine three widely accepted ELT assumptions, namely that:

- ELT pedagogy should be informed by native speaker models.
- The cultural content for ELT should be derived from the cultures of native English speakers.
- The culture of learning that informs communicative language teaching (CLT) provides the most productive method for ELT.

In what follows I shall examine each of these assumptions in reference to EIL curriculum development. Throughout the paper I shall maintain that the increasing number of bilingual users of English, and the de-linking of English from Inner Circle countries, have significant implications for curriculum development.

In the paper I use the term *bilingual users of English* to describe individuals who use English as a second language alongside one or more other languages they speak. Although Jenkins (2000) includes both native and non-native speakers in her use of the term *bilingual English speaker*, in my use of the term I am excluding so-called native speakers of English who speak other languages. I do so because the domains of English for most native speakers tend to be quite different from those of other bilingual users of English, who frequently use English in more restricted and formal domains. I also make use of Kachru's (1985) useful distinction between *Inner Circle* countries where English is spoken as a native language, *Outer Circle* countries where English has official status, and *Expanding Circle* countries where English is a foreign language, though like Yano (2001) and Gupta (2001), I recognize the limitations of these terms.

## Present-day English learning

To begin, it is beneficial to examine why many individuals today are choosing to learn English so that curriculum objectives and approaches can be designed to meet their needs. Some contend that one of the major reasons for the present-day interest in learning English is the extensive promotion of English by Inner Circle countries. One of the major exponents of this view is Phillipson, who in his book *Linguistic Imperialism* (1992) describes the spread of English as a postcolonial endeavor of core English-speaking countries to maintain dominance over periphery (in many cases developing) countries. He coins the term *linguistic imperialism* to describe a situation in which 'the dominance of English is asserted and maintained by the establishment and continuous reconstitution of structural and cultural inequalities between English and other languages' (47).

However, to assume that the active promotion of English is the primary cause of the current interest in learning English is to oversimplify the complexity of the spread of English. Today many individuals desire to learn English not because English is promoted by English-speaking countries, but rather because these individuals want access to scientific and technological information, international organizations, global economic trade and higher education. Knowing English makes such access possible. Indeed Kachru, in his book *The Alchemy of English* (1986), contends that 'knowing English is like possessing the fabled Aladdin's lamp, which permits one to open, as it were, the linguistic gates to international business, technology, science and travel. In short, English provides linguistic power' (1).

There is a variety of evidence to suggest that the current interest in English learning is being fuelled by a belief in the power of English. Chew (1999), for example, argues that the learning of English within Singapore is the conscious choice of Singaporeans who view the use of English as key to their economic survival. She points out that whereas some Singaporeans are concerned that the widespread adoption of English will lead to a loss of ethnic identity and Asian values, many Singaporeans value the material and other rewards that English can bring. As she puts it, among parents there has been a pragmatic realization that their children's lack of a command of English would mean the continued marginalization of their children in a world that would continue to use the language to a greater degree. It would also deny them access to the extensive resources available in English – resources which have developed as a consequence of globalization (Chew 1999, 41).

Bisong specifically challenges Phillipson's theory of linguistic imperialism as it relates to his own country, Nigeria. He notes that presently many Nigerian parents send their children to an international school in which they are sure their children will learn English. However, Bisong maintains that it is important to consider why a parent would make such a decision. For Bisong, a parent does so not as coercion but rather in the secure belief that his/her child's mother tongue or first language is not in any way threatened. There is no way three or four hours of exposure to English in a formal school situation could possibly compete with, let alone threaten to supplant, the non-stop process of acquiring competence in the mother tongue (Bisong 1995, 125).

Bisong concludes by pointing out that Nigerians learn English for pragmatic reasons and are sophisticated enough to know what is in their interest, and that their interest includes the ability to operate with two or more linguistic codes in a multilingual situation. Phillipson's argument shows a failure to appreciate fully the complexities of this situation (131).

Thus, many language learners today are studying English not because they are being coerced to do so by English speakers of Inner Circle countries, but rather because of the benefits which knowledge of English brings. Effective EIL curriculum development, then, must consider the specific goals that lead learners to study English, and not assume that these goals necessarily involve attaining full proficiency in the language.

## Native-speaker models and English learning goals

It has generally been assumed that the ultimate goal of English-language learners is to achieve native-like competence in the language. Stern, for example, maintains that the 'native speaker's "competence," "proficiency" or "knowledge of the language" is a necessary point of reference for the second language proficiency concept used in English teaching theory' (1983, 341). Yet as more and more users of English come to use English alongside one or more other languages, their use of English will be significantly different from that of monolingual speakers of English. Because bilingual speakers of English frequently have different purposes in using English than do monolingual speakers, it is unwarranted to assume that bilingual speakers want or need to attain native-like competence. However, as Cook (1999, 189) notes:

> SLA research has often fallen into the *comparative fallacy* (Bley-Vroman, 1983) of relating the L2 learner to the native speaker. This tendency is reflected in the frequency with which the words

> *succeed* and *fail* are associated with the phrase *native speaker*, for
> example, the view that fossilisation and errors in L2 users' speech
> add up to 'failure to achieve native-speaker competence'.

Sridhar and Sridhar (1994) provide an excellent critique of traditional
English language learning objectives with regard to bilingual users of
English outside of Inner Circle countries. They contend that many
traditional ELT objectives are not relevant to an investigation of these
speakers because they often rest on assumptions that were developed
and tested in reference to the learning of English in the United States,
with little input from the learning of English outside of Inner Circle
countries. The first assumption is that the learner's target in
acquisition of English is native-like competence. However, as Sridhar
and Sridhar point out, many studies of *indigenized varieties of English*
(e.g. Indian English, Nigerian English, Singaporean English) clearly
demonstrate that a variety of English that is too closely aligned with a
native standard can be seen by speakers in the local speech community
to be 'distasteful and pedantic' and 'affected or even snobbish' (1994,
45). As such, many learners of English do not want and may even reject
a native-like pronunciation target. So if, as Richard argues, language
curriculum development must address the needs of the learners, EIL
curriculum development must recognize that many bilingual speakers
of English do not desire native-like competence in English.

A second problem with many currently accepted ELT learning
objectives is that the process of acquisition is not viewed in reference
to the functions that English serves within the local community. As
was pointed out earlier, most bilingual users of English outside of
Inner Circle countries use English alongside other languages they
speak. In some cases English serves primarily as a High variety or
formal register with respect to the other languages of the speech
community. Hence, English does not serve all of the functions it might
serve for learners in the Inner Circle who, in many cases, learn English
as a replacement for their first language. This means that the language-
learning goals of many current users of English are far more limited
than the goals of those who learn English as a result of speaker
migration. Hence, EIL curriculum development must consider the
specific functions for which learners need English today.

As Sidhar and Sidhar point out, the lack of applicability of widely
accepted ELT assumptions for EIL curriculum development is
particularly disturbing in light of the fact that English learners outside
of the Inner Circle 'numerically as well as in terms of the range and
diversity of variables they represent, constitute one of the most
significant segments of second language acquirers in the world today'

(1994, 42). Because of the growing number of such users, the learning needs and goals of bilingual speakers of English in multilingual contexts is a subject that warrants a good deal more research so that appropriate curriculum development for such learners can be designed.

To productively undertake such research, the prevalent assumption that the goal of English language learning is to achieve native-like competence in English must be put aside. It is important to do so for two reasons. First, if – as more and more linguists are recognizing (see, for example, Cook 1999, Davies 1991, Rampton 1990) – the whole notion of defining a native speaker and native-speaker competence is fraught with difficulty, it is unreasonable to take such a poorly defined construct as the basis for EIL curriculum development. Secondly, an approach to curriculum development that is based on the notion that all learners of English need or desire so-called native-speaker competence will do little to contribute to a better understanding of the various ways English is used within Outer Circle countries for intranational communication and for international purposes among speakers or different countries. What, for example, are the functions that English serves within particular Outer Circle countries? How does English fit into the overall linguistic repertoire of bilingual users in these countries? In what contexts does English serve as the unmarked code? How is the use of English within these countries related to educational level, economic status and ethnic background? In addition, far more research is needed on how English is used as a language of wider communication between individuals who use English as their second language. What strategies do such individuals use in solving problems of comprehensibility? What does the use of English in such contexts suggest for linguistic standards and pronunciation models? (See Seidlhofer 2001 for a persuasive argument on the need for such research.)

Clearly, teaching English as an international language requires that curriculum developers thoroughly examine individual learners' specific uses of English within their particular speech community as a basis for determining learning goals, and set aside the native-speaker fallacy whereby bilingual speakers of English, both in research and pedagogy, are constantly compared to native-speaker models.

## Native-speaker models and EIL instructional materials

The role of culture in instructional materials is another area of ELT curriculum development that often reflects a native-speaker model, an approach that once again needs to be reassessed in reference to EIL curriculum development. Cultural knowledge often provides the basis for the content and topics that are used in language materials and classroom discussions. Which culture to use in instructional materials needs to be carefully considered in reference to the teaching of an international language.

Cortazzi and Jin (1999) distinguish three types of cultural information that can be used in language textbooks and materials:

- *source culture materials* that draw on the learners' own culture as content,
- *target culture materials* that use the culture of a country where English is spoken as a first language, and
- *international target culture materials* that use a great variety of cultures in English- and non-English-speaking countries around the world.

Traditionally, many English-language textbooks have used target culture topics. Frequently ELT textbooks use such content because textbooks are often published in Inner Circle countries and because some ELT educators believe such information will be motivating to English-language learners. Whereas it is possible that target cultural content is motivating to some students, it is also quite possible that such content may be largely irrelevant, uninteresting, or even confusing for students. Furthermore, if one of the primary reasons for learners to acquire English today is to provide information to others about their own community and culture, there seems little reason to promote target cultural content in English language classrooms, particularly when such content can result in bilingual teachers of English feeling insecure because they lack specific knowledge about target cultures. (For a more extended discussion of the problems that can arise in using the target culture in EIL pedagogy, see McKay 2002.)

The advantage of using what Cortazzi and Jin call 'source culture' is that such content provides students with an opportunity to learn more about their own culture and to learn the language needed to explain these cultural elements in English. Such a situation also places local bilingual teachers in a position in which they can explain particular cultural events or cultural behaviour to students who may not be familiar with that particular aspect of the culture. It is encouraging to note that today, in a variety of countries in which English is being studied as an additional language, there is a growing recognition of the importance of including the source culture. In the early 1990s, for example, the Moroccan Ministry of Education implemented a textbook project in which Moroccan culture formed the basis for textbook content rather than target culture information.

(See Adaskou, Britten and Fahsi 1990 for a description of this project). More recently, Chile has developed an entire series of textbooks, entitled *Go For Chile*, that includes a good deal of source culture content. (See McKay, forthcoming, for a description of this project.)

There are also many advantages to using what Cortazzi and Jin refer to as an international target culture. Imagine a text in which bilingual users of English interact with other speakers of English in cross-cultural encounters for a variety of purposes. Such materials could have several benefits. They could exemplify the manner in which bilingual users of English are effectively using English to communicate for international purposes. They could include examples of lexical, grammatical and phonological variation in the present-day use of English. They could also illustrate cross-cultural pragmatics in which bilingual users of English, while using English, nevertheless draw on their own rules of appropriateness. They could then provide a basis for students to gain a fuller understanding of how English today serves a great variety of international purposes in a broad range of contexts. There are clearly many advantages to reducing the focus on target cultures in teaching materials, as is evident in the current shift in some countries to doing precisely that.

Ultimately, then, in reference to instructional materials, there are many reasons for putting aside the traditional emphasis on native-speaker cultural content. Chief among these is that, as an international language, English belongs to no one country or culture. In the same way there is no reason why the language teaching methods used in EIL teaching should be informed by native-speaker models.

## Native-speaker models and communicative language teaching

Today many educators, particularly Inner Circle educators, contend that CLT is and should be the dominant method in ELT. Brown (1994), for example, maintains that the generally accepted norms in the field in terms of methodology is CLT. He notes, however, that although CLT is generally accepted, there are numerous ways in which it is defined. Nunan (1991, 279), for instance, maintains that CLT can be characterized by the following features:

1. An emphasis on learning to communicate through interaction in the target language
2. The introduction of authentic texts into the learning situation
3. The provision of opportunities for learners to focus, not only on language, but also on the learning process itself

4. An enhancement of the learner's own personal experience as an important contributing element to classroom learning
5. An attempt to link classroom language learning with language activation outside the classroom

CLT has been largely promoted in ELT in Inner Circle countries, and in private English language institutes in Outer and Expanding Circle countries. In using this method, typically a great premium is placed on using group work to develop students' spoken English.

What has led to the widespread promotion of CLT as the most productive method for teaching English? Tollefson (1991) suggests one reason. He argues that the spread of English is linked to what he terms the modernization theory. According to this theory, 'Western societies provide the most effective model for "underdeveloped" societies attempting to reproduce the achievements of "industrialization"' (83). As applied to ELT teaching, in modernization theory 'Western "experts" ... are viewed as repositories of knowledge and skills who pass them on to elites who will run "modernized" institutions' (97).

Whereas the modernization theory may well be one factor that has led to the spread of CLT, such a view hides the complexity of the issue. Just as the idea of linguistic imperialism can be challenged on the grounds that in many countries English has spread because there is tremendous interest on the part of the people of that country to learn English, so too in many cases CLT has spread not only because of the promotion of the method by Western specialists but also because educators in these countries have advocated the adoption of this method.

Japan is a case in point. In 1989 and 1990, the Japanese Ministry of Education released new guidelines for the study of foreign languages in junior and senior high schools. According to LoCastro (1996), one of the primary aims of the new curriculum was to require teachers to promote speaking and listening skills as a way of developing the communicative language ability of the students. Furthermore, teachers were to strive to adopt CLT methods in their classrooms. Korea is another country that is encouraging the use of CLT. Convinced that the grammatical syllabus does not develop students' communicative competence, in 1992 the Ministry of Education published a new curriculum which clearly stated that CLT should replace the audio-lingual and translation methods currently used in schools.

The above discussion demonstrates that just as the Inner Circle is often looked to for target models of language use, the Inner Circle is frequently looked to for methodology models. Whereas this dependence on the Inner Circle for methodology models may in part be due to a type of pedagogical imperialism on the part of Inner Circle educators, there is no question that, just as with the spread of English, an equally important factor in the spread of CLT has been its conscious selection on the part of local educators. The widespread acceptance of CLT, however, has not gone unchallenged.

Medgyes (1986), for example, a Hungarian teacher educator, has various concerns about the implementation of CLT in his country, even though he has publicly advocated the method in teacher education courses. His primary concern is the burden CLT places on teachers. To begin, teachers of CLT are encouraged to base the syllabus on students' needs and interests. Yet, as Medgyes points out, most Hungarian students, like many EFL students, study English for no obvious reason other than because they are required to do so. Hence, teachers face groups of students who often have very little motivation or interest to use English and uncertain needs for English in the future. Teachers are also asked to develop authentic communicative situations where real messages are exchanged. Hence, 'teachers have to create favourable conditions for such needs to arise and get expressed' (Medgyes 1986, 108). Creating such a context is, of course, particularly difficult in EFL classes in which students would naturally use their mother tongue to communicate in so-called real interactions. In addition, in CLT the textbook is suspect. So teachers are asked to do away with the textbooks and substitute them with a 'wide stock of flexible and authentic "supplementary' material"' (110), an extremely difficult task to undertake in countries in which there is not a wealth of readily available English texts.

Given these difficulties in implementing CLT in Hungary, Medgyes asks who would possibly attempt to implement the method. He contends that perhaps the only teachers who would do this are the elite who have had the opportunity to exchange ideas at conferences and 'on arriving home, they feel obliged to promulgate all the trendy thoughts they have picked up, never doubting that their message is true and will reach the general public' (111). Often such conferences are held in Inner Circle countries, providing a further impetus for the spread of predominant methods of Inner Circle countries to other contexts. In the end, he believes that what is needed are educators who work halfway between 'the zealots and the weary' (112), local educators who are well aware of the complexities of teaching English in the local context.

Indeed, since EIL by definition no longer belongs to any one nation or culture, it seems reasonable that how this language is taught should not be linked to a particular culturally influenced methodology; rather the language should be taught in a manner consistent with local cultural expectations. In short, an appropriate EIL methodology presupposes sensitivity to the local cultural context in which local educators determine what happens in the classroom. As Kramsch and Sullivan (1996, 211) put it:

> Appropriate pedagogy must also be a pedagogy of appropriation. The English language will enable students of English to do business with native and non-native speakers of English in the global world market and for that they need to master the grammar and vocabulary of standard English. But they also need to retain control of its use.

For Kramsch and Sullivan, such a view of an appropriate pedagogy is in keeping with the political motto ' "think globally, act locally," which translated into a language pedagogy might be "global thinking, local teaching" ' (200). This motto is particularly important for the teaching of EIL. Clearly, EIL educators today need to recognize the use of English as a global language, where English is used for a wide variety of cross-cultural communicative purposes. Yet in developing an appropriate curriculum, EIL educators also need to consider how English is embedded in the local context.

The promotion of CLT has been fuelled by the tendency to extend so-called 'centre assumptions' of English language learning to other countries. Unfortunately, the prevalent assumption that CLT is the best method for the teaching of EIL has several negative effects. It often requires students to become involved in language activities that challenge their notion of appropriate language behaviour in a classroom. Its emphasis on an English-only classroom can undermine the productive use of the mother tongue in the learning of English, which is particularly problematic in an era when English is being learned primarily in bilingual classrooms. Most importantly, it can marginalize local teachers who at times are asked to implement a methodology that may be in conflict with their own sense of plausibility. Clearly the first step towards an appropriate methodology must be for local educators, as Kramsch and Sullivan argue, to be involved in a 'pedagogy of appropriation' in which they retain control of the teaching of English. As Canagarajah (1999, 90–1) argues:

> If English teaching in Periphery communities is to be conducted in a socially responsible and politically empowering manner, the authority for conceiving and implementing the curriculum and pedagogy should be passed on to the local teachers themselves.

## EIL curriculum development assumptions

The teaching of EIL takes place in a great diversity of contexts. In some countries like Singapore, English is the medium of instruction. In other countries like Jamaica, students bring to the classroom their own distinct variety of English. In other countries like Japan, the learning of English in public schools is promoted through national examinations. In addition, within each country, great diversity exists so that the teaching of English in, for example, public versus private institutions and urban versus rural institutions tends to be quite different. Clearly, any sound EIL curriculum development must be informed by a theory of language learning and teaching that is sufficiently complex to account for this diversity. However, in closing, let me suggest some of the assumptions that need to inform EIL curriculum development.

Throughout this article, I have argued that the development of English as a global lingua franca has altered the very nature of English in terms of how it is used by its speakers and how it relates to culture. As was pointed out earlier, the current spread of English is largely the result of macroacquisition, leading to more and more bilingual users of English. The growing number of bilingual users of English suggests that a productive theory of EIL teaching and learning must recognize the various ways in which English is used within multilingual communities. Typically these bilingual users of English have specific purposes for using English, employing their other languages to serve their many additional language needs. Often they use English to access the vast amount of information currently available in English, and at times to contribute to this knowledge base. One purpose they all share, however, is to use English as a language of wider communication, resulting in cross-cultural encounters being a central feature of the use of EIL. Hence, one of the major assumptions that needs to inform EEL curriculum development is a recognition of the diverse ways in which bilingual speakers make use of English to fulfill their specific purposes.

The second major assumption that needs to inform EIL curriculum development is that many bilingual users of English do not need or want to acquire native-like competence. Such an assumption, of course, presupposes that there is some agreement as to what constitutes a native speaker, although this is clearly not the case. Nevertheless, current ELT learning objectives frequently posit that the goal of most learners of English is to develop native-speaker grammatical standards, phonological patterns, and discourse competence. There are, however, several reasons why many current bilingual users of English may not see this as their goal. First of all, on a practical level they may not need to acquire the full range of registers that is needed by monolingual speakers of English since their use of English may be restricted to largely formal domains of use. Secondly, there are attitudinal reasons why they may not want to acquire native-like competence, particularly in reference to pronunciation and pragmatics. Third, if, as I have argued throughout the paper, English as an International Language belongs to its users, there is no reason why some speakers of English should be more privileged and thus provide standards for other users of English.

The final assumption that needs to inform EIL curriculum development is a recognition of the fact that English no longer belongs to any one culture, and hence there is a need to be culturally sensitive to the diversity of contexts in which English is taught and used. In terms of materials, this suggests that the traditional use of Western cultural content in ELT texts needs to be examined. There are clear advantages to the use of source culture content. Such content minimizes the potential of marginalizing the values and lived experiences of the learners. Source culture content can also encourage learners to gain a deeper understanding of their own culture so that they can share these insights when using EIL with individuals from different cultures. Perhaps most significantly, source culture content does not place local teachers in the difficult position of trying to teach someone else's culture.

The de-linking of English from the culture of Inner Circle countries also suggests that teaching methodology has to proceed in a manner that respects the local culture of learning. An understanding of these cultures of learning should not be based on cultural stereotypes, in which assertions about the roles of teachers and students and approaches to learning are made and often compared to Western culture. Rather, an understanding of local cultures of learning depends on an examination of particular classrooms. Although it is important to recognize that what happens in a specific classroom is influenced by political, social, and cultural factors of the larger community, each classroom is unique in the way the learners and teacher in that classroom interact with one another in the learning of English. Given the diversity of local cultures of learning, it is unrealistic to imagine that one method, such as CLT, will meet the needs of all learners. Rather, local teachers must be given the right and the responsibility to employ methods that are culturally sensitive and productive in their students' learning of English.

Common assumptions regarding English teaching have been largely based on an instructional context in which immigrants to English-speaking countries learn English, often as a replacement for their first language. Today, however, English is being studied and used more and more as an international language in which learners acquire English as an additional language of wider communication. Hence, the dominance of native speakers and their culture has been seriously challenged. Given this shift in the nature of English, it is time to recognize the multilingual context of English use and to put aside a native-speaker model of curriculum development. Only then can an appropriate EIL curriculum be developed in which local educators take ownership of English and the manner in which it is taught.

(An expanded version of this paper appears in the *International Journal of Applied Linguistics*, Issue 13/1.)

## References

Adaskou, K., D. Britten and B. Fahsi. 1990. 'Design decisions on the cultural content of a secondary English course for Morocco'. *ELT Journal*, 44/1, 3–10.

Bisong, J. 1995. 'Language choice and cultural imperialism: a Nigerian perspective'. *ELT Journal*, 49/2, 122–32.

Brown, H. D. 1994. *Teaching by Principles: an Interactive Approach to Language Pedagogy*. Englewood Cliffs, NJ: Prentice Hall Regents.

Brutt-Griffler, J. 2002. *World Englishes: a Study of its Development*. Clevedon: Multilingual Matters.

Canagarajah, A. S. 1999. 'Interrogating the "native speaker fallacy": non-linguistic roots, non-pedagogical results'. In G. Braine, *Non-native Educators in English Language Teaching*. Mahwah, NJ: Lawrence Erlbaum. 77–92.

Chew, P. 1999. 'Linguistic imperialism, globalism and the English language'. In D. Graddol and U. Meinhof, *English in a changing world. AILA Review 13*. United Kingdom. 37–47.

Cook, V. 1999. 'Going beyond the native speaker in language teaching'. *TESOL Quarterly*, 33/2, 185–209.

Cortazzi, M. and L. Jin. 1999. 'Cultural mirrors: materials and methods in the EFL classroom'. In E. Hinkel, *Culture in Second Language Teaching*. Cambridge: Cambridge University Press. 196–219.

Davies, A. 1991. *The Native Speaker in Applied Linguistics*. Edinburgh: Edinburgh University Press.

Graddol, D. 1999. 'The decline of the native speaker'. In D. Graddol and U. Meinhof, *English in a changing world. AILA Review 13*. United Kingdom. 57–68.

Gupta, A. 2001. 'Realism and imagination in the teaching of English'. *World Englishes*, 20/3, 383–91.

Jenkins, J. 2000. *The Phonology of English as an International Language*. Oxford: Oxford University Press.

Kachru, B. B. 1985. 'Standards, codification and sociolinguistic realism: the English language in the outer circle'. In R. Quirk and H. G. Widdowson, *English in the world: teaching and learning the language and literatures*. Cambridge: Cambridge University Press. 11–30.

Kachru, B. B. 1986. *The Alchemy of English*. Oxford: Pergamon Press.

Kramsch, C. and P. Sullivan. 1996. 'Appropriate pedagogy'. *ELT Journal*, 50/1, 199–212.

LoCastro, V. 1996. 'English language education in Japan'. In H. Coleman, *Society and the Language Classroom*. Cambridge: Cambridge University Press. 40–58.

McKay, S. L. 2002. *Teaching English as an International Language: Rethinking Goals and Approaches*. Oxford: Oxford University Press.

McKay, S. L. 2003. 'Teaching English as an international language: The Chilean context'. *ELT Journal* 57/2, 139–48.

Medgyes, P. 1986. 'Queries from a communicative teacher'. *ELT Journal*, 40/2, 107–12.

Nunan, D. 1991. 'Communicative tasks and the language curriculum'. *TESOL Quarterly*, 25/2, 279–95.

Phillipson, R. 1992. *Linguistic Imperialism*. Cambridge: Cambridge University Press.

Rampton, M. B. H. 1990. 'Displacing the native speaker: expertise, affiliation, and inheritance'. *ELT Journal*, 44, 97–110.

Richards, J. C. 2001. *Curriculum Development in Language Teaching*. Cambridge: Cambridge University Press.

Seidlhofer, B. 2001. 'Closing a conceptual gap: the case for a description of English as a lingua franca'. *International Journal of Applied Linguistics*, 11/2, 133–58.

Smith, L. 1976. 'English as an international auxiliary language'. *RELC Journal*, 7/2, 38–43.

Sridhar, S. N. and K. K. Sridhar. 1994. 'Indigenized Englishes as second languages: toward a functional theory of second language acquisition in multilingual contexts.' In R. K. Agnihotri and A. L. Khanna, *Second language acquisition: socio-cultural and linguistic aspects of English in India*. London: Sage. 41–63.

Stern, H. H. 1983. *Fundamental Concepts of Language Teaching*. Oxford: Oxford University Press.

Tollefson, J. W. 1991. *Planning Language, Planning Inequality*. London: Longman.

Yano, Y. 2001. 'World Englishes in 2000 and beyond'. *World Englishes* 20/2, 119–32.

# A Multi-dimensional Approach to Teaching English for the World

*Brian Tomlinson*
*Leeds Metropolitan University*

## English as an International Language

'Many people feel that the only realistic chance of breaking the foreign-language barrier is to use a natural language as a world lingua franca ... Today, English is the main contender for the position of world lingua franca' (Crystal 1997a, 359). As a native speaker of English I have used English to request an upgrade in a hotel in Malaysia, to complain about a golf club's regulations in Indonesia, to negotiate a course proposal and contract in Vietnam, to travel by bus across a city in Brazil, to discuss music in a jazz club in Thailand, to have clothes altered in Portugal and to run a workshop for curriculum developers in the Seychelles. And my wife, a native speaker of Japanese, has used English in the same countries for the same purposes too.

Not many people would disagree that English has already become a world lingua franca, though many would predict that Spanish will remain a powerful lingua franca in South America and that Mandarin could become the main lingua franca in East and South-East Asia. The big questions in relation to English as a world language seem to be:

- Should the prevailing standard Englishes (i.e. Standard British English and General American) continue to be taught as models of correctness to learners needing English for international communication?
- Should a variety of world Englishes be used as models of effective communication for learners needing English for international use?
- Should it be accepted that an international variety of English is already being evolved by the millions of non-native users of English who communicate with each other in English every day? And should this variety be described and then used as an

appropriate model for learners needing English for international communication?

- How should English as an International Language (EIL) be taught to learners needing English for international communication?

The fourth question has received very little attention in the literature, and I would like to offer my views as to the optimum methodology for the teaching of EIL. First, though, I would like to look briefly at what the literature has to say in answer to the other three questions, and to provide answers to them myself.

## What the experts say

### Standard Englishes

Very few applied linguists these days actually advocate the continuing use of Standard British English or General American as strict models of correctness for learners of EIL whose main need is to communicate in English with other non-native speakers of English. However, most (if not all) Ministries of Education, examination bodies, publishers and language schools still insist on the teaching of a Standard English, regardless of the actual communication needs of the learners of English as an L2; and most learners still seem to maintain that their goal is to speak English with native-like accuracy (Timmis 2002). The reality is that, despite most applied linguists insisting that Standard British English and General American are no longer necessary or desirable models for learners of EIL (e.g. Pennycook 1994), all the coursebooks I know which are sold on the global market still use one of these prestige standards as their model of correctness. It would be a brave publisher who risked financial failure by publishing a global coursebook with an EIL core or a variety of world Englishes as its model(s).

### Varieties of English

As Corder says, 'A speech community is made up of people who regard themselves as speaking the same language' (Corder 1973, 54). But, when a 'language becomes used in all corners of the world, by people from all walks of life, so it begins to develop new spoken varieties which are used by local people as symbols of their identity ... In the course of time these new varieties might become mutually unintelligible' (Crystal 1997, 359). Already speakers of English from different parts of the world speak distinctively different varieties of English (e.g.

**131**

Australian English, Indian English, Zambian English) whilst regarding themselves as speakers of the same language. What many of these speakers do is to speak a globally intelligible variety of English as well as locally intelligible varieties, and to consider them as varieties of the same language (just as I do when I use distinctively different varieties of English to make myself understood and accepted when I watch Liverpool play at Anfield, give a paper at an AAAL Conference in the USA, or order a pint in my local pub in Ilkley in West Yorkshire). A similarly positive view is taken by Graddol (1996, 217) who says that some linguists 'suggest that the designation "English" should now be thought of as that of a language group (like "Germanic" or "Romance") rather than a single language.' He says that 'It may be that English is making the world a more homogeneous place: it may also be that the world is making English more diverse in its forms, functions and cultural associations.'

In my view, lack of mutual intelligibility between different regional varieties of English would not be a major problem, because world users of English would develop two varieties, the local and the global, and they would switch codes in relation to their interlocutors and their purposes for communication. I have experienced this personally when living in Nigeria, Singapore and Vanuatu. In Nigeria academics switched easily from Standard English to Pidgin English when moving from international meetings to their local bar, in Singapore business men switched easily from Standard English to Singlish when leaving their office to go to a Hawker Centre for lunch, and customs officers switched easily from Standard English to Bislama (a Melanesian influenced pidgin English) when playing football in the Efate League.

## English as a common language

Crystal (1997b, viii–ix) states his belief in two linguistic principles by saying:

> I believe in the fundamental value of multilingualism, as an amazing world resource which presents us with different perspectives and insights...
>
> I believe in the fundamental value of a common language, as an amazing world resource which presents us with unprecedented possibilities for mutual understanding...

I agree with him but would add: I believe in the fundamental value of encouraging speakers of any language to use their individual and their cultural voices in ways that respect and include their interlocutors and that, therefore, the English which is taught for world communication should not position speakers of certain of its varieties as models of correct language use. I believe that English as a common language should be characterized by features which are shared by all its varieties and not just by some.

Quirk (1982) advocates teaching a 'Nuclear English', i.e. a restricted code consisting of indispensable structures and vocabulary which would provide the learner with the obligatory minimum of the language for international communication. This follows on from Ogden's (1932) suggestions for teaching a Basic English of 850 words which would serve all the needs of an international language. The remarkable economy of this restricted code was achieved by eradicating all emotive words and words with literary associations, and by using just sixteen verb forms to achieve all linguistic purposes.

Unfortunately people did not succeed in learning it to achieve international communication (I suspect partly because of the highlighting of its restrictive nature and because of the learners' lack of affective engagement in the learning process). A more realistic suggestion for a rich but restricted form of international English has been made recently by Jenkins (2000), who advocates the use of a phonological core, the Lingua Franca Core, in pronunciation teaching, and stresses the importance of helping learners to achieve 'phonological accommodation (convergence) ... in interlanguage talk' (195). She also argues for a change in the way that pronunciation is taught in the classroom (e.g. focusing on the ability to produce the teachable features of the phonological core), the way that pronunciation is taught in English language teacher education (e.g. focusing on how to teach the teachable features of the phonological core and how to understand and analyse the phonological features of a variety of world Englishes) and the way that pronunciation is tested (e.g. testing how well 'speakers are able to adjust their pronunciation appropriately to accommodate their interlocutors' (212)).

Jenkins acknowledges the influence of Jenner (1997), who believes 'that there is, at some level, a single underlying phonological system governing all the many varieties of English used around the world' (127) and that this system (once it has been represented by a substantial corpus) should be used for pedagogic purposes. Jenkins sees such a system as 'the starting point rather than the end point as far as pedagogy is concerned' (Jenkins 2000, 128) and stresses the need to help learners 'to make phonological adjustments (both productive and receptive) in the context of the individual interaction' (128). Seidlhofer (2001a, 2001b), Cook, (2002) and Prodomou (2003) have made cases similar to Jenner and Jenkins for using corpora of International English. Cook's main points are that L2 users have a right to use language differently from monolinguals and that 'students should aim at being proficient L2 users' (335). The distinctive feature of Prodromou's argument, and of his corpus, is that they are based on successful speakers of EIL rather than on learners. He has collected data from samples of 'natural, spontaneous speech produced by *proficient* non-native users of English as a foreign language' (11), and he has found that they have a virtually flawless command of grammar and vocabulary and even seem to have a wider range of lexis than native speakers. However, proficient non-native users of English use less ellipsis and fewer idioms and rarely make use of 'creative idiomaticity'. Prodromou attributes these differences partly to the fact that EIL is 'marked by a "shallow commonality" as opposed to the "deeper commonality" which characterises native-native interaction', and he advocates using his corpus as a model for teachers, learners, syllabus designers and materials writers to make use of.

If what Jenkins says is valid about pronunciation teaching for International English, then it is likely that there are parallels for the teaching of grammar, of vocabulary, of discourse and of pragmatic competence for International English too. However, it should be mentioned that not everybody in the field agrees with Jenkins. Timmis (2002), for example, reports that 67 per cent of a sample of learners of English from 14 countries expressed a desire to 'pronounce English just like a native speaker', and he concludes that 'While it is clearly inappropriate to foist native-speaker norms on students who neither want nor need them, it is scarcely more appropriate to offer students a target which manifestly does not meet their aspirations' (249). Strong opposition to Jenkins' suggestion of teaching a Lingua Franca Core are made by Sobkowiak (2003) who argues, for example, that:

- This would disadvantage learners when they do have to communicate with native speakers.
- This does not follow as a logical conclusion from statistics about the limited number of people who actually speak RP and about the intelligibilty of non-native phonology.
- LFC derives from the 'politically correct self-castigation in the British'. (5)
- LFC is an artificial linguistic model which has no native speakers.
- Numerous research projects have demonstrated that learners of English value RP highly (e.g. Neufeld 2001).
- This would lower learner objectives and achievement.

One obvious rejoinder to these arguments would be that, if LFC was only taught as a basic minimum for productive competence, if learners were taught to accommodate (as Jenkins (2000) argues), and if the learners continued to be exposed to a variety of standard Englishes to develop receptive competence, then standards could not be seen to be lowered, learners would be able to develop the ability to communicate with native speakers as well as non-native speakers, and the possibility of acquiring a native-like accent would still be there. This is basically my position on the question of the Lingua Franca Core. Its description and its use as a basic productive model would be extremely useful providing it was never viewed as the only goal for learners of EIC.

Pennycook (1994) argues against the assumption that English can be the 'neutral language of global communication' (301) and advocates a critical pedagogy which encourages learners to be political in their evaluation of the cultural assumptions implicit in the standard Englishes they aspire to learn. He argues that 'a critical practice in English language teaching must start with ways of critically exploring students' cultures, knowledges and histories in ways that are both challenging and at the same time affirming and supportive' (311). He also argues persuasively that:

> ...we need to make sure that students have access to those standard forms of the language linked to social and economic prestige; second, we need a good understanding of the status and possibilities presented by different standards; third, we need to focus on those parts of language that are significant in particular discourses; fourth, students need to be aware that those forms represent only one set of particular possibilities; and finally, students also need to be encouraged to find ways of using the language that they feel are expressive of their own needs and desires, ... so that they can start to claim and negotiate a voice in English. (317–18)

In my view, all the positions referred to above have something to recommend them but they all make the mistake of assuming that what learners learn is what teachers teach, and that a language can be defined by an inventory of linguistic forms and functions. What is needed is both a curriculum and a methodology for teaching English for global communication which identifies what its learners need and want to do in that language, which predicts the contexts in which they will need and want to do it, and which helps them to learn to do so in ways which will facilitate both language acquisition and the development of a global and a personal voice. One of the problems is that there is a universal school culture of conservatism, convergence and control, which discourages diversity and discovery and encourages transmission of knowledge and values (Tomlinson 1988). This is a culture which makes it difficult for experientially inclined learners to learn another language successfully regardless of whether it be a standard prestige language, a standard local language or a specially restricted global language for international communication.

## My position

Here is a summary of my position on the issue of English as an International Language. It is the result not only of my critical reading of the literature but of my experience as a teacher, teacher trainer, curriculum developer and university lecturer in Indonesia, Japan, Nigeria, Singapore, the UK, Vanuatu and Zambia.

### Language description

I think it is very important that applied linguists follow the lead set by Jenner, Jenkins, Cook, Prodromou and others in constructing corpora which will provide us with the data we need to describe a Lingua Franca Core. This could then act as a resource for designing syllabuses for the teaching of basic interactive competence in EIL. My view is that these corpora should be derived from successful interactions amongst proficient non-native users of English in a variety of contexts, for a variety of purposes and in a variety of genres and text types. So, for example, we need to know what non-native proficient users of EIL *do* when talking to each other in formal meetings, at social events and in informal conversation, and when writing to each other in letters, by fax, by e-mail and in documents. My emphasis on the word 'do' reflects my view that the main distinctive characteristics of EIL as a variety of English relate to its restricted set of intended outcomes and the strategies used to achieve them and that, therefore, we need to know about the pragmatic and discourse features of EIL as well as about its linguistic and paralinguistic features.

In addition to describing the characteristic pragmatic, discourse, lexical, phonological and grammatical features of the Lingua Franca Core, we also need to describe the characteristics of the Basic EIL Business Core, the Basic EIL Media Core, the Basic EIL Travel Core, the Basic EIL Entertainment Core, and many other specific basic EIL cores. Only then will we have reliable sources of information on which to base the productive teaching points for syllabuses and materials for specific groups of learners of EIL.

## Language planning

Language planners need to consider the actual and potential needs of their country, region, company or association and to ask and answer such questions as:

- Who must be able to use English?
- Who needs to be able to use English?
- Who wants to be able to use English?
- Who will each of the above groups use English with?
- What will each of the above groups use English for?
- Which varieties of English will each of the above groups need to be able to understand and which will they need to be able to produce?

When these questions have been answered, the planners will be in a position to recommend who English should be taught to, what English should be taught to them and when it should be taught.

Language planners have traditionally diverged in answering questions about whether to teach English to everybody or only to selected sections of the population, whether to teach English to young children, and/or to teenagers and/or to adults, whether to teach English as a second language, an additional language or a foreign language, and whether or not to use English as a medium of instruction, as a medium of media communication and even as an official language. But, as far as I know, whatever recommendations language planners have made, they have made them on the assumption that the variety of English taught will be a 'correct' and prestigious standard English. And in some countries governments have insisted that learners are taught only a 'pure' standard English and are protected from the corrupting influence of exposure to non-standard varieties of English. For example, the Government of Singapore currently insists on Standard British English being taught in Singapore primary and secondary schools and has forbidden the use of Singlish in schools (thus preventing the classroom use of local literature which includes dialogues in Singlish). However, as more descriptions of the Lingua Franca Core of EIL are provided, and as more and more people realize the inevitability and value of the development of a variety of EIL which differs from the prestige standard Englishes but facilitates international communication, there is the possibility that even conservative language planners (as most of them inevitably and suitably are) might come up with recommendations something like the following example of a possible language policy for a country in which English is not normally used as a medium of communication:

| Lower Primary | No teaching of English but exposure to some songs, rhymes and cartoons. |
|---|---|
| Upper Primary | English taught to all pupils with the emphasis on receptive competence and on fun, enjoyment and the development of positive attitudes towards both English and their L1. |
| Junior Secondary | English taught to all pupils with the emphasis on further developing receptive competence from exposure to a variety of Englishes, on learning to achieve productive competence in a Lingua Franca Core of Basic EIL and on the maintenance of positive attitudes to both English and their L1. |
| Senior Secondary | 1. Pupils without the inclination to continue to learn English are no longer taught English but are sometimes exposed to English through news broadcasts, songs, films, the Internet and sports commentaries. 2. Selected groups of pupils are taught English with the emphasis on further developing receptive competence from exposure to a variety of Englishes, on learning to achieve productive competence in a more elaborated Lingua Franca Core of EIL and on the maintenance of positive attitudes to both English and their L1. 3. 'Elite' groups of successful English learners to be taught all their subjects in English, as well as being taught English with the same objectives as those of the groups in 2 above. |
| Tertiary Education | 1. Students not studying English are taught Basic EIL Academic English plus the Basic EIL Cores relevant to their subjects of study (e.g. Basic EIL Travel English, Basic EIL Hotel English, Basic EIL Business English, etc). 2. Students studying English are taught to develop receptive and productive competence in a number of standard Englishes as well as to develop their understanding of how EIL cores are described and used. |

## Curriculum development

Dhamija (1994) explains why English is the most widely used language in the world by listing its world functions as:

English as a link language
English as a medium of literary creativity
English as a medium of science and technology
English as a language of reference and research
English as a resource language
English as a media language

We could easily emphasize how important English has become by adding the following EIL functions:

English as a conference language
English as an academic language
English as an Internet language
English as a business language
English as a commercial language
English as an industrial language
English as the language of air and sea control
English as a language of social intercourse
English as a diplomatic language
English as a language of sport
English as a language of entertainment
English as the language of popular songs
English as a travel language
English as a language for migration
English as a holiday language
English to provide access to news and views
English as a language of self-expression

It is important to consider these functions when designing a curriculum for global English but it is equally important to accept that each learner will only need and want to acquire competence in a limited number of these functions, and that global English curricula need to be individualized. I would argue, though, that, regardless of how restricted the perceived needs and wants of the learners, all learners of English as a global language need to learn it as a language of self-expression. If you are at a conference, at a dinner, in a meeting or on a plane and you are using English as a lingua franca you are going to feel diminished and frustrated if you are not able to express your views, opinions and feelings in English. And you are going to lose confidence and credibility too. One question on an EIL course would be where does the language of self-expression come from, and I would agree with Timmis (personal communication) that it will need to come 'from native varieties because, as a general rule, NS use English for a wider range of purposes than LFC users: jokes, anecdotes, endearments, abuse, nursery rhymes etc.' and 'NS use English more often for affective purposes than LFC users'.

Depending on what the learners are going to need to do in English and who they are going to need to do it with, national, institutional, group and even individual curricula could be developed that specify which varieties of English should be learned for both receptive and productive competence, and which should be learned for receptive competence only. For example, an English course for a group of medical students in a Japanese university could be based on a syllabus which features:

- exposure to a variety of World Englishes so as to develop receptive competence and the ability to achieve accommodation.
- the learning of a Lingua Franca EIL Core for receptive and productive competence.
- the learning of Basic EIL Medical, Academic and Conference Presentation Cores for receptive and productive competence.
- the learning of English for Self-Expression for receptive and productive competence.

## The teachers

The best teachers of EIL would be successful learners of EIL, as they would be proficient users of the variety they are teaching and would be sensitive to the needs and wants of their learners. Native speakers of English, on the other hand, are less likely to be proficient users of EIL and are unlikely to be as sensitive to the needs and wants of the learners. They are also more likely to teach features of standard Englishes which are not relevant for learners of EIL, and to correct 'errors' which are actually characteristic features of EIL. This position seems to me to be a logical conclusion of any decision to teach EIL. But how many language schools would be willing to employ non-native English speakers in preference to native speakers? And how many learners would be happy to pay a lot of money to be taught by teachers whom they do not perceive to be native speakers of the language they are learning? My experience as a Director of Studies of language schools tells me that it would take a lot of 'education' to persuade owners, principals and users of language schools (especially sponsors) to accept the argument that the best teachers of EIL are proficient users of it.

Ultimately, what matters most will not be whether EIL teachers are native or non-native speakers, but whether they:

- make effective communication their main objective.
- are open-minded in their acceptance (and even encouragement) of any variety of English which achieves effective communication.
- are able to use themselves and teach to others 'the communicative strategies of tolerance of variation and participant cooperation' (Kirkpatrick 2004).

## Methodology

The debate about whether standard Englishes, world Englishes or EIL should be taught to non-native speakers who will need to use English with other non-native speakers seems to have ignored the obvious point that learners do not learn what teachers teach. Learners learn what they need, want and are ready to learn (Ellis 1994, Pienemann 1985, Schmidt 1992, Tomlinson 1998a), and they only learn anything durable at all if the conditions are right for acquisition. It seems they learn best if they are motivated, stimulated, challenged, supported and engaged (Tomlinson 1998a). Affective engagement seems to be a prerequisite for durable learning (Arnold 1999, Tomlinson 1998b) and successful learning is best facilitated by the achievement of self-esteem, by positive attitudes to the language and to the context of learning it, and by emotional engagement in the learning process. In my experience, the last point is the most important. Learners need to laugh, to be excited, to be exhilarated, to be provoked, to take a position, to empathize, and even to be disturbed, in order to achieve the deep processing required for acquisition (Craik and Lockhart 1972). It is even better that they are angered by a text rather than totally neutral towards it. Blandness does not engage; controversy does. The teaching of a restricted code of Core Lingua Franca features could only succeed if the methodology promoted affective engagement and if the learners were also exposed to the cognitive and affective richness offered by other elaborated codes.

We also need to keep in mind that learners differ in needs and wants, in contexts of learning, in previous experience, in expectations, in goals, in language learning aptitude and, in particular, in preferred learning styles. Whilst the academic debate about World English(es) has been conducted mainly in large generalizations at a language planning/curriculum level, the actual teaching of World English would have to be carried out in specific contexts of learning with groups of specific individuals. The methodology of EIL would have to cater for variability and could not be based on such absolutes as represented by the polarized proponents of the 'teach everybody the correct standard' approach, or the 'teach everybody a core lingua franca' approach. The methodology of EIL (if such a thing is desirable and feasible) must be flexible and must be capable of catering for all learners who are likely to need to use English for international communication.

In order to cater for the needs and wants of the learners of EIL, I would propose the following components of a flexible methodology for teaching EIL.

## Objectives

To help learners to:

- develop positive attitudes towards EIL and to the environment in which they are learning it.
- develop self-esteem as users of EIL.
- develop the ability to achieve their intended outcomes when communicating with other non-native users of English.
- develop the ability to achieve their intended outcomes when communicating with native users of English.
- accommodate their use of English in order to communicate successfully in English with users of differing varieties of English.
- develop the skills required to understand users of differing varieties of English (including Standard Englishes).

## Principles

Learners of EIL:

- will only learn what they need and want to learn.
- have a restricted number of instrumental needs but need and want to express themselves as individual human beings too.
- have both short-term and long-term needs and wants (e.g. giving a conference presentation at an international conference vs feeling comfortable and confident whenever communicating

with other non-native speakers in English).
- have individual wants, which can vary from wanting to get a good deal when booking a hotel to wanting to write poetry in English.
- can be helped to discover (and even modify) their needs and wants and to develop readiness to learn.
- need to be both cognitively and affectively engaged in the learning process.

## Procedures

Procedures for teaching EIL should:

- be humanistic in the sense of respecting and catering for the instrumental, intellectual, creative and affective needs and wants of the individual learners (e.g. by including tasks encouraging personal reflection and connection (Tomlinson 2003a, 2003b, 2003d) and by offering choice of learning routes, texts and tasks (Maley 1998, 2003)).
- follow a multidimensional approach which promotes the use of sensory imaging, inner speech, emotional connections and cognitive analysis in the learning process (Masuhara 2000, Tomlinson 2001a).
- concentrate initially on helping the learner to develop a fluent inner voice in EIL so as to develop confidence, facilitate self-expression and facilitate preparation for outer voice expression (Tomlinson 2000, 2001a, 2003c).
- use both text-driven approaches (Tomlinson 2003b) to achieve cognitive and affective engagement, and task-driven approaches (Willis 1996) to achieve a focus on the successful achievement of outcomes.
- make use of language awareness, pragmatic awareness, cultural awareness and critical awareness activities to help the learners to discover for themselves some of the characteristic features of EIL (Bolitho and Tomlinson 1995, Bolitho et al. 2003, Tomlinson 1994).

## Materials

In order to help teachers to teach EIL, materials are needed which:

- teach different types of target learners those features of the EIL core which are relevant, teachable and useful.
- give learners opportunities to interact with other EIL users in order to achieve intended outcomes.
- expose learners in meaningful ways to a rich variety of language use in a variety of genres and text types from a variety of Englishes (including Standard English, General American, EIL and various regional Englishes).
- help learners to notice and respond to implications signalled by native speakers on the assumption of 'deep commonality'.
- help learners to accommodate their English both receptively and productively when interacting with native speakers or with speakers of regional Englishes.

Ideally these materials would be presented through print, audio, video, computer and face-to-face channels in order to replicate the contexts of use likely to be experienced by EIL users, and it would be very important that the voices and personas of the 'characters' in the materials represent a varied sample of successful EIL users (Cook 2002). It would also be important that the settings of the texts and tasks are multinational and multicultural, and either that they are authentic or that they replicate very faithfully the characteristic features of EIL communication.

Ideally the writers and editors of EIL materials would be proficient users of EIL rather than (or at least in addition to) native-speaker users of English.

## Examinations

None of my suggestions above could be implemented without a radical change in evaluation and assessment, and in particular in the policies of the major examiners of English as an L2. At the moment such examinations as the Cambridge First Certificate, IELTS and TOEFL insist that their candidates need to demonstrate the ability to use a Standard English with accuracy and effect in order to be successful in the examination. They would need to be persuaded that it would be justifiable, popular and profitable to change their policy. What I would ask them to consider, though, would be the introduction of a series of additional examinations assessing the ability of the candidates to achieve intended outcomes when using English as an International

Language. Such examinations would be at different levels of outcome achievement (rather than at different levels of linguistic difficulty and complexity), and would include tasks requiring:

- the successful production of EIL in spoken and written tasks involving the achievement of outcomes in contexts typical of EIL use.
- the successful production of EIL in spoken and written tasks involving the expression of self in contexts typical of EIL use.
- the successful understanding of EIL in listening and reading tasks involving the achievement of outcomes in contexts typical of EIL use.
- the ability to achieve accommodation to achieve successful communication with users of EIL from different L1s.
- the successful understanding of standard Englishes in listening and reading tasks.
- the successful understanding of a variety of world Englishes in listening and reading tasks.

Ideally there would be a Core Examination of Proficiency in English as an International Language at different levels of outcome achievement, plus supplementary examinations in proficiency in the use of specific sub-varieties of EIL (e.g. The Examination of Proficiency in English as an International Language for Business Communication). Obviously such examinations would only be viable if they were accepted by the world as being different from but also equivalent to the existing prestige examinations of English as an L2. Without such acceptance the examinations would be unattractive to learners of English as an L2, and their 'failure' would be a disincentive to applied linguists, language planners and curriculum developers to take the description and teaching of EIL seriously.

## Conclusion

At the beginning of this chapter I posed some questions about English as an International Language. Here are my answers to those questions:

Should the prevailing standard Englishes (i.e. Standard British English and General American) continue to be taught as models of correctness to learners needing English for international communication? One answer to this question would be that EIL is developing as a distinctive variety of English anyway, regardless of decisions made by language planners and methodologists. So why not leave things as they are and allow the teaching of standard Englishes to make sure that EIL does not diverge too far? However, *my* answer is that this would continue to disadvantage, and even stigmatize, effective users of EIL who are not accurate users of a Standard English. Learners of EIL should continue to be exposed to input in Standard British English and General American but these varieties of English should not be considered to be superior to other varieties of English, and the learners' production of spoken and written English should not be evaluated exclusively against these standards.

Should a variety of world Englishes be used as models of effective communication for learners needing English for international use? Learners should be exposed to input in a variety of world Englishes, but none of them should be considered as models of correctness for learners to emulate. Learners' production of spoken and written English should be evaluated in relation to the outcomes (or potential outcomes) in the context in which it is produced.

Should it be accepted that an international variety of English is already being evolved by the millions of non-native users of English who communicate with each other in English every day? And should this variety be described and then used as an appropriate model for learners needing English for international communication? This Lingua Franca Core should be described and then used as a source for the syllabuses of courses aimed at helping learners to achieve a threshold level of productive effectiveness in EIL.

How should English as an International Language (EIL) be taught to learners needing English for international communication? It should be taught in ways determined by the intended outcomes and the length and intensity of the course, but even the shortest and most instrumental course should pay attention to the learners' need for affective and cognitive engagement in the learning process.

But, are we not being rather arrogant in assuming that it is we as applied linguists, language planners, curriculum designers, teachers and materials developers who will determine the characteristics of a World Standard English? Is it not the users of English as a global language who will determine these characteristics as a result of negotiating interaction with each other? We can facilitate the process by making sure that our curricula, our methodology and our examinations do not impose unnecessary and unrealistic standards of correctness on our international learners, and by providing input and guiding output relevant to their needs and wants. But ultimately it is they and not us who will decide. To think otherwise is to be guilty of neo-colonialist conceit and to ignore all that we know about how languages develop over time. As Graddol (1996, 186) asks, 'has such an international English already emerged as a natural consequence of the increasing use of English as a medium of communication between speakers of different languages?'

Maybe our most important contribution will be to 'seek to find positive ways of ensuring that our students are aware of their rights – and their responsibilities – in owning their English' (Hayhoe and Parker 1994: xii).

What we need in order to facilitate the acquisition of a universally beneficial EIL is:

- the construction of easily accessible corpora for all the varieties of EIL identified above.
- a description of a Core EIL common to all the varieties of EIL.
- the development of a pedagogy which provides exposure to a rich and varied sample of Englishes being used for a multiplicity of purposes, whilst at the same time teaching for productive use those features of the Core EIL and of relevant varieties of EIL which are considered to be teachable and to be important for international communication for the target learners.
- the development of materials both for teaching Core EIL and for each variety of EIL (a textbook series could be designed, for example, in which each book includes materials to facilitate the learning of Core EIL, of English for Self-Expression, and of one other variety of EIL (e.g. English for Business).
- the development of EIL examinations which assess the candidates' ability to use Core EIL, English for Self-Expression, and another relevant variety of EIL in order to achieve international communication. Such an examination could also include sections assessing the ability of candidates to understand and respond to communication in a variety of regional Englishes.

Above all, what we need is to encourage awareness that communication between speakers of different varieties of English is typically characterized by mutual understanding and cooperation even when the speakers make 'errors' (Kirkpatrick 2004), and that we should rejoice in this as a positive rather than lament the speakers' failure to achieve native-speaker norms.

# References

Arnold, J. 1999. (ed.) *Affect in Language Learning*. Cambridge: Cambridge University Press.

Bolitho, R. and Tomlinson, B. 1995. *Discover English* (New edition). Oxford: Heinemann.

Bolitho, R., R. Carter, R. Hughes, R. Ivanic, H. Masuhara and B. Tomlinson 2003. 'Ten questions about language awareness'. *ELT Journal* 58/2, 251–9.

Cook, V. 2002. *Portraits of the L2 User*. Clevedon: Multilingual Matters.

Corder, S. P. 1973. *Introducing Applied Linguistics*. Harmondsworth: Penguin.

Craik, F. I. M. and R. S. Lockhart 1972. 'Levels of processing: a framework for memory research'. *Journal of Verbal Learning and Verbal Behaviour* II, 671–84.

Crystal, D. 1997a. *The Cambridge Encyclopedia of Language* (second edition). Cambridge: Cambridge University Press.

Crystal, D. 1997b. *English as a Global Language*. Cambridge: Cambridge University Press.

Dhamija, P. V. 1994. 'English as a multiform medium'. In M. Hayhoe and S. Parker, *Who Owns English?* Buckingham: Open University Press, 62–7.

Ellis, R. 1994. *The Study of Second Language Acquisition*. Oxford: Oxford University Press.

Graddol, D. 1996. *Redesigning English: New Texts, New Identities*. London: The Open University and Routledge.

Hayhoe, M. and S. Parker 1994. *Who Owns English?* Buckingham: Open University Press.

Jenkins, J. 2000. *The Phonology of English as an International Language*. Oxford: Oxford University Press.

Jenner, B. 1997. 'International English: an alternative view'. *Speak Out!* 15, 15–16.

Kirkpatrick, A. 2004. 'English as an ASEAN lingua franca: implications for language teaching'. IAWE Conference, Syracuse University, 16–18 July 2004.

Maley, A. 1998. 'Squaring the circle – reconciling materials as constraint with materials as empowerment'. In B. Tomlinson (ed.), *Materials Development in Language Teaching*. Cambridge: Cambridge University Press, 279–94.

Maley, A. 2003. 'Creative approaches to materials writing'. In: B. Tomlinson (ed.), *Developing Materials for Language Teaching*. London: Continuum, 183–98.

Masuhara, H. 2000. 'Experiencing literature through language'. In S. H. Chan, M. A. Quayam and T. Rosli (eds), *Diverse Voices: Readings in Language, Literature and Culture*. Serdang: Penerbit UPM, 104–11.

Neufeld, G. G. 2001. 'Non-foreign-accented speech in adult second language learners: does it exist and what does it signify?' *ITL Review of Applied Linguistics*, 133/134, 185–206.

Ogden, C. K. 1932. *The Basic Dictionary*. London: Kegan Paul, Trench, Trubner.

Pennycook, A. 1994. *The Cultural Politics of English as an International Language*. London: Longman.

Pienemann, M. 1985. 'Learnability and syllabus construction'. In K. Hyltenstam and M. Pienemann (eds), *Modelling and Assessing Second Language Acquisition*. Clevedon: Multilingual Matters.

Prodromou, L. 2003. 'In search of the successful user of English: how a corpus of non-native speaker language could impact on EFL teaching'. *Modern English Teacher* 12/2, 5–14.

Quirk, R. 1982. 'International communication and the concept of Nuclear English'. In R. Quirk, *Style and Communication in the English Language*. London: Edward Arnold, 37–53.

Schmidt, R. 1990. 'The role of consciousness in second language learning'. *Applied Linguistics* 11/2, 129–58.

Seidlehofer, B. 2001a. 'Towards making "Euro-English" a linguistic reality'. *English Today* 68, 14–16.

Seidlehofer, B. 2001b. 'Closing a conceptual gap: the case for a description of English as a lingua franca'. *International Journal of Applied Linguistics* 11/2, 133–58.

Sobkowiak, W. 2003. 'Why not LFC?' In: W. Sobkowiak and E. Waniek-Klimczak (eds), *Dydaktyka fonetyki – teorie a praktyka. Zeszyty naukowe Państwowej Wyższej Szkoły Zawodowej w Koninie nr 1/2003 (2). Proceedings of the Wasosze Conference on Teaching Foreign Pronunciation, 10–12.5.2002*, 114–24 (available in English translation at: *http://elex.amu.edu.pl/~sobkow/*).

Timmis, I. 2002. 'Native-speaker norms and International English: a classroom view'. *ELT Journal* 56/2, 240–49.

Tomlinson, B. 1988. 'Conflicts in TEFL, reasons for failure in secondary schools'. In: V. Bickley (ed.), *Language in Education in a Bi-Lingual or Multi-Lingual Setting*. Institute of Education, Education Department, Hong Kong. 103–10.

Tomlinson, B. 1994. 'Pragmatic awareness activities'. *Language Awareness* 3 & 4, 119–29.

Tomlinson, B. 1998a. Introduction. In B. Tomlinson (ed.), *Materials Development in Language Teaching*. Cambridge: Cambridge University Press, 1–24.

Tomlinson, B. 1998b. 'Affect and the coursebook'. *IATEFL Issues* 145, 20–21.

Tomlinson, B. 2000. 'The role of inner speech in language learning'. *Applied Language Learning* 11/1, 123–54.

Tomlinson, B. 2001a. 'The inner voice: a critical factor in L2 Learning'. *The Journal of the Imagination in Language Learning and Teaching*. V1, 26–33.

Tomlinson, B. 2001b. 'Connecting the mind: a multi-dimensional approach to teaching language through literature'. *The English Teacher*, 4/2, 104–15.

Tomlinson, B. 2003a. 'Humanising the coursebook'. In B. Tomlinson (ed.), *Developing Materials for Language Teaching*. London: Continuum, 162–74.

Tomlinson, B. 2003b. 'Developing principled frameworks for materials development'. In B. Tomlinson (ed.), *Developing Materials for Language Teaching*. London: Continuum, 107–29.

Tomlinson, B. 2003c. Helping learners to develop an effective L2 inner voice. *RELC Journal*. 34/2, August, 178–94.

Tomlinson, B. 2003d. 'Humanising the language class'. *RELC Guidelines*, 25/2, December, 2–9.

Willis, J. 1996. *A Framework for Task-Based Learning*. London: Longman.

# Teaching EIL – Teaching *International* or *Intercultural* English? What Teachers Should Know

*Nicos Sifakis*
*Hellenic Open University*

## Introduction

The term EIL (English as an International Language) has been used in a wide variety of different contexts in and beyond language teaching by a wide variety of different scholars, who have used it (together with 'global' or 'world' English or 'English as an international lingua franca') to discuss the status of the English language in the globalized, postmodern era (Ammon 2001, Block and Cameron 2002, Brutt-Griffler 2002, Clyne 2003, Crystal 2003, De Swaan 2001, Jenkins 2003, McKay 2002, Swales 1997, Widdowson 1997; for a wider perspective, cf. Maurais and Morris 2003), relating it to native and non-native speakers' and teachers' linguistic, national and cultural identities (Arva and Medgyes 2000, Braine 1999, Brutt-Griffler and Samimy 2001, Seidlhofer 1999), linking it with the notions of linguistic and cultural diversity and their impact on the linguistic human rights movement (Del Valle 2003, Skutnabb-Kangas 2000), questioning its ownership by native and non-native speakers alike (Widdowson 1994), or even making predictions about the future of English (Crystal 2003, chapter 5, Graddol 1997, 2001).

Other scholars also raise concerns related to ethnolinguistics, anthropology, educational sociology and educational linguistics, and discuss language policy and language planning, critical pedagogy and discourse analysis (Phillipson 1992 and 2003, Pennycook 1994 and 1998, Ricento 2000; for a review of these and similar issues, cf. Author et al., 2003).

While such discussions have been forthcoming in these matters, what has not been made entirely clear until now is what sense a teacher interested in teaching EIL can make of it in practical, tangible terms. In this article, I concentrate on drawing some pedagogical implications from the wider discussion about EIL and, taking on board a number of theoretical and practical concerns raised in the relevant research, attempt to draw some awareness-raising considerations for the prospective EIL teacher.

I begin by offering a working definition of EIL and briefly reviewing the current position of the EIL debate by distinguishing the domain into three areas – 'theory', 'reality' and 'application'. 'Theory' is concerned with the delineating and defining of the EIL paradigm. 'Reality' is related to observations of actual EIL communication and an understanding of the various cognitive and communicative processes involved. Finally, 'application' is related to the teaching of EIL and refers to those pedagogical considerations that the EIL teacher should be aware of. This triangulation of the EIL domain is particularly important since, as we will see, a coherent and cohesive discussion of the pedagogical implications of EIL is very much dependent upon the various interpretations of the uses of English in international communication. We therefore need first to concentrate on these uses (and their interpretations) before we embark on discussing any specific pedagogical implications. Having said that, however, it should be stressed that my aim in this paper is not to provide ready-made solutions to well-known problems, but to raise my fellow teachers' awareness of a number of characteristics of a pedagogical area that is increasingly trendy and ever-fascinating, but still remains largely under-explored.

## Introducing the tools of our analysis: the *N-bound* and *C-bound* perspectives

The distinctions between theory, reality and application correspond to three different ways of studying the English (or any other) language: namely, in terms of language analysis (where intrinsic linguistic properties are of interest), language communication (where socio-cultural and pragmatic patterns of interaction and transaction are studied) and language teaching (where pedagogical standards of language learning are accounted for). In order to draw out implications for the EIL teacher, it is important to pinpoint similarities and differences between the way that EIL and other perspectives (i.e. those that view English as a first, second, foreign, additional or auxiliary language) perceive English in terms of these three viewpoints.

I suggest that this can be done by drawing a continuum along which two distinct points of view can be placed (Sifakis et al. 2003). At one end we have a perspective which emphasizes matters of regularity, codification and standardization. Let us call this the norm- or N-bound perspective. At the other end we find those analyses that focus on 'a pattern of learned, group-related perceptions – including both verbal and non-verbal language, attitudes, values, belief systems, disbelief systems, and behaviors – that is accepted and expected by an identity group' (Singer 1998, 96). This perspective prioritizes the process of cross-cultural comprehensibility between learners as a communicative goal in itself rather than notions of accuracy and standards. Let us call this the C-bound perspective, since the three operative words (communication, comprehensibility, culture) start with 'c'.

Let us see how the terms 'N-bound' and 'C-bound' can facilitate the drawing up of a list of characteristics of EIL that teachers can refer to.

## The EIL domain

### *'Theory'*

Traditional N-bound approaches generally correlate the languages around the world with their native speakers (NSs) – in fact, this seems to be a strong, 'natural' tendency of most 'unsuspected', ordinary people that is psycholinguistically accounted for (e.g. Timmis 2002). For this reason, it is common for most people learning foreign languages to want to find out about and adapt to all aspects of the native speakers' uses of these languages. It is interesting to note in this regard that, in most cases, the standardization principles adhered to by language planners typically exclude variability (as it is evidenced, for example, in the different dialects and accents of different NSs) and nominate a central variety as the 'standard norm' of the language (cf. Bruthiaux 2002, Crowley 2003, Downes 1998, 32–45, Fairclough 1992, 202, Mugglestone 2003).

Furthermore, N-bound interaction between native and non-native speakers (NNSs) is understood as communication between NNSs/ 'learners' and NSs/'owners' of the target language (Table 1). In such situations, all aspects of the NNSs' own L1 (e.g. the phonological and grammatical characteristics) are, in principle, looked down upon as obstacles that can hinder communication. Norm-bound approaches respond to this phenomenon by providing codified (or rule-based) accounts of languages by means of a lexical, syntactic, morphological, phonological, socio-cultural etc. analysis of the various uses of languages by their various native speakers.

**Table 1.** N-bound and C-bound approaches to language and communication

|  | **N-Bound approach** | **C-Bound approach** |
|---|---|---|
| **Basic language 'rules' (e.g. grammar, pronunciation)** | Codified | Not (easily) codified |
| **Target language 'ownership'** | By its native speakers | By native and non-native speakers alike |
|  | Learners 'adapt' to NS norms | No need for learners to 'adapt' to NS norms |
|  | Native speakers central | Non-native speakers central |
| **Language communication** | Seen primarily as competency (addressor-oriented) | Seen primarily as comprehensibility (addressee-oriented) |
|  | Interaction between non-native speakers/'learners' and native speakers/'owners' | Interaction between speakers/'owners' |
|  | Interlocutors' L1 'suppressed' | Interlocutors' L1 'basic' |
|  | Target use of English easily specified | Target use of English not easily specified |

With C-bound situations quite the reverse is the case. What singles English out as a natural language is the fact that it is essentially the first choice for communication between non-native speakers (Crystal 2003). This means that, in descriptive terms, the very notion of a 'native speaker of English' fails to act as a measure for the many different forms of communication among monolingual/multilingual English speakers from the Inner and Outer Circles (Kachru 1985), and among fluent or less fluent multilinguals from the Expanding Circle. Thus, C-bound interaction is understood as communication among speakers/'owners' of the target language, for whom their L1 (or experience in communicating in other languages) is not only an inescapable, but also a very welcome and 'desired' feature of their projected cultural identity (Table 1).

Language communication in the N-bound paradigm is seen primarily from the point of view of the addressor, or producer of the message to be communicated. In C-bound terms, what matters more is not whether an interlocutor is a NS of English but whether their communication is intelligible or comprehensible to their interlocutors (thus emphasizing the key function of the addressee/receiver of that message – Jenkins 2000). Comprehensibility (also known in cognitive science as normalization) is one of the key elements in all forms of communication between people, and refers to the natural ability of speakers/listeners to overcome the problems of speech variability by adapting (or accommodating, or normalizing) their discourse to the linguistic, expressive or cultural characteristics inherent in their interlocutors' communicative performance (Giles et al. 1991).

Thus, in successful EIL communication NNSs manage to over-come potential comprehensibility problems by sharing the ability to process each other's performance to account for the needs of the specific situation and of one another. Such accommodation and normalization techniques have been the subject of extensive study by various discourse analysis, pragmatics, sociolinguistics and inter-cultural accounts (e.g. Braidi 2002, Derwing and Munro 2001, Munro and Derwing 1999, O'Sullivan 1994, Tyler 2001, Wierzbicka 2003, Wong 2000), form a central part of recent language learning reference frameworks (e.g. the Common European Framework – cf. Council of Europe 2001) and need to be further investigated.

Such variability in the communication between different NNSs renders any attempt at codifying the various uses of English in EIL situations difficult, since we would have to know in advance many things that are situation-specific and user-dependent. Nevertheless, codification of different facets of comprehensible EIL use is one of the targets of applied linguistics research, with the 'lingua franca core' of EIL phonology suggested by Jenkins (2000, 2002) being one of the most coherent recent suggestions.

## 'Reality'

If we look at what actually takes place in real communications in English among NNSs we will see that the great variety that characterizes such discourse is very close to what we understand today as global or international English. In real world (and out-of-the-ELT-classroom) NNS performance, highly valued in-class notions such as fluency or competence in a particular skill (or combinations of skills) are accomplishments that are far from absolute and depend on a multitude of circumstances, only a fraction of which are under the language user's conscious control (James 1998). In fact, this phenomenon is not restricted to NNSs but extends to all speakers of English, be they native or competent bilingual.

What characterizes such EIL communication is the need for mutual comprehensibility. From an N-bound point of view, this often results in an abundance of pronunciation, syntax and expression errors and lapses of intelligibility that are nearly always situation-specific, and usually have very little to do with the way the language has been taught/learned in the ELT classroom (Ellis 1997). What is more, such communication is fraught with non-linguistic communication (e.g. gestures, grimaces, etc.) that is known to greatly facilitate comprehensibility (and is also not generally taught in classes).

In this light it can be argued that, while in-class learning may be N-bound, real life NNS–NNS and NNS–NS communication, and communication between fluent and less fluent bilingual speakers is, and has always been, C-bound. This means that when these people communicate in English, their communication has key non-linguistic features and their discourse takes forms that are dependent on many parameters. These parameters include people's reasons for and modes of communicating, their personal training or talent in individual language skills (e.g. pronunciation or syntax), their attitudes towards the English language and the reasons for using it, their preconceptions about their interlocutors' cultural and linguistic background, and their predispositions towards their interlocutors' social status (Byram 1997, Samovar and Porter 1994).

## ElcL: English as an *Intercultural* Language

In this light it is perhaps more useful, when considering real-life English language communication, to shift the emphasis from its *international* usage to its *intercultural* use by all speakers, native and non-native. The former centres on N-bound analyses of comprehensibility that focus on the non-native speaker. The latter focuses on a C-bound analysis of the interlocutors' ability to handle all sorts of communicative situations, as well as their attitudes to and beliefs about English.

The essential difference between the two is that the description of *international* English (EIL) follows an N-bound route that aims at delineating that variety (or varieties) of English that are globally comprehensible, whereas the description of *intercultural* English (ElcL) follows a C-bound route according to which each communicative situation appropriates the use of widely different varieties with elements that are not necessarily readily regularized. In this regard, EIL is norm-oriented and refers to a finite set of descriptive or prescriptive varieties of world English (cf. Crystal 2003, Smith and Foreman 1997), whereas EIcL is much more expansive: it transcends the linguistic standardization of such communication and refers to those aspects that are situation-specific and cannot necessarily be standardized (e.g. Alred et al. 2002, Byram et al. 2001).

**Figure 1** EIcL

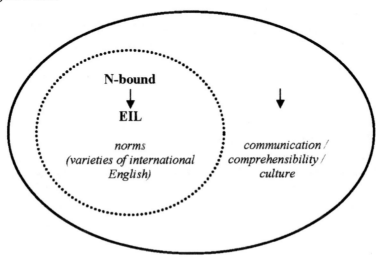

How then are the N- and C- bound perspectives related? It can be argued that the various codified varieties of international English (EIL) are only a subset of the many more forms that real communication between NNSs can take (Figure 1). It should be possible to account for the linguistic varieties adopted, but such an account is far from being an exhaustive appreciation of such communication. What this means for the EIL teacher is that teaching a norm of world English to a group of NNS learners would not necessarily guarantee that any and all future communications between these learners and other NNSs or NSs would be equally successful and unproblematic. Learners should be exposed to and become actively aware of as many and diverse samples of NNS discourse as possible, and acquire training in making themselves comprehensible in as many different communicative situations and with as many different types of NNSs as possible. In this way, they will become skilful at rendering their discourse comprehensible to their interlocutors by making repairs, asking questions, shortening utterances, changing the tempo of their speech output, etc. (Byram et al. 2001). EIcL incorporates those issues that make a communication successful, and these certainly include the usage of some kind of norm. However, that norm can change in the process of communicating, as interlocutors become aware of certain linguistic and non-linguistic elements that make their communication 'tick'.

It is therefore important for teachers to appreciate that a coherent understanding of communication involving NNSs necessitates *both* an N-bound and a C-bound analysis, as follows (Table 2):

**Table 2.** The two different facets of international/intercultural English

| | **Theory** | **Reality** |
|---|---|---|
| | English as an International Language | English as an Intercultural Language |
| **Which variety?** | One maximal variety of English | Many 'varieties' of English |
| **Non-linguistic features** | Not of primary importance | Of primary importance |
| **Orientation** | Predominantly N-bound | Predominantly C-bound |
| **Strengths** | Suggested variety is readily teachable | Each variety used is appropriated by each communicative situation and the participants' attitudes to and awareness of many parameters |
| **Weaknesses** | Suggested variety neither the one used by NSs, nor one that NNSs might 'identify' with as 'owners' | Suggested varieties are not (?) readily teachable |

## N-bound matters

- The linguistic (syntactic, semantic, phonological) proximity of NNSs' L1;
- that certain languages are 'closer' together than others (for example, English is nearer to Dutch phonologically and syntactically than to, say, Japanese – cf. Jenkins 2000);
- the corresponding 'systemic' competence of NNSs with respect to English – i.e. their knowledge about and skill 'related to the way the language works as a system' (Johnson 2001, 16);
- that different speakers exhibit different degrees of fluency or non-fluency in a particular language, which may be due to many diverse factors, such as exposure to NSs' use of that language, private study, talent, etc.

## C-bound matters

- The corresponding communicative competence of the speakers (Canale and Swain 1980) with respect to English, i.e. the extent to which they are able to handle the various conditions of use and discourse;
- the corresponding 'languaculture', or inherent cultural baggage, of words and expressions of English and NNSs' L1 (Agar 1994);
- the corresponding 'strategic competence' of the speakers with respect to the languages involved: this involves the 'verbal and non-verbal communication strategies that may be called upon to compensate for breakdowns of communication' (Canale and Swain 1980);
- the nature of the communication (in the Hallidayan sense of channel, tenor and manner) and participants' awareness of it;
- participants' awareness of and beliefs about the 'appropriate' sociolinguistic behaviour dictated by each communicative situation (this brings up the issue of politeness in intercultural communication – cf. Boxer 2002, Kasper 1998 and 2001, Wierzbicka 2003);
- participants' sense of belonging to a particular identity group and its corresponding culture (Singer 1998), and their sense of being an outsider/insider with regard to the English language and its intercultural uses (Gubbins and Holt 2002, Keating 1998);
- participants' beliefs about and attitudes towards the use of English for international/intercultural communication.

## The EIL domain – 'application'

Clearly, as far as the EIL/EIcL teacher is concerned, these considerations should ultimately be construed as different types of competence that EIL/EIcL users portray and EIL/EIcL learners have to be aware of and acquire. It is also important to understand, however, that it is extremely difficult to describe, classify and ultimately codify all the different facets of EIcL communication, precisely because all these parameters have widely different values for different speakers.

In terms relevant to our discussion so far, the problem facing the EIL/EIcL teacher can be restated as follows: how to create a comprehensive syllabus (i.e. one that has codified, or N-bound, characteristics of English-as-an-international-language use) and integrate it with material from a C-bound understanding of the many different real-life facets of English-as-an-intercultural-language use (see Table 3).

**Table 3.** Norm-bound and culture-bound approaches to language teaching

| | **N-Bound approach** | **C-Bound approach** |
|---|---|---|
| **English language teaching situations** | ESL, EFL, EAL, EIL etc. | EIcL |
| **Extensive applied linguistics research** | Available | Not available |
| **Coursebooks** | Available | Not available |
| **Supplementary teaching materials** | Teachers can easily choose/adapt/create them | Teachers cannot easily choose/adapt/create them |
| **Accuracy/fluency polarity** | Crucial | Non-crucial |
| **Testing techniques** | Available | Not available |
| **Teacher education techniques** | Available and widely trialled | Available (arguably) but not widely trialled |

ESOL practitioners are usually familiar with, trained for and experienced in teaching predominantly N-bound classes – i.e. classes that concentrate on teaching English as a second or foreign language. Current attempts at presenting codified accounts of EIL use are also available, albeit scant (cf. Jenkins 2000). This means that there is a plethora of applied linguistics research, curricular and testing documents, coursebooks and potential supplementary material (in the form of newspaper and magazine articles, books, etc) that teachers can use in the classroom in an N-bound way. To teach in such a way means to focus learners' attention and creative powers, via appropriate communicative activities, on producing and understanding written and spoken discourse along the familiar lines of, for example, the fluency/accuracy polarity (Brumfit 1984).

On the other hand, to teach in a C-bound way would mean to concentrate on and get learners involved in the creation and under-standing of NNS communicative discourse that is comprehensible. This would necessarily imply the learners' exposure to as many authentic NNS ways of communicating as possible and, as a result, to discourses that often sacrifice linguistic precision (or 'correctness') for the benefit of intelligibility. It can be easily assumed that there is no availability for syllabi and coursebooks that adopt this route, and that the EIcL teacher would not know either where to look for the appropriate inputs or how to construct the appropriate activities (for a discussion of these issues cf. Bardovi-Harlig 2001, Judd 1999, McKay 2003).

## Advice for the EIL/EIcL teacher

In light of the above, what follows are a number of considerations that every teacher eager to teach EIL/EIcL should consider (in this regard, cf. also O'Sullivan 1994, Timmis 2002).

### Learner attitudes

Learners' attitudes regarding the ownership of English and its status in international/intercultural communication are paramount, and need first to be investigated. It is important for the EIL/EIcL teacher to find out (e.g. by carrying out a short needs analysis with their adult learners) whether learners adopt a predominantly N-bound or a C-bound viewpoint regarding both the communication and the teaching domains. One area that is likely to yield such information is pronunciation. What do learners believe about 'standard' English accents (i.e. RP or General American)? Is a 'native-like' English pronunciation important for them? How aware are they of other NS varieties? How do they view their own accent? How do they react to other NNSs' accents? To find out about learners' views, the teacher can ask them to listen to recordings of different NS and NNS varieties (they can be easily retrieved from most Web-based newspaper or radio sites). Also, s/he can record a teaching session and play back the tape asking learners to note down their immediate response to their own (and their peers') accents.

Another area to consider is learners' attitudes regarding teacher feedback and correction techniques. If, for example, learners ask to be corrected whenever they make a mistake (which is very likely, especially with exam-oriented situations, and even more so with adult learners), then it is obvious that matters related to an accurate/fluent performance is a priority for them – these learners adopt a norm-bound approach.

It is important to try to find out as much as possible about such attitudes. Do learners prefer their national/cultural identity to be evident (C-bound) or concealed (N-bound) through their accent? Why do they learn English – to pass an exam (N-bound) or to be able to communicate with other people around the world (C-bound)? On which occasions do they use English? Are they equally 'happy' when they use English with both NSs/NNSs (C-bound), or are they afraid that their possible 'mistakes' might be 'criticized' by NSs or fluent bilingual NNSs (N-bound)? Are they aware that NSs also make mistakes (e.g. in writing)? These questions can provide the teacher with adequate information regarding the extent to which individual learners are willing to be taught the C-bound way. If their perspective is N-bound, it might be practically difficult to teach EIcL and a more 'traditional' approach would probably have to be undertaken. The teacher can try to raise learners' awareness of (a) the relationship between EIL and EIcL and (b) the 'reality' of EIL and EIcL in all communications that involve NNSs (see above).

## Teaching monolingual/multilingual/multicultural classes

In this light, the 'best' EIcL teaching situations are those that exhibit variety in the learners' cultural and linguistic backgrounds. This essentially means that classes whose learners' L1 are different serve better for EIcL tuition. The same is the case with classes of bilingual or multilingual learners, or learners who have travelled outside their own country and are eager to use English to find out about other cultures. The key aim in these situations is to prompt learners to communicate with their peers in English, but the use of their L1 (and of any other language that would enhance mutual intelligibility) is also encouraged – the main emphasis being on communication (Baxter 1983). With monolingual classes, the use of technology should prove very useful, since the teacher can encourage learners to seek communication with learners from other countries via e-mail or teleconferencing (so that all skills are practised – Warschauer and Healey 1998, Watts 1997).

## Teaching EIL/EIcL in the Inner, Outer and Expanding Circles (Kachru 1985)

The statutory role of English and its NSs may also play a definitive role in the extent to which individual ESL/EFL classes can be 'turned into' proper EIL/EIcL classes. Most ESL (i.e. Inner Circle) situations operate in domains where the native speakers of English are the majority, and the same is the case with most EFL (i.e. Outer and Expanding Circles) situations, where N-bound viewpoints may dominate. On the other hand, it is in these areas (in particular, in ESL situations) that one is likely to find the multicultural and multilingual classes mentioned above. It is then up to the EIL/EIcL teacher to reflect on how to find ways to raise these learners' awareness of the C-bound perspective.

In certain domains, looking at the bigger picture might be helpful. For example, EIcL is the *de facto* situation in the expanding European Union (EU) (Labrie and Quell 1997, Wright 2000) – thus, the English used for communication between, say, a Dutch person and a German will typically be different from that used between a Greek and a Spaniard, and those will be different from the English used in a company of people from all these nationalities (Cenoz and Jessner 2000). This means that the use of English as a lingua franca in this domain certainly has features that can render it the status of a standard norm (or a variety of EIL), but that such a norm cannot easily be agreed upon (cf. Grin 2003). It is very probable that the reason for this lies with the predominantly C-bound dimension of such communication. It also means that EU English, itself an international variety of English, will not be the same with other international varieties (e.g. the English used in Asia or South America). Therefore French, Italian, German, Greek and other EU learners should be made aware of this growing phenomenon (i.e. using English in communication), but should be trained to develop a reflective mentality in their communication with other NNSs and to take into consideration those issues that characterize C-bound communication (see above; also cf. Alred et al. 2002, Byram et al. 2001, Guilherme 2002, Phillipson 2003).

## EIcL tasks and task inputs – drawing up the learning syllabus

Due to the scarcity of C-bound material, the EIcL syllabus should be created by the teacher with the active help of the learners themselves. In appropriately designed in-class and out-of-class activities, learners can be prompted to write or speak about themselves and their national and cultural background, while becoming actively engaged in and aware of the normalization techniques they use in making their messages comprehensible (for ways of achieving this, cf. Alred et al. 2002, Brady and Shinohara 2000, Byram 1997, Byram et al. 2001, Jenkins 2003, Kasper 1998 and 2001, Liaw and Johnson 2001). This involves training learners to concentrate on the communication itself, by

- monitoring their own communication techniques and dealing with breakdowns of communication (e.g. by making repairs);
- recognizing miscommunication resulting from misattribution of meaning and making adjustments (O'Sullivan 1994); and ultimately,
- learning about one another's personality and culture.

EIcL teachers are urged to make the best of existing coursebooks but should have a critical eye for dominant N-bound features in them (see above). Tasks:

- *must* have a genuine communicative orientation;
- *must* be realistic, challenging and motivating – depending on the circumstances, learners can be asked to air their views on language matters by discussing, for example, the function of minority and majority languages in their region, or the effects the growing spread of English has on their L1;
- *must not* ask learners to 'be someone else' (e.g. a NS);
- *must not* treat learners as cultural stereotypes – learners should be treated as individuals with their own distinct identity and ideas.

Due to the scarcity of C-bound material, and provided s/he has the learners' approval, the teacher can record such discussions and keep learners' assignments for future use with other EIcL classes. Ultimately, the best resource of genuine EIcL material are EIcL learners themselves, and in particular those who have been exposed to real-life EIcL situations and tasks.

## Conclusion

It is important that EIcL-oriented research sheds light on the ways learners from different speech communities and cultural backgrounds communicate with other NNSs in English. This article has presented a means of analysing such communication by separating it into codifiable linguistic norms and more elaborate ways of establishing mutual comprehensibility, while maintaining speakers' cultural identities. On this basis, suggestions have been made for teachers wishing to identify and teach EIL/EIcL classes.

# References

Alred, G., M. Byram and M. Fleming (eds). 2002. *Language in Intercultural Communication and Education*. Clevedon: Multilingual Matters.

Ammon, U. (ed.). 2001. *The Dominance of English as a Language of Science: Effects on Other Languages and Language Communities*. New York: Mouton de Gruyter.

Árva, V. and P. Medgyes. 2000. 'Native and non-native teachers in the classroom'. *System* 28/3, 355–72.

Agar, M. 1994. *Language Shock: Understanding the Culture of Conversation*. New York: William Morrow.

Bardovi-Harlig, K. 2001. 'Evaluating the empirical evidence: Grounds for instruction in pragmatics?' In K. R. Rose and G. Kasper (eds), *Pragmatics in Language Teaching*. Cambridge: Cambridge University Press. 13–32.

Baxter, J. 1983. 'English for intercultural communication'. In D. Landis and R. W. Brislin (eds), *The Handbook of Intercultural Communication Training* (Volume 2), Oxford: Pergamon Press. 290–324.

Block, D. and D. Cameron. 2002. *Globalization and Language Teaching*. London: Routledge.

Boxer, D. 2002. *Applying Sociolinguistics: Domains and Face-to-Face Interaction*. Amsterdam: John Benjamins.

Brady, A. and Y. Shinohara. 2000. 'Principles and activities for a transcultural approach to additional language learning'. *System* 28/2, 305–22.

Braidi, S. M. 2002. 'Re-examining the role of recasts in native-speaker/non-native-speaker interactions'. *Language Learning* 52/1, 1–42.

Braine, G. (ed.). 1999. *Non-native Educators in English Language Teaching*. Mahwah, NJ: Lawrence Erlbaum.

Brumfit, C., 1984. *Communicative Methodology in Language Teaching: The Roles of Fluency and Accuracy*. Cambridge: Cambridge University Press.

Bruthiaux, P. 2002. 'Predicting challenges to English as a global language in the 21st century'. *Language Problems and Language Planning* 26/2, 129–57.

Brutt-Griffler, J. 2002. *World English: A Study of its Development*. Clevedon: Multilingual Matters.

Brutt-Griffler, J. and K. Samimy. 2001. 'Transcending the nativeness paradigm'. *World Englishes* 20/1, 99–106.

Byram, M., 1997. *Teaching and Assessing Intercultural Communicative Competence*. Clevedon: Multilingual Matters.

Byram, M., A. Nichols and D. Stevens (eds). 2001. *Developing Intercultural Competence in Practice*. Clevedon: Multilingual Matters.

Canale, M. and M. Swaine. 1980. 'Theoretical bases of communicative approaches to second language teaching and testing'. *Applied Linguistics*, 1, 1–47.

Cenoz, J. and U. Jessner (eds). 2000. *English in Europe: The Acquisition of a Third Language*. Clevedon: Multilingual Matters.

Clyne, M. 2003. *Dynamics of Language Context: English and Immigrant Languages*. Cambridge: Cambridge University Press.

Council of Europe 2001. *Common European Framework of Reference for*

*Languages: Learning, Teaching, Assessment*. Cambridge: Cambridge University Press.

Crowley, T. 2003. *Standard English and the Politics of Language*. London: Palgrave Macmillan.

Crystal, D. 2003. *English as a Global Language* (second edition). Cambridge: Cambridge University Press.

Del Valle, S. 2003. *Language Rights and the Law in the United States: Finding Our Voices*. Clevedon: Multilingual Matters.

Derwing, T. and M. J. Munro. 2001. 'What speaking rates do non-native listeners prefer?' *Applied Linguistics* 22/3, 324–37.

De Swaan, A. 2001. *Words of the World: The Global Language System*. Oxford: Blackwell.

Downes, W. 1998. *Language and Society*. Cambridge: Cambridge University Press.

Ellis, R. 1997. *The Study of Second Language Acquisition*. Oxford: Oxford University Press.

Fairclough, N. 1992. *Discourse and Social Change*. Cambridge: Polity Press.

Giles, H., N. Coupland and J. Coupland. 1991. 'Accommodation theory: communication, context and consequences'. In H. Giles, J. Coupland and N. Coupland (eds), *Contexts of Accommodation*. Cambridge: Cambridge University Press. 1–68.

Graddol, D. 1997. *The Future of English*? London: The British Council.

Graddol, D. 2001. 'The future of English as a European language'. *The European English Messenger*, 10/2, 47–50.

Grin, G. 2003. *Language Policy Evaluation and the European Charter for Regional or Minority Languages*. London: Palgrave Macmillan.

Gubbins, P. and M. Holt (eds). 2002. *Beyond Boundaries: Language and Identity in Contemporary Europe*. Clevedon: Multilingual Matters.

Guilherme, M. 2002. *Critical Citizens for an Intercultural World: Foreign Language Education as Cultural Politics*. Clevedon: Multilingual Matters.

James, C. 1998. *Errors in Language Learning and Use*. London: Longman.

Jenkins, J. 2000. *The Phonology of English as an International Language*. Cambridge: Cambridge University Press.

Jenkins, J. 2002. 'A sociolinguistically based, empirically researched pronunciation syllabus for English as an international language'. *Applied Linguistics* 23/1, 83–103.

Jenkins, J. 2003. *World Englishes: A Resource Book for Students*. London: Routledge.

Johnson, K. 2001. *An Introduction to Foreign Language Learning and Teaching*. London: Longman.

Judd, E. L. 1999. 'Some issues in the teaching of pragmatic competence'. In E. Hinkel (ed.), *Culture in Second Language Teaching and Learning*. Cambridge: Cambridge University Press. 152–66.

Kachru, B. B. 1985. 'Standards, codifications, and sociolinguistic realism: The English language in the outer circle'. In R. Quirk and H. Widdowson (eds), *English in the World: Teaching and Learning the Language and Literatures*. Cambridge: Cambridge University Press.

Kasper, G. 1998. 'Interlanguage pragmatics'. In H. Byrnes (ed), *Learning Foreign and Second Languages: Perspectives in Research and Scholarship*. New York: Modern Language Association. 183–208.

Kasper, G. 2001. 'Learning pragmatics in the L2 classroom.' In L. F. Bouton (ed.), *Pragmatics and Language Learning* (Volume 10). Urbana, IL: University of Illinois at Urbana-Champaign. 1–25.

Keating, M. 1998. *The New Regionalism in Western Europe*. Cheltenham: Edward Elgar.

Labrie, N. and C. Quell. 1997. 'Your language, my language or English? The potential language choice in communication among nationals of the European Union'. *World Englishes* 16/1, 3–26.

Liaw, M.-L. and R. J. Johnson. 2001. 'E-mail writing as a cross-cultural learning experience'. *System* 29/2, 235–51.

Maurais, J. and M. A. Morris (eds). 2003. *Languages in a Globalising World*. Cambridge: Cambridge University Press.

McKay, S. L. 2002. *Teaching English as an International Language: Rethinking Goals and Approaches*. Oxford: Oxford University Press.

McKay, S. L. 2003. 'Toward an appropriate EIL pedagogy: re-examining common ELT assumptions'. *IJAL* 13/1, 1–22.

Mugglestone, L. 2003. *Talking Proper: the Rise and Fall of the English Accent as a Social Symbol*. Oxford: Oxford University Press.

Munro, M. J. and T. M. Derwing. 1999. 'Foreign accent, comprehensibility, and intelligibility in the speech of second language learners'. *Language Learning* 49/1, 285–310.

O' Sullivan, K. 1994. *Understanding Ways: Communicating Between Cultures*. Sydney: Hale & Iremonger.

Pennycook, A. 1994. *The Cultural Politics of English as an International Language*. New York: Longman.

Pennycook, A. 1998. *English and the Discourses of Colonialism*. London: Routledge.

Phillipson, R. 1992. *Linguistic Imperialism*. Oxford: Oxford University Press.

Phillipson, R. 2003. *English-Only Europe? Challenging Language Policy*. London: Routledge.

Ricento, T. (ed.). 2000. *Ideology, Politics and Language Policies: Focus on English*. Amsterdam: John Benjamins.

Samovar, L. E. and R. E. Porter (eds). 1994. *Intercultural Communication: A Reader*. Belmont, California: Wadsworth.

Seidlhofer, B. 1999. 'Double standards: teacher education in the expanding circle'. *World Englishes* 18/2, 233–45.

Sifakis, N. et al. 2003. 'Facing the globalisation challenge in the realm of English language teaching'. *Language and Education*, 17/1, 59–71.

Singer, M. R. 1998. *Perception and Identity in Intercultural Communication*. Yarmouth, Maine: Intercultural Press.

Skutnabb-Kangas, T. 2000. *Linguistic Genocide in Education – or Worldwide Diversity and Human Rights?* Mahwah, NJ: Lawrence Erlbaum Associates.

Smith, L. E. and M. L. Foreman (eds). 1997. *World Englishes 2000*. Honolulu, HI: University of Hawaii Press.

Swales, J. 1997. 'English as Tyrannosaurus rex'. *World Englishes* 16/3, 373–82.

Timmis, I. 2002. 'Native-speaker norms and international English: a classroom view'. *ELTJ*, 56/3, 240–49.

Tyler, M. D. 2001. 'Resource consumption as a function of topic knowledge in non-native and native comprehension'. *Language Learning* 51/2, 257–80.

Warschauer, M. and D. Healey. 1998. 'Computers and language learning: an overview'. *Language Teaching* 31, 57–71.

Watts, N. 1997. 'A learner-based design model for interactive multimedia language learning packages'. *System* 25/1, 1–8.

Widdowson, H. G. 1994. 'The ownership of English'. *TESOL Quarterly* 28/2, 377–89.

Widdowson, H. G. 1997. 'EIL, ESL, EFL: global issues and local interests'. *World Englishes*, 16/1, 135–46.

Wierzbicka, A. 2003. *Cross-Cultural Pragmatics*. New York: Mouton.

Wong, J. 2000. 'Delayed next turn repair initiation in native/non-native speaker English conversation'. *Applied Linguistics* 21/1, 244–67.

Wright, S. 2000. *Community and Communication: The Role of Language in Nation State Building and European Integration*. Clevedon: Multilingual Matters.

# Standard Englishes, Pedagogical Paradigms and their Conditions of (Im)possibility

*T. Ruanni F. Tupas*
*National University of Singapore*

## Introduction

This paper deals with the politics of Standard Englishes: Standard English (SE), World Englishes (WE), and English as an International Language (EIL). It argues that the social bases (or epistemologies) of these Standard Englishes are strikingly similar: yes, the shift of power from 'native' to 'non-native' speakers of English, from speakers in the Inner Circle to speakers from the Outer and Expanding Circles (Kachru 1986) may have legitimized different cultures and local uses of English around the world, but the issue of *who* among the speakers and/or learners of English in their respective localities have access to any of these Standard Englishes in the first place is still not adequately addressed. '... English is ours', proclaims Filippino writer Gemino Abad (Abad et al. 1997, 170). 'We have colonized it too'. But who are the 'we' who have colonized English? Certainly not the majority of Filippinos whose English according to the government, education officials, and creative writers like Abad, is 'deteriorating'.

The problem of standards (of SE, WE and EIL) is a problem of class: class-based issues that accrue to English in many societies in the world remain marginalized or ignored.

While Kachru refers to the Inner Circle of English as largely belonging to its 'native' speakers, and the Outer Circle as the province of 'non-native' speakers whose Englishes are as legitimate as the 'native' ones, I argue that such a sociolinguistic configuration essentially ignores an important social reality: that the power to (re)create English ascribed to the Outer Circle is mainly reserved only for those who have been invested with such power in the first place (the educated/the rich/the creative writers, etc.) such that the Inner/

Outer dichotomy is demolished by the fact that no matter what standards of English are used, the power to deploy such standards is shared by both 'native' and 'non-native' speakers who enjoy particular social privileges such as wealth, symbolic power, education, and so on, in their respective communities or societies.

In other words, 'legitimate' Englishes are 'standard' Englishes inaccessible to the majority of the Outer Circle. There are *inner circles* everywhere, in 'native' and 'non-native' English-speaking countries, whose speakers enjoy the privilege of having much access to Standard Englishes. Similarly, there are *outer circles* everywhere, whose speakers, because of positions of relative powerlessness, are largely unable to gain access to such standards – and they are the much larger social groups, usually the majority in their respective communities, with much less access to quality education, and with whom the socio-economic, cultural and political impacts of globalization have been severe. Will there then be a 'democratization' (Jenkins 2000) of English language use through English as an International Language? What kind of 'liberation' (Kachru 1991) is possible or not possible through World Englishes?

This paper explores these questions in the light of the *conditions of (im)possibility* within which Standard Englishes are located. Simply put, these conditions are socio-economic, political and ideological conditions that influence the classroom practices of teachers. We will look at how these conditions generate teaching practice by examining the position taken by seven Philippino teachers after they have recently been introduced to some of the current major issues in second language teaching. Unlike most teachers of English, perhaps, these teachers have been introduced formally to a broad array of perspectives on second language teaching – from pragmatic/liberal to critical positions, for example – but whose 'informed' decisions have nevertheless complicated the choices available and have therefore forced us to take a second look at these perspectives from the conditioned practices of these teachers. The main finding of this paper, thus, is as follows:

> While the teachers seem critically aware of the competing paradigms of teaching English, their choices are also constrained by socio-economic, political and ideological conditions which are largely not of their own making. These conditions help prevent the teachers from practising what in theory are sociolinguistically and politically legitimate ways to deal with English.

However, because of their critical awareness of the competing paradigms, such conditioned choices do not go back simply to the teaching of 'Standard English'. The (im)possibility of conditions is such that while these conditions help prevent teachers from implementing their choices of paradigm(s), the teachers nevertheless are able to create spaces of agency or action within such limiting conditions. Data from the teachers' essays and other works reveal the painful process by which they deal with 'Standard English', and the way forward for them is to use culturally appropriate content and – to a lesser extent – codeswitching, to teach SE. In other words, they *idealize* their work: mainly teaching SE through a 'Philippinized' content because it is through this that English will ultimately be localized. Whether or not this is possible is beside the point, and may be subject to future research, but what the teachers wish to do is to justify their work on SE by arguing that the very act of teaching it through the use of localized content and/or codeswitching already changes its form.

## Preliminary discussions

During the first semester of Academic Year 2002–3 at the University of the Philippines Open University, the textbook *Second Language Teaching* (Tupas 2002) was pilot-tested among seven students of the Diploma/Master in Language Studies Education degree course. The textbook was designed to enable the students to grapple with theoretical and practical issues in the field of Second Language Teaching (SLT) as it is implicated in broad social and political questions concerning globalization, nationalism and identity, (neo) colonialism and postcolonialism, development, and the problems of class, race, and gender. The three major units and nine modules of the textbook are the following:

| | |
|---|---|
| UNIT I | Clearing the Ground: Basic Issues |
| | Module 1 Perspectives on Second Language Teaching |
| | Module 2 Popular Issues in Second Language Teaching |
| UNIT II | Focus on the Classroom: Usual Considerations |
| | Module 3 Theories of Language |
| | Module 4 Language Theories in Action |
| | Module 5 Methods and Approaches in the Classroom |
| UNIT III | Contexts of Teaching: Critical Dimensions |
| | Module 6 The Problem of Culture |
| | Module 7 The Politics of Second Language Teaching |

Module 8 Linguistic Imperialism and Practices of
Resistance

Thus, major issues in SLT (e.g. standards, ownership of English,
politics of knowledge) are discussed as they appear through popular
discourses in the media and state politics. Language theories that
underpin language teaching approaches are evaluated, while the
historical discussion of methods from the late nineteenth century to
the late twentieth century (Richards and Rogers 2000) is viewed
through the conceptual and political haziness of 'methods'. Second
language teaching in the Philippines is discussed within Phillipson's
(1992) framework of linguistic imperialism, although the possibility of
agency is equally emphasized through World Englishes (Kachru 1986),
counter-discourses (Pennycook 1998), and codeswitching practices
(Canagarajah 1999).

## The data

Throughout the semester, the teacher-students (henceforth, TSs) were
required to attend monthly meetings at a designated regional centre
with an assigned tutor and to submit five tutor-marked assignments
(TMAs) derived mainly from activities in the textbook. Here is a
summary of the five TMAs:

| | |
|---|---|
| TMA 1 | Consciousness-raising: an essay on the teachers' own classroom practice |
| TMA 2 | Language assumptions about language teaching material: a critique |
| TMA 3 | Cultural issues in the teaching of grammar: re-writing a grammar exercise |
| TMA 4 | Classroom observation: a critical evaluation |
| TMA 5 | (Re)visions of SLT in the Philippines: political dimensions |

The topic of this paper has emerged from the five TMAs of the seven
teachers in the course. I do not claim that the statements and opinions
taken from the TMAs represent those of all other English teachers in
the country, and furthermore do not wish to say that these data are
sufficient to make definitive statements about second language
teaching around the world, but the emerging issues surely need
immediate and serious attention as they not only come from voices 'on
the ground', but they also interrogate the fine borders of contending
positions emanating from recent sociolinguistic and pedagogical
studies of English around the world.

## The issues

The teachers' responses to the issues raised in the textbook expose the porousness of the academic line between WE and EIL and bring us closer to the politics of standardization where SE, WE and EIL constitute themselves into Standard Englishes, sociolinguistically different from each other and with varying levels of political and ideological legitimacy, but all enmeshed in conditions of (im)possibility within which the choice of one over the others does not really bring about any sort of liberation (Kachru 1991) or democratization (Jenkins 2000) on the part of many learners of English around the world. English, after all, whether we like it or not, continues to help stratify many societies in the world (Mazrui 2002, Tupas 2001b, Bunyi 2001, Lin 2001, Azman 2002, Neville 2000).

The TSs have consistently written about the difficulty of teaching SE because their pupils bring with them their own way of using the language, which is legitimate on political and cultural grounds. On the other hand, they set out to continue to teach SE because it is what is needed. It is not necessarily the correct form of the language, but it is nevertheless what their students need. Such 'contradictions' – incompatibilities (Seidlhofer 1999) or ambiguities (Canagarajah 1993) – are perfectly explicable if viewed from the specific locations of the teachers' teaching experiences, locations generated by structuring conditions which are largely beyond their control. It is these structuring conditions which have been marginalized in the academic discussions concerning the sociolinguistic and pedagogical dimensions of WE and EIL. Viewed from locations of constriction, such discussions appear to be what Butler calls 'naïve forms of political optimism' (Butler 1997, 17). While it is true that 'the logic of the spread of English has invested ... "non-native speakers" with "authority" – or what is more adequately called "agency in language change"' (Brutt-Crifflor 1998, 381, emphasis in original), such authority is conditioned agency. Teachers work and live in conditions of (im)possibility, historically positioned to generate both the status quo and change in education and, more generally, in society.

How do we explain the logic of such conditioned practice?

## The logic of conditioned practice

To answer this question I will undertake to do the following:

(1) I will show how the TSs demonstrate a critical awareness of the competing paradigms in the teaching of English through

their relatively progressive views on Philippine English and codeswitching in the classroom.

(2) I will show with the same data how the TSs refuse to take up any of the positions available from the competing paradigms, arguing that cultural strategies like codeswitching and the use of culturally appropriate content (through which Philippine English may emerge) can actually be used to teach SE.

(3) I will show how certain socio-economic, political and ideological conditions help generate such a position on the teaching of SE.

(4) I will argue that the way to go is to intensify teacher training programs by broadening the teachers' range of options for paradigms of teaching, without necessarily limiting them to any of such options.

In a sense, the TSs provide us with a different view of pedagogical standards that are somehow different from the frameworks provided by the proponents of SE (e.g. Quirk 1990, Honey 1997), WE (e.g. Kachru 1994, 1986, Brown 2002, Brown & Peterson 1997), and EIL (e.g. McKay 2002, Jenkins 2000, Hino 2001). The TSs propose to teach SE (even if their own English does not always conform with it) through cultural strategies like codeswitching, as well as the use of content that speaks of the 'ills of society, the bad affect of colonization' (TS2, TMA4) and 'enlighten[s] our people that we have our own culture' (TS7, TMA5) because, *in the process*, this will help create 'Philippine English' in both its form and content. The TSs do not wish to go back to an uncritical teaching of SE, but would like to engage with it on a different platform where the teaching of content vis-à-vis SE is of paramount importance, and through which SE ceases to become one, but theirs and their students'. The symbolic power (Bourdieu 1996, 1992, 1990, 1973) of SE continues to govern the TSs' daily teaching practice, but the very act of teaching it through culturally appropriate practices *de*standardizes it.

For example, the TSs have identified practices of resistance in their own classrooms and that of their peers. In their individual observations of classroom teaching as required by TMA 4, the TSs have argued for the positive appraisal of 'Philippine standards' (TS7), 'the Philippine version of English' (T4), 'the practice of World Englishes' (T5), 'counter culture' (TS2), 'Taglish' (mixture of Tagalog and English, TS3) or 'code-switching' (TS4). They accompany such appraisal with specific descriptions of particular teaching or learning practices in the observed classrooms. For example, in TS3's chosen class of 'around 50' Grade Six pupils, 'it is obvious that pupils speak in a Philippine English way':

That is, they have tendencies to follow their Filipino accent and their sentences are patterned after the structures of the sentences in Filipino. Their English is a translation of their language. Some pupils invent their own English words which are derived from some Filipino terms like 'kalkalize' as in 'The children failed to kalkalize their things due to lack of time'. This is happening when the pupils can no longer think of the English equivalent of a certain Filipino word (TS3, TMA4).

In TS4's case, the use of the mother tongue to facilitate information and accelerate pupils' understanding of the subject matter is the focus of positive assessment. The observation occurs in a Grade Two class located in a public school in a poor province in the Northern Philippines. There are 28 pupils, the majority of whom are poor and whose parents are farmers and fishermen. TS4 accompanies her analysis with a long transcription of an interaction between the teacher and the pupils. The content of the transcribed lesson is concerned with the teacher's review of capitalization. The following is an excerpt from the transcription (with my English translation in brackets):

T –     All right. Now let us have a practice. (She writes a sentence on the board: mrs. amansec is our principal.)
        Tama ba ang pagkasulat? (*Is it correctly written?*)
S –     (chorus) Hindi po! (*No!* – note that *po* is a cultural marker for respect which is untranslatable)
T –     Why? Bakit mali? (*Why wrong?*) Pwede mo bang sabihin kung ano ang mali sa isinulat, Renan? (*Can you tell what's wrong with what has been written, Renan?*)
S –     Kasi po yung pangalan ng tao hindi naka-big letter ang simula. (*Because 'po' the start of the name of the person is not in a big letter.*)
T –     Very good! Go to the board, Aileen, at isulat mo nang tama ang mga pangalan (*and write the name correctly*). (Aileen goes to the board, then applies the needed changes.)
        Is Aileen correct, Mary Joy?
S –     Yes, ma'am.
T –     Correct! So, kailan natin ginagamit ang capital letter? (*When do we use the capital letter?*) Yes, Jerome?
S –     Kapag isinulat po ang pangalan ng tao. (*When we write names of people*). (TS4, TMA4)

Commenting on this excerpt and the rest of the transcription, TS4 says that 'codeswitching' and 'the use of the vernacular' are necessary in the transmission and negotiation of meaning in the classroom. This is a fairly radical position (something shared by all other TSs), considering the fact that the monolingual fallacy in English language teaching continues to inform the positions of many, if not most, teachers of English around the world (Phillipson 1992). TS4's justifications are clear. In the case of codeswitching, where 'the teacher poses questions in English then translates them in Filipino or in Ilocano (the vernacular in the place)', it 'makes it easier for the students to understand and answer the question. Using the language of the home helps students facilitate the information they acquire'. She concludes:

> In totality, the teacher's method of managing her classroom is not a failure case. Though still confined with the traditional approach, her attempts to inject new techniques is apparent ... By using the common culture she shares with the students, (through the vernacular), she is able to bridge the content of the English subject with the ability and background of the learners. (TS4, TMA4)

## Cultural strategies in the teaching of SE

Yet, amidst such non-mainstream positions, the TSs consistently agonize over the felt real need to teach SE. Early on in the semester, TS7 describes the goals of her teaching which she keeps until the end of the semester because 'Proficiency in English offers opportunities of economic and professional advancement, English is a global language' (TS7, TMA5). Some of these goals are:

> A focus on the correct expression/pronunciation of words *in the target language*. It enables the children (to) communicate effectively in the language. It can be done through the phonetic approach, (learning the correct expression of the short/long vowel sounds by teacher modeling) listening from cassette and video tapes stories, songs, poems, verses in English and follow the expressions and intonation patterns listened to.
> A focus on speaking following *sentence patterns*. Learning the language through listening and speaking skills. Teacher provides sentence pattern, through drills and exercises children supplies other parallel to the pattern, like I can *swim*. (run, jump)
> A focus on social rules and functions to develop *the proper behavior* and learn the social amenities in appropriate social situations. This will enable them to develop the cultural behavior and gestures that go with language learning. Ex. The waving of the hand as we say Goodbye, *the proper intonation* in greetings like

> Good Morning/Good afternoon, Hello/Hi etc. This can be learned
> through *role playing*. (TS7, TM1, italics supplied)

The teachers' way out of this seemingly neoconservative position is to
employ fairly defined roles for cultural strategies in the classroom. The
use of the vernacular and/or codeswitching, therefore, is mainly a
cognitive and practical way to bring learners closer to English or, more
specifically, to make them learn 'correct English'. On the one hand,
through the use of the vernacular it is hoped that 'sooner or later, the
minds of ... students will be more attuned to learning English aided by
having a positive outlook about the language' (TS4, TMA1). On the
other hand, such use can help learners clarify concepts and to 'ask
confirmation on the correctness of ... sentences' (TS5, TMA4). In the
end, both English and the vernacular are positively appraised and used
in the classroom.

In the case of Philippine English which the TSs all agree is a
cultural manifestation of English language use in the country, the
argument could be more nuanced. The TSs recognize Philippine
English as legitimate but they do not wish to teach it, at least explicitly
or intentionally. In this case, the way out of this other potentially
neoconservative position is to create a crucial line (no matter how
tenuous) between the symbolically powerful forms of English,
idealized 'rules' in teaching the language, which therefore must be
taught, *and* the equally abstract strategy of demolishing such rules
through the teaching of culture, with the hope that cultural (and
political) content will produce 'Philippine English': 'The language
used may be foreign but its content is localized and cultural' (TS3,
TMA3); 'we could play with English terminologies easily and we could
even express our thoughts in that language. While making us
linguistically competent, we also come [to] value our own heritage in
the process' (TMA5, TS4).

The TSs tend to believe that residues of local culture are
inextricably part of everyday classroom experience, manifested in
the meanings, forms and ideologies of English language use, but whose
legitimacy does not mean they should be taught explicitly or
intentionally, but simply left to emerge as they will – and do –
through the teaching of content. Some strands of the structure of this
argument can be gleaned through the following 'visions' of the TSs:

(1) We should Filipinize our books to portray Phil. cultures.
    Writings in English should conform to Filipino standards to
    instill our identity. Through writing we should infuse great
    sense of Filipinism that features our desirable traits like

        hospitality, bayanihan, etc. (TMA5, TS7)

(2)  Integrate through writing about the life, aspirations of the Filipino people. Use the language (English) within the context of the Philippines – Filipino setting – the values – and the dreams to be really be independent, not idolizing the principles – the culture of the elite. Use sentences which are within the experiences of the Filipinos. (TMA5, TS3)

The TSs' quite intricate position simultaneously for *and* against Philippine English demonstrates how some local practitioners of English language teaching, fairly aware of the sociolinguistics and politics of their classroom work, may grapple sensitively with various positions and compromises that come their way. They do not simply espouse the teaching of (cultural) content to resist English in the form of counter-discourses (Pennycook 1998) but, more importantly, they do it to escape being pigeon-holed into currently available positions in the teaching of English, including the postcolonial paradigm of discursive resistance. They acknowledge the power of SE and wish to continue teaching it, but theirs is not a neoconservative position in the sense that they are uncomfortable with such a position and are working around it to address the problem.

On the other hand, they acknowledge the cultural appropriateness of local forms of English, but they stop short of recommending teaching them in the classroom. Politically, they wish to hang on to the power of SE but, ideologically, they wish to move away from it by justifying their position on grounds that they can teach content through which, they claim, local forms of English can emerge. While sharing with many scholars the same sentiment that there should still be a 'standard of standards' in school (Bautista 2000, 17) despite the proliferation of local forms of English worldwide (also Pakir 2002, Crystal 2001), the TSs deal with their dilemma by envisioning a content-centred, culturally sensitive English language pedagogy out of which English (specifically, SE) will continue to be localized. The TSs do not show how, indeed, content can change form; which is understandable since, as Gupta (2001) asserts, the amount of change culture can exert upon English is '*not much* – (because) Standard English is so powerful that it sticks' (378, emphasis as original). But such positioning demonstrates the teachers' way of acknowledging *and*, at the same time, repudiating the pedagogical frameworks provided by the teaching of SE, WE and EIL. Such 'logic' responds to all these frameworks without necessarily being completely appropriated by any of them.

## Conditions of (im)possibility

The next big question, therefore, is: What produced this logic? Or: Why does this logic take the shape that it does now? The answer may lie in conditions of (im)possibility or those socio-economic, political and ideological conditions within which the TSs work.

### The global market of SE ideology

For example, the TSs cannot ignore SE because the Philippines, as the 'best producers of human resources' needs it to 'compete globally' (TS3, TMA5). This is, of course, not an isolated position since 'English linguistic culture' around the globalizing world, while supporting polycentrism, has always been firm on the central role of SE and its main features (Gupta 2001). In the case of formerly colonized countries like the Philippines, the tradition of teaching SE has its colonial beginnings: only American and/or British English was correct, and local uses were marginalized and stigmatized (Ashcroft et al. 1989, Mazzon 2000).

So the combined forces of SE ideology and the push of the global market towards English proficiency due to labour demand, (re)produced explicitly and/or implicitly in materials production and export of expertise from 'expert' countries like the United States and Great Britain (Phillipson 1992), largely condition teachers towards supporting the teaching of SE. SE is invested with power and ideology which cannot be ignored. National examinations, university admissions, job requirements and social prestige are mostly structured towards mastery of SE. Varying degrees of proficiency in English, in fact, correlate positively with the positions of speakers in the socio-economic hierarchy (Mazrui 2002, Lorente & Tupas 2002, Sibayan and Gonzalez 1996). Although the teaching of SE cannot for most students assure freedom from poverty – since access to quality education where SE is mostly being taught is unequal to start with – the support for SE has always been overwhelming, as this is supposedly what will help extricate many students from poverty. Never mind if there is actually a lack of clarity as to what SE is. This has not diminished its own authority (Davies 1999, 171): 'Those who are in actual charge of the education system, the politicians and the officials, seem, as far as I can tell, to be totally in favour of Standard English as the medium of instruction' (177). Ideologically, politically and socio-economically, therefore, local practices of English language teachers are largely conditioned by the expressed and real power of SE.

## Back to class: the social epistemologies of WE and EIL

But what about WE and EIL? At the outset, both paradigms could offer alternative ways to deal with the issue of pedagogical standards. But, while they may be different in some respects – WE and EIL are primarily concerned with 'intranational domains' and 'international settings', respectively (Hino 2001, 35) – they nevertheless share similar epistemologies. Vis-à-vis SE, they do not have enough symbolic power to enable teachers to legitimize their own work should they opt for either of them. They may be sociolinguistically legitimate but they largely remain politically unacceptable to most people. Vis-à-vis the '(p)romotion of linguistic equality' (Hino 2001, 41) which is a fundamental tenet of both positions, access to either WE or EIL is still unequal. Both paradigms are social constructs premised on the unassailability of 'educated' English (Parakrama 1995, Tupas 2001a). Villareal (2002), for example, asserts that:

> ... although much scholarly discussion and literary experimenta-
> tion have been done on the concepts of hybridity, the appropria-
> tion of English, and the development of our varieties of English, it
> is too facile to speak of equality in language and culture. Note, for
> instance, the concern to capture the notion of a Filipino variety of
> English, and the 'standardization of the grammatical features of
> Filipino English' or Singlish, or other varieties of English.
> Languages are documented mainly by the educated and standards
> set by them. Thus, English, even when appropriated, eventually
> becomes exclusionary and divisive (33–4).

So what really happens (or may happen) in the 'liberation' or 'democratization' of English through WE or EIL is the diffusion of the symbolic power of English beyond Kachru's (1986) Inner Circle and across the socially-marked *inner circles* of so-called 'non-native' English-speaking countries. We may grant that both WE and EIL are political attempts to wrest power from 'native' speakers of English to define what is or is not 'good' or 'standard' English, but both paradigms nevertheless offer only alternative standards access to which will still be largely determined by one's proximity to education and, for that matter, all other related symbolic goods in the social market (Bourdieu 1996, 1973). Kachru's concentric circles may not be helpful in this alternative configuration of relations brought about by the need to introduce the similarity of the two alternative paradigms in our discussion. There are inner circles everywhere which have much access to the symbolic power of English, whether this be SE, WE, or EIL. These are socially-defined inner circles both in 'native' or 'non-native' contexts. Similarly, there are outer circles everywhere, and these are much larger social groups whose English or Englishes have been largely marginalized in our search for 'the Standard' (Davies 1999, 181). McKay (2002), one of the major proponents of EIL, affirms the same position: among the criticisms hurled against the spread of English in the world which she has adequately addressed with counter-arguments in her pioneering book *Teaching English as an International Language*, there is only one position she shares with other critics: 'the growing relationship between English proficiency and economic resources' (24):

> In many countries around the world English is being learned only by those who can afford instruction in it. Not being able to afford such instruction can close many doors, particularly with regard to accessing higher education. (ibid.)

The symbolic power of SE may be undeniable, but both WE and EIL as alternative standards can also be potentially disempowering. In other words, precisely because the idea of a standard is closely linked with 'lengthy education, (which) puts it out of reach of the majority' (Davies 1999, 176), not all these Standard Englishes can offer broad spaces of democratization.

## Pedagogical paradigms as a range of choices in teacher education

The TSs, therefore, have very little space (although such space is there and is available) to manoeuvre with their newly-found knowledge of various paradigms of English language teaching, and their way out, it seems, is to teach SE through culturally appropriate teaching strategies with the hope that this will further create 'Philippine English'. Their ideological position is justified by what *should*, and not on what *is*. Their pedagogical practice is defined by what *can* happen, and not by what *is* happening. They are uncomfortable with all paradigms, but they also seem sympathetic to all of them. Their ideological comfort zone rests not exclusively on any of the paradigms available, but on adherence to an ideal that is nevertheless generated by the conditions surrounding it. What we need at this point, therefore, is not a paradigm of teaching English (see Petzold 2002, Brown 2002, Hino 2001), but a paradigm of ways to introduce all teachers into existing theories and debates (see Seidlhofer 1999), and to equip them with the necessary skills and questions for them to be able to grapple with the complexity of their teaching practices. It is in this sense that Seidlhofer (1999), arguing for a critically-informed English language education in EFL contexts, is also very relevant to our discussion:

To what extent different and competing claims are reconcilable will depend on specific circumstances, and only the teacher concerned will be in a position to take local decisions. The critical criterion for how informed these local decisions can be will be the quality of teacher education. EFL teachers who have a good idea as to what options are in principle available to them, and have learnt to evaluate these critically, skeptically and confidently, are unlikely to be taken in by the absolute claims and exaggerated promises often made by any one educational philosophy, linguistic theory, teaching, or textbook. (240)

## Conclusion

The pedagogical frameworks that may emerge from practice, therefore, are those generated by a broad array of choices with which teachers wrestle within sociopolitical, economic and ideological conditions largely not of their own making. On the one hand, these are not simply (pragmatic) choices (e.g. Savage 1997, Li 2002) under the cloak of 'laissez-faire liberalism' whose pedagogical implication is 'business as usual: give people what they want' (Pennycook 2002, 222). This broad range of options also deals with critical perspectives on, say, 'the larger context of what we are doing, the cultural, political, social and economic implications of language programs' (237). On the other hand, these are not simply 'critical' frameworks since they are enmeshed in choices of (im)possibility and, therefore, may transform themselves through inescapable compromises along the way. Therefore the contours of critical English language pedagogies, I believe, have not yet emerged, although well-documented critical descriptions of ELT classroom practices in many parts of the world have already started to proliferate (e.g. Canagarajah 1999, 1993, Holliday 1994, Lin 1999). They will come from teaching practices informed by all current competing paradigms, and generated by all sorts of conditions saturating such practices.

## References

Abad, G., S. Butler, M. Evasco and C. P. Hidalgo, 1997. 'Standards in Philippine English: The writers' forum'. In M. L. S. Bautista (ed.), *English is an Asian language: The Philippine context*. Manila: The Macquarie Library. 163–76.
Ashcroft, B., G. Griffiths and H. Tiffin, 1989. *The Empire Writes Back – Theory and Practice in Post-colonial Literatures*. London and New York: Routledge.
Azman, H. 2002. 'Multilingual practices in rural Malaysia and their impact on English language learning in rural education'. In A. Kirkpatrick (ed.), *Englishes in Asia: Communication, Identity, Power and Education*. Australia: Language Australia. 303–13.

Bautista, M. L. S. 2000. *Defining Standard Philippine English – Its Status and Grammatical Features*. Philippines: De La Salle University Press, Inc.

Bourdieu, P. 1973. 'Cultural reproduction and social reproduction'. In R. Brown (ed.), *Knowledge, Education and Cultural Change: Papers on the Sociology of Education* London: Tavistock. 71–112.

Bourdieu, P. 1990. *The Logic of Practice* (trans. R. Nice). Cambridge: Polity Press.

Bourdieu, P. 1992. *Language and Symbolic Power* (J. B. Thompson, ed.; trans. G. Raymond and M. Adamson). Cambridge: Polity Press.

Bourdieu, P. 1996. *The State Nobility – Elite Schools in the Field of Power* (trans. Lauretta C. Clough). UK: Polity Press.

Brown, K. 2002. 'Ideology and context: world Englishes and EFL teacher training'. *World Englishes* 21/3, 445–8.

Brown, K. and J. Peterson. 1997. 'Exploring conceptual frameworks: framing a world Englishes paradigm'. In L. E. Smith and M. L. Forman (eds), *World Englishes 2000*. Hawai'i: University of Hawai'i. 32–47.

Brutt-Griffler, J. 1998. 'Conceptual questions in English as a world language: Taking up an issue'. *World Englishes* 17/3, 381–92.

Bunyi, G. 2001. 'Language and educational inequality in primary classrooms in Kenya'. In M. Heller and M. Martin-Jones (eds), *Voices of Authority: Education and Linguistic Difference*. Westport, Connecticut and London: Ablex Publishing. 77–100.

Butler, J. 1997. *The Psychic Life of Power*. California: Stanford University Press.

Canagarajah, A. S. 1993. 'Critical ethnography of a Sri Lankan classroom: ambiguities in student opposition to reproduction through ESOL'. *TESOL Quarterly*, 27/4, 601–26.

Canagarajah, A. S. 1999. *Resisting Linguistic Imperialism in English Teaching*. Oxford: Oxford University Press.

Crystal, D. 2001. 'The future of Englishes' (first published in *English Today* 15/2, 1999). In A. Burns and C. Coffin (eds), *Analysing English in a Global Context*. London and New York: Routledge. 53–64.

Davies, A. 1999. 'Standard English: discordant voices'. *World Englishes* 18/2, 171–86.

Gupta, A. F. 2001. 'Realism and imagination in the teaching of English'. *World Englishes*, 20/3, 365–81.

Hino, N. 2001. 'Organizing EIL studies: Toward a paradigm'. *Asian Englishes*, 4/1, 34–65.

Holliday, A. 1994. *Appropriate Methodology and Social Context*. Cambridge and New York: Cambridge University Press.

Honey, J. 1997. *Language is Power: The Story of Standard English and its Enemies*. London: Faber and Faber.

Jenkins, J. 2000. *The Phonology of English as an International Language: New Models, New Norms, New Goals*. Oxford: Oxford University Press.

Kachru, B. B. 1986. *The Alchemy of English: The Spread, Functions and Models of Non-native Englishes*. Oxford: Pergamon Press.

Kachru, B. B. 1991. 'Liberation linguistics and the Quirk concern'. *English today* 25, 3–13.

Kachru, B. B. 1994. 'The speaking tree: A medium of plural canons'. In J. E. Alatis (ed.), *Educational Linguistics, Cross-cultural Communication and Global Interdependence*. Washington, DC: Georgetown University Press. 1–17.

Li, D. 2002. 'Hong Kong parents' preference for English medium education: passive victims of imperialism or active agents of pragmatism?' In A. Kirkpatrick (ed.), *Englishes in Asia: Communication, Identity, Power and Education*. Australia: Language Australia Ltd. 29–62.

Lin, A. M. Y. 1999. 'Doing-English-lessons in the reproduction or transformation of social worlds?', *TESOL Quarterly*, 33/3, 393–412.

Lin, A. M. Y. 2001. 'Symbolic domination and bilingual classroom practices in Hong Kong'. In M. Heller and M. Martin-Jones (eds), *Voices of Authority: Education and Linguistic Difference*. Westport, Connecticut and London: Ablex Publishing. 139–68.

Lorente, B. P. and T. R. F. Tupas. 2002. 'Demythologizing English as an economic asset: the case of Filipina domestic workers in Singapore'. *The ACELT Journal* 6/2, 20–32.

Mazrui, A. M. 2002. 'The English language in African education: dependency and decolonization'. In J. Tollefson (ed.), *Language Policies in Education – Critical Issues*. New Jersey and London: Lawrence Erlbaum Associates. 267–81.

Mazzon, G. 2000. 'The ideology of the standard and the development of Extraterritorial Englishes'. In L. Wright (ed.), *The Development of Standard English 1300–1800*. Cambridge: Cambridge University Press. 73–92.

McKay, S. L. 2002. *Teaching English as an International Language*. Oxford: Oxford University Press.

Neville, A. 2000. *English Unassailable But Unattainable. The Dilemma of Language Policy in Education in South Africa*. (*PRAESA Occasional Papers*, No.3). Cape Town: Praesa/University of Cape Town.

Pakir, A. 2002. 'The matter of English, the matter with English: maintaining language standards in teaching of English in the 21st century'. In Low and Teng (eds), *The Teaching and Use of Standard English*. Singapore: Singapore Association for Applied Linguistics. 59–80.

Parakrama, A. 1995. *De-hegemonizing Language Standards – Learning from (Post)colonial Englishes about 'English'*. London: Macmillan Press.

Pennycook, A. 1998. *English and the Discourses of Colonialism*. London and New York: Routledge.

Pennycook, A. 2002. 'Ruptures, departures and appropriations: postcolonial challenges to language development'. In: C. D. Villareal, L. R. R. Tope and P. M. B. Jurilla (eds), *Ruptures and Departures: Language and Culture in Southeast Asia*. Philippines: Department of English and Comparative Literature, University of the Philippines in Diliman. 212–41.

Petzold, R. 2002. 'Toward a pedagogical model for ELT'. *World Englishes* 21/3, 422–6.

Phillipson, R. 1992. *Linguistic Imperialism*. Oxford: Oxford University Press.

Quirk, R. 1990. 'What is Standard English?' In R. Quirk and G. Stein (eds), *English in Use*. London: Longman. 12–25.

Richards, J. C. and T. S. Rodgers. 2000. *Approaches and Methods in Language Teaching*, 2nd edn. Cambridge: Cambridge University Press.

Savage, W. 1997. 'Language and development'. In B. Kenny and W. Savage (eds), *Language and development: teachers in a changing world*. London and New York: Longman. 283–325.

Seidlhofer, B. 1999. 'Double standard: teacher education in the Expanding Circle'. *World Englishes*, 18/2, 233–45.

Sibayan, B. P. and A. B. Gonzalez. 1996. 'Post-imperial English in the Philippines'. In J. A. Fishman, A. W. Conrad and A. Rubal-Lopez (eds), *Post-imperial English – Status Change in Former British and American Colonies, 1940–1990*. Berlin and New York: Mouton de Gruyter. 139–72.

Tupas, T. R. F. 2001a. 'Global politics and the Englishes of the world'. In J. Cotterill and A. Ife (eds), *Language Across Boundaries*. London and New York: BAAL/Continuum. 81–98.

Tupas, T. R. F. 2001b. 'Linguistic imperialism in the Philippines: reflections of an English language teacher of Filipino overseas workers'. *The Asia-Pacific Education Researcher*, 10/1, 1–40.

Tupas, T. R. F. 2002. *Second Language Teaching*. Philippines: University of the Philippines Open University.

Villareal, C. D. 2002. 'Re-searching language teaching'. *The ACELT Journal*, 6/2, 33–7.

# English in the World does not mean English Everywhere: The Case for Multilingualism in the ELT/ESL profession

*Michael Joseph and Esther Ramani*
*University of the North, South Africa*

## Introduction

The practice of English in the world today is situated within multilingual contexts. It is clear from the work of numerous scholars (Alexander 2000, Agnihotri 1996, Auerbach 1993, Barkhuizen and Gough 1996, Cummins 2000, Heugh et al. 1995, Pennycook 1994, Ngũgĩ 1981) that globally, multilingualism is the norm rather than the exception. Yet the practice of English has been informed by a monolingual consciousness and a curiously apolitical agenda. Amongst applied linguists and language specialists dealing with language pedagogy, the concern has been with a search for more powerful theories of language acquisition and learning, and the development of English language curricula in tune with these theories. There seems to be little awareness of what might be the role of English in these multilingual contexts and little concern for the devastating effect that English has had on local, indigenous languages.

## Effects of the global role of English on multilingualism

We need to say here that several scholars have written on the impact that the global spread of English has had on local languages, but we do not see the ELT/ESL profession engaging with their observations and arguments. Our aim in this section is therefore not to offer new insights, but to reiterate earlier observations as a background to our proposals for a multilingually-sensitive profession.

It is important, as we will argue later, to acknowledge explicitly the right of people to have access to English – the language of modernity and globalism. Our concern, however, is with the spread of

English, which has led increasingly to two alarming phenomena. The first is the danger of educated, middle-class people worldwide becoming monolingual in English. The second is the social exclusion and isolation from mainstream life for many people in 'the developing world' who have inadequate levels of competence in English. This latter phenomenon is linked to the rapid displacement of local languages by English, and lack of support for maintenance and promotion of these languages.

The dominance of English (first as an instrument of colonization, but entrenched by globalization) in education, science, technology, communications, industry, commerce and international diplomacy has led to its occupying a hegemonic position in relation to other languages, especially indigenous languages, which are not used beyond provincial or national boundaries. The dominance of English in these domains, while entrenching and spreading the use of English, is also unfortunately eroding the linguistic diversity so central to the maintenance of cultural identities. It is clear from the work of Pennycook (1994) that the loss of indigenous languages is a form of 'linguistic genocide'.

It is also clear that English is the language of the educated middle class in many parts of the world, and plays a gatekeeping function. More and more people wanting to enter that gate are prepared to abandon the use of their own languages even in domains where they were exclusively used, for example in social interaction in private and familial settings. In South Africa, where we currently work, as in India, from where we originate, many young people in the urban centres claim English to be their mother tongue or home language. We have discussed this phenomenon in an earlier paper (Joseph and Ramani 1998). As a direct result of language loss, these young adults are increasingly alienated from their counterparts from more rural or provincial backgrounds.

Our experience in South Africa shows that there is a widespread belief that a knowledge of and competence in English will ensure increased status, job opportunities and social mobility. Multilingual campaigns, meant to conscientize people about the value of local languages, seem to be largely unsuccessful in many developing countries.

## The need for a politics of language for the ELT/ESL profession

Yet the ELT/ESL profession does not seem to problematize the relation between English and local languages. Except for a few scholars, some of whom we have mentioned earlier in this paper, the 'hegemony' of English does not seem to be an issue to be engaged with or debated.

We believe that we, as ELT/ESL scholars and practitioners, need to acknowledge the multilingual realities within which we carry out our profession, and to examine the effects of the demand for English on the languages of our learners. This means that we have to develop a political view of the roles of the different languages in our students' lives and to examine the power relations between these languages. This necessarily means that we have to take an informed and self-critical view of the role of English and its impact on multilingualism. We cannot avoid an engagement with the politics of language, namely the asymmetrical power relations between English and other languages.

In other words, a theory of language must include a theory of the politics of language, which in today's world requires an understanding of the hegemony of English and the universal demand for it as an instrument of upward social mobility.

## A theory of a politics of language

The question we need to ask in developing a theory of the politics of language is: Can we accept that English is a global language and therefore provide the best possible access to it, yet challenge its hegemony? Is this a contradiction in terms?

We sought to address this issue in an earlier paper (Granville et al. 1998) in which we addressed three important considerations:

- The politically-neutral view of global English that needs to be challenged, and the multilingual reality of the world that needs to be affirmed
- The recognition of people's right to, and English language professionals' obligation to provide, competence in English
- The critical distinction between the 'symbolic' versus the 'real' power of English

The first of these views, namely the hegemony of English, has been described in the early sections of this paper.

The second view, namely the 'right to English', is based on Bourdieu's notion of 'cultural capital' (1991). English is undoubtedly cultural capital. To increase students' awareness of the politics of English is not enough. We also have a responsibility to enable the vast majority of people, deprived of modernism and cultural capital, to have access to this capital that the middle class (and English language specialists do belong to this middle class, wherever they are in the world) take for granted. In other words, we have to challenge the hegemony of English while at the same time granting people their right to access this capital. We note in passing that increasing access to English 'de-elitizes' it. We have discussed the idea of de-elitization more fully in Granville et al. (1998).

What is more important is the dilemma posed by the first and second views, namely anti-hegemony and the right of access to English. This dilemma has forced us to move beyond a simplistic politics of English to a more complex view of hegemony called the 'access paradox', to which we now turn.

As English language specialists, we are obliged to provide access to English for our learners. However, we need also to be aware that in fulfilling this obligation we are empowering English further and increasing its hegemonic power. In addition, in carrying out this obligation we are consciously or unconsciously encouraging our learners to devalue their own languages.

Janks (1995) discusses this contradiction. She shows that if you provide access to the dominant language, you entrench its dominance. If, on the other hand, you deny students' access to the language of power, you entrench their marginalization in a society which continues to accord value and status to that language. Lodge (1997) refers to this as the 'access paradox'. The 'access paradox' is an important concept to help to re-evaluate some of the well-intended but simplistic attacks on the hegemony of English often advanced by supporters of multilingualism. It is also a concept that enables progressive English language professionals to overcome the paralysis of guilt that a simplistic politics of English can induce. The access paradox allows us to expand rather than abandon our role as English language specialists.

The third view to be included in a theory of the politics of language is the concept of 'symbolic power' (Bourdieu 1991). Using Bourdieu again, we showed how the education system, while seeking to teach *competence* in a language, at the same time also teaches the *social values* attached to the language, English being the language of power in the present world. However, in many parts of the developing world the education system *fails* to provide real access to the language of power (due to poor schooling, inadequate training of teachers, lack of resources and infrastructure). Instead, what the education system does *succeed* in doing is to 'teach' students that the language of power has status and legitimacy, creating thereby an unfulfilled longing for real competence in English. Those who do 'succeed' in getting into

**189**

English medium schools still do not have access to the 'best' teaching in English.

The school-leaving results of non-mainstream children the world over show that the major cause for their failure at school has to do with their low proficiency in English. The high failure rate of students in their school-leaving exams in the Limpopo Province (one of the poorest of the nine provinces in South Africa) has largely to do with poor levels of competence in English. Desai (1999, 46) observes that 'proficiency in English remains an unattainable goal for most learners. This applies not only to English as a subject, but also to it as a language through which learners can access knowledge'. Yet the craze for English-medium education continues unabated. Uninformed parents demand that even primary school education (which in many developing countries is conducted through the local languages) now be carried out in English. The demand for a 'straight for English' policy rather than 'a gradual transfer to English' is becoming the norm among the rapidly-growing black middle class in South Africa (LANGTAG 1996).

This shows that while we are not really able to develop actual competence in English and thus ensure real power, we are entrenching in people's minds the symbolic power that Bourdieu writes about.

## Going beyond the access paradox

But we also need to ask these questions: Is awareness of the access paradox enough? What action emanates from it? Are campaigns to make government, educationists and parents aware of the access paradox enough?

In addition, we also need to ask: Should students be made aware of the politics of English through curricularized courses (Kapp 1998)?

To this last question, we want to acknowledge that the *practice* of the politics of English has started in English language programmes that include topics such as the hegemony of English, multiliteracies, multilingualism, and Critical Language Awareness (Janks 1990). These courses meet the twin requirements of challenging the hegemony of English, while providing 'access' to English to students from marginalized language backgrounds. They represent an advance against the traditional 'neutral' view of English, which is still widespread. They empower students to uncover the deceptiveness of the 'neutral view' and see the marginalization of their languages and cultures as a product of the hegemony of English.

However, these curricular practices of the politics of language, with a special emphasis on the access paradox, do not go far enough. They still evade the issue of the *medium of instruction* (MOI) or *language of learning and teaching* (LOLT). We may ask of such courses why it is that only English (notwithstanding its politically-driven content) continues to be used in the prestigious arena of tertiary education, and why indigenous languages are not. Or to press the point to its political limits we may ask: Is it politically adequate for English language professionals to empower learners with a critical conscious-ness through English as MOI/LOLT (with CALP status) but allow, through inaction, the indigenous languages of their students to remain at their present BICS level (the terms are from J. Cummins 1980)?

Overcoming the limitation of all awareness campaigns and curricula means making a change, even if a small one, in the *practice* of multilingualism, namely the development of the marginalized home languages of our learners through their use as a medium of instruction in tertiary education.

But even this is not enough. We need further to find a place in our curricula for indigenous languages as vehicles of rational and creative thinking. This means that the ELT/ESL profession needs to be engaged in debates about the roles of the indigenous languages in the world today, and discussions on what it can do to promote these languages. To do this we need to clarify an educational role for these languages, and specifically the role of these languages in the cognitive develop-ment of our learners.

## Language and cognition

We have argued so far that an educational perspective based on a political approach to languages is necessary to right the imbalance between English and indigenous languages. Such an approach/theory must include the three perspectives: challenging the hegemony of English, upholding in theory and practice people's right to have access to English, and going beyond the symbolic value of English to its real value. These perspectives culminate in the concept of the access paradox which problematizes a simplistic view of the hegemony of English.

However, while a political theory underpinned by the access paradox is necessary, it is not a sufficient condition to ensure the status of indigenous languages for cognitive and academic purposes, or what Cummins (1980) and Cummins and Swain (1986) have called Cognitive Academic Language Proficiency (or CALP). That is to say, even if indigenous languages are realized across the educational spectrum, from primary to tertiary levels, both as subject and medium, there is still the issue of whether these languages are being used for cognitively challenging purposes.

In making a case for indigenous languages that have been forced by the hegemony of English to remain at the Basic Interpersonal Communication Skills (BICS) level to now be deployed for CALP purposes, there is a danger in assuming that English curricula (as subject or medium) are not in need of development, and that indigenous languages have to catch up with a perfected system.

Recent research studies into classrooms in South Africa (Taylor and Vinjevold 1999) show that even in English-medium schools, teaching and learning activities are limited to lower-level cognitive skills. In terms of Bloom's taxonomy (Bloom 1956), these activities involve rote learning, lower-order comprehension requiring formulaic responses, and simple information-gap tasks. It is clear that using a language as medium does not automatically ensure the deployment of higher-order skills such as hypothesizing, predicting, developing and applying criteria, analysing, synthesizing and evaluating information.

Therefore, the use of English for CALP purposes does not automatically guarantee its being used in cognitively challenging ways. The 'C' of CALP may involve making cognitive demands on learners without necessarily providing the support they need to achieve these demands. A CALP-driven curriculum endows English with symbolic value as it is then seen as a vehicle for modern knowledge, but may only partially deploy the higher-order skills necessary for processing such knowledge. Often it is a case of thinking processes being taken for granted by mainstream teachers of the disciplines, and hapless students being left to sink or swim! Students then fail to develop the 'elaborated code' in English (Bernstein 1971) associated with formal schooling, and are left only with the symbolic status of an 'English' education.

The weakness of the teaching of English or any other language, either as a subject or a medium, might have to do with the absence of a cognitively-driven linguistics. Western linguistics has tended to be largely structural despite the shift from sentence-based to discourse-based studies. The value of human agency in language has consequently been seriously eroded. Speech Act theory is the first attempt in linguistics to bring agency (i.e. the subjective intentions of the speaker) into language studies, making it thereby an important resource for a multilingual curricular practice. However, a more powerful notion of agency is one in which human beings act upon the world through language as a tool for thinking. Such a view has been articulated by Vygotsky (1986). The intrinsic connection between language and cognition shown to exist by Vygotsky makes his theory, we believe, a more satisfactory basis for the development of languages in education.

## Integrating a politics of language with a cognitive role for indigenous languages

We now give one example of integrating a political view of language with deploying an indigenous language for CALP purposes, from a newly-approved undergraduate degree that we have started at the University of the North. The three-year bilingual BA degree programme comprises two programmes, Contemporary English Language Studies (CELS) and Multilingual Studies (MUST). Both programmes focus on language in all its aspects: syntactic structure, discourse analysis, language policy, sociolinguistics, the politics of language, translation, language teaching, critical language awareness, and workplace literacies. But the two programmes, though broadly similar in content, differ in the language medium: CELS uses English and MUST uses Sesotho sa Leboa – the dominant indigenous language of the Limpopo province in the northernmost part of South Africa.

The aim of such a bilingual degree is to turn out bilinguists who are competent in both a modern language (English in this case) and in their home language. We believe, as affirmed in our collective paper (Granville et al. 1998) that students (and their parents) will only opt for a programme of African medium instruction if they are simultaneously guaranteed an excellent English language programme.

Such bilingual programmes create an alternative to the dominant models of 'straight for English' or 'English only' curricula. The absence of excellent bilingual programmes of education explains why English lures people. The weak efforts to provide mother tongue as a subject and the limited use of the mother tongue as medium (by restricting it to the early years of schooling) do nothing to enhance its status, by contrast with the use of English as a medium throughout schooling and tertiary education.

The lure of English is thus based on the denial of options, which in turn reinforces the hegemony of English. That is why research into people's language preferences that is carried out in the absence of real options (between an English only versus an English plus indigenous language programme) tends to discover the obvious, namely that people 'opt' for English. In actuality, hegemony is achieved (beyond its early coercive phase) when people consent to something hegemonic because they have no choice.

But hegemony becomes virtually unassailable when the knowledge of the absence of choice is itself hidden from people. English then becomes desirable because it is assumed to be the 'natural' language of higher education. This naturalizing of the role of English is given academic (and applied linguistic) respectability, for instance by the well-known applied linguist Widdowson (1996), who argues for a 'domains' view of languages or 'everything in its proper place', following Swift's 'proper words in their proper places'. English is to be used in the educational domain and indigenous languages in the hearth and home, thus preserving all the languages. Such a view is a modern reincarnation of the 'neutral' view that legitimizes itself by incorporating multilingualism into it. However, it ignores the asymmetry between English, which occupies prestigious domains that have a CALP status, and indigenous languages that have a socially and economically lower BICS status. Fairclough (1989) challenges this view, but this potential debate appears not to have caught the imagination of the ELT profession.

We need therefore to reflect on this issue. Widdowson's perspective reinforces the notion of the 'naturalness' of English by presenting a deterministic view of the multilingualness of the world and the role of English in it. There is no admission that our present world, in which English dominates, is a world that has been constructed by human beings and is therefore changeable by them.

The anonymous power of the 'culture' of the hegemony of English, backed by widespread silence from the ELT community, and reinforced by occasional articulated support for it by ELT specialists, might seem quite daunting for anyone attempting to support a counter-culture redefining the role of English and therefore of globalism. It is against this background that the role of practice becomes effective. We believe the hegemony of English needs to be challenged through a small practice embodied in a bilingual programme set in the multilingual context of global English. Such a practice creates a real option for people, and a feeling of the 'politics of the possible' among practitioners.

Campaigns against the hegemony of English can finally only be effective if, in addition to a country's multilingual policies on paper, there is also a practice-based campaign. These practices, we reiterate, must comprise excellent indigenous language programmes coupled with excellent English language programmes.

To use a metaphor, we think of such curricular practices as based on a policy of 'walking with two legs' as against the dominant practice of 'hopping with one leg'. As we have said, the power of the hegemony of English lies in making us believe that English is not only desirable but also natural. The analogy of 'hopping with one leg' being better than 'walking with two legs', however, shows up the ridiculousness of monolingualism – which is a strong basis for the hegemony of English. The monolingual view that argues that 'concentrating' on one thing at a time, rather than being 'distracted' by doing two things at a time, seems logical and economical. But no human being would accept such a view when it is applied to the natural human state of walking. The argument that the more we practise hopping, the better we become at it, holds good only if we have one leg. But because hopping has not achieved hegemonic status in the way English has, and is not in danger of ever doing so, it is much more difficult to convince people that walking is a clumsy act.

Returning to global English in a multilingual world, it is high time we started walking. The first steps in walking that one takes after the long historical stage of hopping is bound to be awkward, slow and even painful. But just because we are naturally able to walk on two legs (talk in two or more languages), it is not hard to imagine we will get better at it in time. Perhaps after some experience of developing and implementing bilingual programmes, we may even begin to wonder how we ever believed that an English-only education was the best imaginable. For us as formerly 'English-only' professionals, our new bilingual programme has shown that not only should we, from the dominant language group, transfer the best resources from English to indigenous languages (argued in Ramani and Joseph 1998), but that this is also possible and excitingly challenging as well. Many of the old, tired insights and ideas of ELT/ESL take on a new life when tried out with indigenous languages, thus revitalizing the profession.

Further, indigenous languages also acquire a modern status when modern systems of analysis (such as discourse analysis), with their accompanying technologies (like online learning) are applied to these languages. Thus the 'traditional' African languages (which were limited to BICS) now come to be experienced as 'modern' languages by students of these languages. This symbolic status of indigenous languages is important in developing a counter-hegemonic conscious-ness. At the same time, the programme we are developing seeks to go beyond this symbolic status of modernity, by challenging learners to engage in the actual development of their indigenous languages to levels comparable to English.

To summarize: the ELT/ESL profession needs to be engaged in debates about the roles of the indigenous languages in the world today, and in discussions of what it can do to promote these languages. To our traditional responsibility of providing excellent access to English, we need to respond creatively and proactively, in order to increase access for students from historically marginalized groups who are seeking to enter hitherto elitist spheres of higher education, and to offer them cognitively stimulating, modern bilingual programmes.

## A perspective on the relation between policy and implementation

In this final section, we would like to present our view of the relation between policy/theory and implementation/practice.

South Africa has one of the most progressive multilingual policies in the world. The South African Constitution (1996) grants official status to eleven languages, nine of which are black languages, but one of the greatest challenges facing the country is the implementation of this policy.

We all know that progressive policies based upon progressive theories of language do not in themselves guarantee change. Unless the relation between policy and practice is clarified, language practitioners are likely to experience the paralysis of guilt and defeat from knowing what is the right thing to do without knowing *how* to do it.

Our practice of multilingualism at the University of the North is based not only on politically and cognitively driven theories of language, but also on a theory of practice. Such a theory has been described by Prabhu (1987) as 'professional activism', and we adhere to this term, though we will take the liberty of developing it in ways beyond what its author intended.

The gap between theory/policy on the one hand and practice/ implementation on the other is often noted as a major crippling factor in educational change. We believe the difficulty lies in the way we think policy is supposed to be implemented. It is often assumed that a policy must be implemented *in toto*, and that a symmetrical relation exists between the policy and its implementation. This assumption sets up implementation for failure and leads to a culture of blame, where implementation is often the responsibility of a vague 'other'. Language practitioners thus prevent themselves from becoming agents of change. Such an approach to implementation breeds a defeatist attitude to change and a feeling of hopelessness.

We believe that the relation between policy and its implementation is *asymmetrical*, i.e. practice does not have to be an implementation of all aspects of policy. Nor does practice have to be large-scale. Practice is best achieved in small-scale, local, low-risk efforts that are within the reach of the existing powers of a practitioner. Thinking big while acting small has been the theory of practice behind our own multilingual efforts. This is a theory of practice that calls for an analysis for one's own power, and an effort to bring policy within the scope of one's power. Policy thus personalized becomes a powerful driver of practice.

We are operating with a view of professional activism that rejects a symmetrical approach to the relation between policy and practice, and operates instead with a notion that 'small is beautiful' (Schumacher 1973), and therefore 'manageable'. We believe that professional activism needs to be socially motivated, just as it is in any other form of activism. In the language teaching context this means a *moral* concern with the needs of students in a multilingual world where English is both a desirable learning goal and also paradoxically a destroyer of indigenous languages. But in addition to social goals backed by a moral consciousness, we think a less known but equally important one is an *epistemological* goal, i.e. by engaging with practice, language specialists can theorize/create knowledge. Such notions as 'the teacher as reflective practitioner', 'action research', 'professional activism' and 'role reversals by teachers' are well known in education and the ELT profession. These are notions, we believe, that the ELT profession needs to transfer to multilingual education.

Our own efforts over the years to deepen the concept and practice of professional activism argues for role-reversal by teachers (English language teachers learning marginalized languages), as a way of theory construction through changing one's ontological status: from teacher to learner.

To summarize, small pockets in which policies are implemented are a viable, legitimate and productive way of generating both new practices and new theories. Such a view of implementation, combined with an enriched politics of English and a powerful theory of cognition in language studies, can help us arrive at a changed identity in an English-speaking world. This identity, while challenging a monolithic, monolingual view of culture, will also create a new form of globalism, which values and upholds diversity.

## References

Agnihotri, R. 1996. 'Sociolinguistic aspects of a multilingual classroom'. Paper presented at the International Seminar on Language in Education, University of Cape Town, South Africa.

Alexander, N. 2000. 'English unassailable but unattainable: the dilemma of language policy in South African education', *PRAESA* Occasional Paper No 3. Cape Town: PRAESA.

Auerbach, E. 1993. 'Re-examining English only in the ESL classroom'. *TESOL Quarterly* 27/1, 9–32.

Barkhuizen, G. P. and D. Gough. 1996. 'Language Curriculum development in South Africa: what place for English?' *TESOL Quarterly* 30/3, 453–70.

Bernstein, B. 1971. *Class, Codes and Control, Vol I*. London: Routledge and Kegan Paul.

Bloom, B. S. 1956. *Taxonomy of Educational Objectives: The Classification of Educational Goals. Handbook I, Cognitive Domain*. London: Longman.

Bourdieu, P. 1991. In J. Thompson (ed.), *Language and Symbolic Power*. Cambridge: Polity Press.

Cummins, J. 1980. 'The cross-lingual dimension of language proficiency: implications for bilingual education and the optimal age issue'. *TESOL Quarterly* 14/1, 75–87.

Cummins, J. and M. Swain. 1986. *Bilingualism in Education*. London and New York: Longman.

Cummins, J. 2000. *Language, Power and Pedagogy: Bilingual Children in the Crossfire*. Clevedon: Multilingual Matters.

Desai, Z. 1999. Enabling Policies, Disabling Practices. *Per Linguam* 15/1, 42–53.

Dowling, T. and P. Maseko. 1995. 'African language teaching at universities'. In K. Heugh, A. Siegruhn and P. Pluddemann (eds), *Multilingual Education for South Africa*. Johannesburg: Heinemann. 100–6.

Fairclough, N. 1989. *Language and Power*. London and New York: Longman.

Granville, S., H. Janks, M. Joseph, M. Mphahlele, E. Ramani, Y. Reed and P. Watson. 1998. 'English with or without g (u) ilt'. *Language and Education* 12/4, 254–72.

Janks, H. 1990. 'Contested terrain: English Education in South Africa 1948–1987'. In I. Goodson and P. Medway (eds), *Bringing English to Order*. London: Falmer Press.

Janks, H. 1995. 'The research and development of Critical Language Awareness materials for use in South African secondary classrooms'. Unpublished PhD thesis, Lancaster University, UK.

Joseph, M. and E. Ramani. 1997. 'Making monolinguals multilingual'. *AD Issues* Vol 5, No 1, 15–17.

Joseph M. and E. Ramani. 1998. 'The ELT specialist and linguistic hegemony: A response to Tully and Mathew'. *ELT Journal* 52/3, 214–22.

LANGTAG. 1996. *Towards a National Language Plan for South Africa*. Cape Town: Final Report of the Language Plan Task Group.

Lodge, H. 1997. 'Providing access to academic literacy in the Arts Foundation Programme at the University of the Witwatersrand in 1996: the theory behind the practice'. Unpublished Masters research report, University of the Witwatersrand.

Macdonald, C. A. 1990. *Crossing the Threshold into Standard 3*. Main report of the Threshold Project. Pretoria: Human Sciences Research Council.

Pennycook, A. 1994. *The Cultural Politics of English as an International Language*. London: Longman.

Prabhu, N. S. 1987. *Second Language Pedagogy*. Oxford: Oxford University Press.

Ramani, E. and M. Joseph. 2002. 'Breaking new ground: introducing an African language as medium of instruction at the University of the North'. *Perspectives in Education*. Special issue on Multilingualism, 20/1, 233–40.

Republic of South Africa. 1996. *Constitution of the Republic of South Africa (Act 108 of 1996)* Pretoria: Government Printer.

Schumacher, E. F. 1973. *Small is Beautiful: Economics as if People Mattered*. New York: Harper and Row.

Taylor, N. and P. Vinjevold (eds). 1999. *Getting Learning Right: Report of the President's Education Initiative Research Project.* Johannesburg: Joint Education Trust.

Vygotsky, L. S. 1986. *Thought and Language.* Cambridge, MA: MIT Press.

wa Thiong'o, Ngũgĩ. 1981. *Decolonising the Mind: The Politics of Language in African Literature.* Nairobi, Kenya: Heinemann.

Widdowson, H. G. 1996. In T. Hedge and N. Whitney (eds), *Power, Pedagogy and Practice.* Oxford: Oxford University Press.

# An Interview with Suresh Canagarajah

*Rani Rubdy*
Nanyang Technological University, Singapore
*Mario Saraceni*
University of Portsmouth, UK

**Q1**  *Can you tell us something about your own special interest with regard to English as a world language?*

**A1**  I am interested in the poetics and politics of local varieties of English. It is their politics that I was first interested in. While I read much about English as a 'killer language' that causes the extinction of local languages (in addition to colonizing local cultures, knowledge, and value systems), I became sensitive to the ways in which postcolonial speakers of English creatively negotiate the place of English in their lives. By appropriating this language for their local uses according to their preferred cultural and linguistic practices, postcolonial communities were initiating subtle changes in the grammar and discourse of English. Codemixing, bilingual communicative strategies like codeswitching, and the use of local accents and idioms are manifestations of this process of nativization. Making English serve local interests by adopting new communicative practices and ideologies is what I consider the 'mircopolitics' of postcolonial resistance.

Such considerations as the changes in the grammar and discourse of English relate essentially to its 'poetics'. But I am interested in the poetics of World Englishes in a broader sense also: the new patterns of writing in academic communication and research publishing, and the creative alterations of genre rules, style, and metaphor in literary writing. Combining both notions, I see this kind of *poetics* as basically *political*.

I am, of course, open to the criticism that resistance in these micro-social domains of text, grammar and interpersonal relations leaves unchanged the social and material factors that undergird the dominance of English. I am interested in exploring the limitations as well as the possibilities of such micropolitics.

**Q2**  *What would you say are some 'burning issues' in the area of English as a World Language today?*

**A2**  The World Englishes notion has forced us to redefine many linguistic constructs and pedagogical practices. Here are some of the questions that need to be explored:

If all varieties of English have equal status, how do we pluralize our notion of norms and standards? Are there new norms of usage developing from 'within' global communities of English? How do we codify these new norms? Can we thus develop an orientation to English as a multinational language with a heterogeneous and hybrid grammatical system that accommodates the features of different local varieties – not a homogeneous system based on the norms of one community or the other?

If the notions 'native speaker/non-native speaker' don't have meaning any more (as postcolonial subjects are native to their own variety of English, if not those of the British or American variety), how do we distinguish between speakers with different levels/types of competence (without invoking notions of birth, nationality, or ethnicity and without imposing non-linguistic forms of inequality)? Even notions like Inner Circle, Outer Circle, and Expanding Circle impose hierarchies that aren't valid for many speakers (as they have been using English as their sole or dominant language for some generations even outside the Innner Circle).

How can we teach English for shuttling between diverse English-speaking communities worldwide, and not just for joining a single community (i.e. a native-speaker community in UK or USA) as we did hitherto? Postmodern subjects are compelled to move fluidly between different dialects and discourses today in the domains of work, media and education. How can we teach English as part of a communicative repertoire (that includes various dialects of English – both local and global – in addition to the vernacular and local regional languages)?

How do we facilititate intercultural communication in English where people can retain their preferred styles, discourses and conventions in order to represent their identity, but also to effectively negotiate the differences and ensure smooth communication? Can we formulate meta-discursive guidelines that will help us transcend (or at least navigate) our cultural and sociolinguistic diversity?

**Q3** *At present, English has reached a dominant position of extraordinary proportions, especially with the USA enjoying the exclusive status of being the only superpower. Is there any likelihood that this powerful position of the English language will be challenged in the future?*

**A3** I am not interested in seeing another language overtake English. What purpose would that serve? We have to then start theorizing resistance against the newly powerful language all over again! Nor do I believe in a neutral playing field where all languages enjoy equal status. Power is real. A more effective strategy is to constantly negotiate, modify, and resist power to achieve the interests of dominated communities. Therefore I am more interested in discerning and developing challenges to English from *within*. And such a resistance to English has been going on from the day it was introduced in colonized communities (as I illustrate in Canagarajah 1999 and 2000). I am thinking here of practices that appropriate the language to serve local interests according to local values, through the linguistic and sociolinguistic processes I mentioned earlier. These processes are not insignificant; they are ideologically loaded. Purists (in the communities that claim ownership over English) know well that these changes in grammar and discourse make the language impure. They know that these changes alter the character of the language. Eventually, such changes lead to pluralizing the system of English. The changes even have the potential of democratizing the language, preventing any one community from claiming monopoly over the language. I do believe that such processes of appropriation weaken (if not sever) the ties between English language and the United States (or Britain, for that matter).

We have to also note here the 'death of the native speaker'. Not only is this exclusivist identity not valid any more, there are literally more multilingual speakers of English from traditionally non-English communities than the Inner Circle communities today (as statistics from Graddol 1999 and Crystal 1997 prove). So who owns the English language? English is not the language of the UK or USA any more. Consider also the developments in postmodern communication and culture. Technological features such as the Internet and multimedia communication, social developments like diaspora communities, and the internationally networked economy have created conditions whereby English has to exist side by side with many other languages. English doesn't go unscathed in this process of close contact. It is becoming a hybrid language, mixed with elements from other languages. It is enough for me that diverse communities can find such textual and linguistic spaces within English to represent their identities, voices and interests.

**Q4** *Some (e.g. Phillipson 1992) have argued that the unprecedented spread of English in the last half a century is a result of deliberate policy on the part of core English-speaking countries to maintain dominance over the periphery, which in many cases comprise the developing countries. Others (McKay 2002) maintain that to assume that the dominance of English is a function of the language itself, or its active promotion, is to oversimplify the complexity of the phenomenon of language-spread. What are your views on this extremely controversial topic?*

**A4** The relationship between deliberate policy and impersonal socio-economic forces in the linguistic exercise of power is always quite complex. But pointing out the more abstract social factors in the dominance of a language should not be used to obfuscate the sources of power (i.e. the people who directly and indirectly benefit from the hegemony of that language). We can't think of language as having a life of its own, spreading globally by its own sweet will. The role of the speakers of that language needs to be interrogated. Sometimes, the speech community strives for economic and political power, which then has implications for the privileged status of its language. It is also the case that once certain basic infrastructural conditions are established (i.e. political and economic institutions that favour the dominant group), then language goes on to derive certain advantages without visibly seeming to depend on the machinations of the people concerned. For example, given the status of the USA in business, technology, mass media and popular culture, it is not surprising that English enjoys a privileged life among languages.

While acknowledging these impersonal processes of power, we mustn't also forget the well-documented cases of linguicism during the colonial and the Cold War periods, when agencies first in Britain and then the United States deliberately imposed English on certain communities in order to exercise their power. The oft-quoted statements of Macaulay and the recent policy documents of the British Council are evidence of such a conscious policy (see Phillipson 1992 for examples). Of course, in the post-Cold War period and the days of late capitalism, scholars may consider socio-economic conditions as too diversified to benefit any one language group. But English still serves as linguistic capital (relative to the other languages) partly benefiting from its earlier history and institutions, providing advantages to its speakers. Perhaps, as Stuart Hall (1997) argues, it is through this new strategy of accommodating other languages and communities in its practices, and popularizing discourses like linguistic hybridity and social fluidity, that English now exercises power in more subtle ways.

**Q5**  *In your writings, you have suggested that the spread of English has resulted in the devaluing of non-Western cultures and knowledge paradigms, and particularly in the way people of these cultures perceive themselves and the world. Is there a way to reverse this trend while English continues to be a dominant world language?*

**A5**  Yes, there are ways. And neither are they new. While I have documented ways in which the spread of English has resulted in devaluing other cultures and knowledge paradigms, I have also exemplified the ways in which colonized people have creatively adopted English for critical expression and authentic representation. In my home town, the nineteenth-century Hindu reformist Arumuga Navalar adopted the English language and the discourse practices of the missionaries (such as evangelistic pamphlets, apologetics, inter-faith debates, and popularization of Hinduism) to proselytize new converts and reconvert those whom the missionaries had converted to Christianity. These are examples of appropriating the master's tools to bring down his house – or to build one's own! Of course, the English language had to go through some changes (in the form of codemixing and new styles of writing) as it was adopted for such purposes. Nowadays, local scholars have begun adopting new forms of research writing as they publish their knowledge in mainstream academic journals in English. Here, again, they have to reconstruct the dominant conventions and discourses of academic communication in order to represent local knowledge (see examples in Canagarajah 2002). These are what I consider counter-discourses in English, that challenge the cultural and intellectual hegemony exercised by the English language.

But an important qualification has to be made. The cultures and knowledge paradigms of local communities are not 'non-Western' (if by this term you are referring to an exclusive and absolute construct). The culture and knowledge of a local community have always been in contact with those belonging to other communities (including those of the West). These constructs are even more hybrid today, and postcolonial communities are finding critical ways of representing the forms of culture and knowledge practised in their local settings in and through English. So there is no contradiction in representing local cultures and knowledge in the English language – they have always been in contact with other cultural and intellectual traditions, even as they maintained their relative autonomy.

and Mario Saraceni

e in ESL contexts is social, it may be merely individual and
in EFL contexts.) However, it is possible that localized norms
will develop socially over time in these Expanding Circle
ties as individuals continue to use them according to their
preferences.

*the one hand, it is undesirable, and also not feasible, to
a single monochrome native-speaker Standard form on non-
eakers of English because the burden they will have to bear in
learning forms of pronunciation (and even syntax) associated
ive-speaker varieties will be enormous. On the other hand, if
mmunity of non-native speakers develops its own distinct
there is a fear of loss of intelligibility and eventual fragmenta-
the language. Therefore, a middle ground being proposed
ys is that, arguably, non-native speakers will be well catered for
gua franca English made up of common core features that
he usage of all the non-native varieties. How do you react to
a?*

s difficult to imagine what form this lingua franca English will
this variety is similar to what Crystal (1997) proposes as the
Standard Spoken English, I have already expressed my
tions about this (see Canagarajah 1999, 179–81). There is a
on that the core features will still come from the politically
ul communities. (When have language norms been divorced
ower?) Besides, this manufactured variety will be another
mative norm, imposed from outside, and not developed locally
communities of usage. Furthermore, this variety will have its
thos – it will be 'marked' (perhaps as a more cosmopolitan
) and will exist parallel to or in opposition to existing local
es.

envision other ways of coping with issues of intelligibility and
ntation. It is important to develop a practice of negotiating
rses (or dialects, registers and codes for that matter). I think
ers of any language already negotiate their differences in actual
ctions of communication. If not socio-lectal differences, we all
o negotiate at least idio-lectal differences all the time. So if
ers of a specific variety of English come to a communicative event
he assumption that they have to negotiate differences as they talk
speakers of another variety, they will overcome problems of
gibility. Negotiation may take different forms. We know from
es in speech accommodation that speakers make mutual
ications in their speech to facilitate intelligibility. We also know

**Q6** *In many cases English is spreading primarily among those with greater economic resources, thus contributing to and reinforcing existing social inequalities and driving an even deeper wedge between the 'haves' and 'have nots'. In this sense, English acts as a gatekeeper to positions of wealth and prestige both within and between nations. What concrete steps can governments and educators take to empower the powerless under these circumstances?*

**A6** This is not surprising. Since the days of colonialism, the English language has rewarded local people unequally. It has served to stratify local societies hierarchically. It is by limiting the distribution of the language that those in power get to enjoy the benefits it affords. Sadly, even after decolonization the local elite haven't shown a readiness to lose control over their vested interests. Ironically, even the discourse of nationalism – promoting the vernacular and denigrating English – only serves to strengthen the power of those who already 'have' English.

To combat the advantages English seems to provide selectively to people in postcolonial societies, governments and educators have to universalize the teaching of English. In this case at least, more is better (even if it is a threatening language like English)! We have to take care, however, to encourage an additive bilingualism (or additive multi-lingualism). This means that English should not be allowed to replace the individual's or society's local languages. This unequal distribution has geopolitical implications as well: countries with a healthy multilingualism (where English proficiency is more advanced) enjoy greater possibilities of using this language in their favour to negotiate symbolic and material rewards for themselves. English is a linguistic capital and we ignore it at our peril. So it is important for governments to develop more effective bilingual programs and/or ESL programs consistent with additive multilingualism.

Of course, there are practical problems now, such as the inadequacy of trained teachers of English. Therefore, the available few teachers and educational resources are concentrated in urban areas, benefiting those who have always been blessed with a higher proficiency in English. From my experience in Sri Lanka, I know that many rural schools cannot provide the English classes that are mandated for state examinations because they don't have anyone to teach English. A radical solution is to shift the resources and teachers to rural areas, as there are ample opportunities in urban settings for the classroom and social acquisition of English. Or, more idealistically, resources and teachers have to be increased in order to serve all the communities in a country without disparities.

**Q7** *Some countries, such as India, not only accept but actually support the widespread promotion of local varieties of English. In other countries, such as Singapore, the belief among educational leaders that schools must actively promote the Standard variety is so strong that not only are local innovations frowned upon but vigorous campaigns are also launched for the promotion of Standard English. What is it that has brought about such divergent views and attitudes towards local varieties of English?*

**A7** I am not sure that differences among postcolonial nations in their attitude to nativized Englishes have been empirically studied and compared. All I can say is that all the communities (almost universally) have developed localized varieties of English from the earliest times of colonial intrusion as part of the normal processes of language contact; and yet, all communities equally despise their local varieties in deference to 'native' or 'standard' varieties (which attitude shows the power of internalized colonial values). This is an inconsistency that postcolonial communities are now beginning to address in favour of developing the status and currency of their local varieties. The difference in attitudes to local varieties may only be relative – relative to the extent of dependence on Western communities, the depth of anti-colonial resistance, and attitudes towards multilingualism.

It seems to me that India has had a long and vibrant history of multilingualism, that it has become natural for diverse communities to maintain and use their own dialects of English. India has also had a mass movement of anti-colonial struggle that has made the people sensitive against colonial values. Singapore, on the other hand, is more tightly integrated into the Western market/economy, and displays the presence of a more cosmopolitan community. Perhaps Singapore cares more about using the 'standard' variety as it treats the 'native English community' as its frame of reference. In fact, India has such a huge local bilingual community (with English as the link language for many communities) that it has a more indigenous frame of reference. To give an example from literature, writers from my own country, Sri Lanka, display a stronger commitment to the standard variety in comparison to Indian writers, although our history of colonization is similar. Sri Lankan creative writers in English have not displayed the scope and depth of experimentation with the use of local varieties of English that we see among Indian writers. A probable explanation is that our bilingual community is limited in number; therefore, local writers are thinking of the Western or global community of readers as their audience. But Indian writers have a well-developed local readership,

and adopt a different orientation to their
comfortable with their local varieties.

**Q8** *Ideological concerns suggest that giv*
*varieties of English (i.e. American or Bri*
*reinforce economic, political and social i*
*where English has begun to be owned by*
*teachers and students are more likely to re*
*this kind because of the strong link be*
*national identity. By contrast, in EFL co*
*lacking, teachers and students find it qui*
*exonormative models that are readily avail*
*at the centre. How can these ideologic*
*imperialism and resistance be reconciled wi*
*of EFL contexts?*

**A8** I think the differences between ESL
Outer Circle and Expanding Circle in K
sociolinguistically significant, and need
pedagogical practice. In the communities
English as an additional language and w
norms of usage, the model that is taught will
in EFL contexts, English is used primarily fe
outside the community (with issues of id
importance). Such 'Expanding Circle' commu
established tradition of local usage or norn
contexts, teachers will orientate students to n
other Inner Circle communities where they h
or receive education.

The ideological implications for both grou
different. Those who use English as an additi
community interactions have a stronger need
practices that reproduce centre interests. But th
a limited way, for purely instrumental reasons
lities for detaching themselves from the values a
the language. They face less danger of intern
However, at an individual level, EFL students w
language in their own way – according to their
discourses. Though the level of divergence from
be pronounced, and speakers may not draw from
set of local norms (which is not available to them
feel free to adopt English in ways that are su
purposes and represent their preferred identitie

resistanc
personal
of usage
commur
personal

**Q9** On
*impose*
*native s*
*terms o*
*with no*
*each co*
*variety,*
*tion of*
*nowado*
*by a li*
*reflect*
*this ide*

**A9** It
take. If
World
reserve
suspici
power
from
exonor
within
own e
variety
varieti

fragm
disco
speak
intera
have
speak
with
with
intell
studi
modi

from conversation analysis that speakers skilfully employ strategies of repair, clarification and paralinguistic interpretation (that includes gestures, tone and other cues) to negotiate differences. These are the strategies we are all already using in the global community of English speakers to negotiate our differences.

As for fragmentation, I think we need to orientate to English as a hybrid language. It is a multinational language that constitutes diverse norms and systems, represented by the global community of English speakers. While there are subtle differences, this hybrid system is also characterized by underlying similarities. (How this is different from Crystal's model or the model proposed in your question is that this is not artificiality constructed or externally imposed; this global system constitutes the varieties that are already in existence in postcolonial communities, and develops from within.) Creating an appreciation of differences and a readiness to negotiate diversity will see to it that this hybrid system of World Englishes bridges communities rather than fragments them.

**Q10**  *In some countries of Asia and Africa, English has become 'nativized' and begun to be considered an Asian or African language, and not one that is owned exclusively by any one speech community. For this reason some sociolinguists are of the view that it may be more realistic to recognize a plurality of standards. Given this view, if 'the English language' needs to be pluralized into 'the English languages', what does ELT stand for?*

**Q11**  *On the other hand, pedagogy tends to be ill at ease with multiple and/or flexible standards. How then can the ELT profession cope with such multiplicity of standards?*

**Q12**  *Teachers already have a hard time dealing with the differences between British and American English. If further pluralization of Englishes is to be accepted, would this not add to their difficulty, particularly where English is largely learnt as a foreign language, as, say, in Thailand? What can teachers do about this in the classroom?*

**A10, 11, 12** To address all these questions, we need a paradigm shift in the teaching of English. We don't have to teach each and every variety of English in the world (or the standard Englishes of Inner Circle communities); we simply have to change our understanding of language learning. To begin with, we have hitherto taught English in terms of a 'target language'. The target has been defined in terms of a 'native' variety, such as British or American English. Now we should teach in terms of a *repertoire* of language competence. While we focus on the variety of immediate relevance (in the ESL context of Sri Lanka, this will be 'educated' Sri Lankan English), we must make students sensitive to other varieties of English. Students should be ready to transfer their knowledge and competence in the underlying deep structure of their variety to the other varieties they will confront (including standard American and British English). They will confront even more diverse varieties in the world of computers, Internet, technology, and pop culture, which are not remote for any community in the context of globalization today. It is important for everyone – including those in the Inner Circle communities – to be multidialectal (or even multilingual) in today's society. While we treated language learning before as a way of joining a community (typically the 'native'- speaker community in the Inner Circle), now we will help students to think about shuttling between communities. To teach towards developing a repertoire is not to teach each and every dialect of the English-speaking communities students are going to confront. That is an impossibility in the world today, where linguistic and cultural fluidity and people's mobility are pervasive. What we need are changes in our approach that orientate students to issues of 'process' rather than 'product' (i.e. grammar, correctness, system, etc.) I like to chart such pedagogical changes as follows:

| FROM: | TO: |
| --- | --- |
| mastery of grammar rules | meta-linguistic awareness |
| focus on rules/conventions | focus on strategies |
| correctness | negotiation |
| language/discourse as static | language/discourse as changing |
| language as homogeneous | language as hybrid |
| language as context-bound | language as context-transforming |
| language as transparent/ instrumental | language as representational |
| L1 or C1 as problem | L1 or C1 as resource |

In the new approach, we will not focus on teaching surface level rules of grammar, syntax, pronunciation and spelling. We will focus on creating a deeper language awareness – a skill students will be able to apply to other dialects and varieties they confront. (There is already the school of language awareness that we can learn from.) Further- more, insisting rigidly on rules and correctness is misleading, as there are divergences across varieties. We have to focus on strategies and processes of language negotiation. Students can be trained to be sensitive to the contextual variation of language rules and conventions. (Here again, schools of learner strategy training can help us operationalize this approach – see Wendon 1991, Kumaravadivelu 2003.) A readiness to negotiate variation can help our students in another way – they must think of language as changing rather than static. Unfortunately, many pedagogical grammars adopt a prescriptive and conservative approach to language – partly motivated by convenience.

A more radical approach, to take this pedagogy a step further, is to think of language as context-transforming. This focus diverges from the traditional axiom that language is context-bound. Our students have to realize that making strategic decisions in deploying unconventional grammatical choices or discoursal features (motivated by their social and rhetorical interests) will help them in the path towards changes in power relations. If what is considered deviant enjoys social uptake, it will gradually begin to contest the norm, replacing the previous norms or pluralizing the social environment. To use language critically, students also have to realize that language is representational. One cannot suppress one's values, identities and interests in language and communication. In this struggle to represent our identities and interests in a language, one's first language (L1) or culture (C1) can be a resource rather than a problem. Ironically, such assumptions are not radical or new in our field. We simply have to develop appropriate pedagogical practices motivated by these assumptions.

## References

Canagarajah, A. S. 1999. *Resisting Linguistic Imperialism in English Teaching.* Oxford: Oxford University Press.

Canagarajah, A. S. 2000. 'Negotiating ideologies through English: strategies from the periphery'. In Tom Ricento (ed.), *Ideology, Politics, and Language Policies: Focus on English.* Amsterdam, Philadelphia: John Benjamins. 107–20.

Canagarajah, A. S. 2002. *A Geopolitics of Academic Writing.* Pittsburgh: University of Pittsburgh Press.

Crystal, D. 1997. *English as a Global Language.* Cambridge: Cambridge University Press.

Graddol, D. 1999. 'The decline of the native speaker.' *AILA Review*, 13, 57–68.

Hall, S. 1997. 'The local and the global: globalization and ethnicity'. In A. D. King (ed.), *Culture, Globalization, and the World System.* Minneapolis, MN: University of Minnesota Press. 19–40.

Kumaravadivelu, B. 2003. *Beyond Methods.* New Haven: Yale University Press.

Wenden, A. 1991. *Learner Strategies for Learner Autonomy.* New York: Prentice Hall.

# Name Index

Fahsi, B., 122
Fairclough, N., 153, 194
Firth, A., 32, 41, 59
Fishman, J., 57
Foreman, M. L., 157
Giles, H., 155
Gonzalez, A. B., 179
Gorlach, M., 75, 76
Gough, D., 186
Graddol, D., 5, 114, 132, 146, 151, 202
Gramley, S., 98
Granger, S., 59
Granville, S., 188, 189, 193
Greenbaum, S., 59
Grin, G., 163
Gubbins, P., 159
Guilherme, M., 163
Gupta, A. F., 6, 95, 96, 99, 104, 116, 178, 179
Hall, R. A. Jr., 86
Hall, S., 86, 203
Harkins, J., 80
Hayhoe, M., 147
Healey, D., 162
Hino, N., 174, 180, 181
Holliday, A., 182
Holm, J., 86
Holt, M., 159
Honey, J., 174
House, J., 96
Hung, T., 38, 74
Irujo, S., 65
James, C., 156
Janks, H., 189
Jenkins, J., 7, 9, 17–18, 32, 36, 40–1, 43–4, 46, 49, 55, 78, 86, 88, 96, 116, 133–6, 151, 155, 159–60, 164, 170, 173–4
Jenner, B., 133, 136
Jessner, U., 163
Jiang, Y., 5
Jin, L., 121, 122
Johnson, K., 159, 164
Johnson, R. J., 159, 164
Joseph, M., 13, 112, 186, 187, 195
Judd, E. L., 161

Kachru, B. B., 7, 13, 19, 21, 32, 35, 40, 43, 52, 71, 84, 85, 95, 115, 117, 154, 163, 169, 170, 172–4
Kahane, H., 86
Kahane, R., 86
Kasper, G., 159, 164
Kaufman, T., 95
Keating, M., 159
Kirkpatrick, A., 6, 8, 12, 14, 19, 71, 77–80, 84, 141, 147
Knapp, K., 44
Korea, 76, 80, 123
Kramsch, C., 44, 52, 125
Krasnick, H., 79
Kumaravadivelu, B., 211
Labrie, N., 163
Laufer, B., 65
Leith, D., 87
Leitner, G., 8, 85
Li, D. C. S., 71, 80, 182
Liaw, M.-L., 164
Lin, A. M. Y., 173, 182
LoCastro, V., 123
Lockhart, R. S., 141
Lodge, H., 189
Loewenberg, I., 67
Lorente, B. P., 179
Lowenberg, P., 32
Maley, A., 8, 143
Masuhara, H., 143
Maurais, J., 151
Mazrui, A. M., 173, 179
Mazzon, G., 178
McArthur, T., 17, 21, 88, 96, 112
McKay, S. L., 7, 14, 84, 110, 114, 121–2, 151, 161, 174, 181, 203
Medgyes, P., 62, 76, 124, 151
Melchers, G., 11
Milroy, J., 7, 86–7
Milroy, L., 7, 87
Minkova, D., 86
Modiano, M., 52, 85, 88
Moon, R., 63
Morris, M. A., 151
Mufwene, S., 34, 43
Mugglestone, L., 153

# Subject Index

American English, *see United States*
Australia, 26, 58, 71, 74, 103–4, 106,
  115
  English in, 26, 31, 74, 77, 80, 132
bilingualism, 26, 44, 115–16, 118–22,
  125–6, 156, 200, 205–6
  bilingual classrooms, 125
  bilingual learners, 162
  bilingual programmes, 112, 193–4,
    205
  bilingual teachers, 38
  the "successful bilingual", 12, 18,
    51–60, 66
  *see also multilingualism*
British English, *see Great Britain*
Canada, 26, 29, 58, 97, 103, 104, 106,
  115
  English in, 26, 31, 96
canonical grammar, 12, 55, 58, 62
Caribbean, The, 10, 26
  English in, 28, 96
China, 5, 25, 76–8
  English in, 77
code mixing, 204
code switching, 174, 176
codification, 11, 43, 72, 75, 153, 155
colonization, 23, 169, 171, 174, 179,
  187, 205–6 *see also postcolonialism*
  colonial societies, 75, 203–4
  colonial values, 98, 206
  colonized English, 169
  English as a colonizing language,
    200
Council of Europe, 155
cultural imperialism, 24
disempowerment, 6, 25, 74, 181, *see
  also empowerment*
empowerment, 125, 205

of learners, 14, 58, 190–91
of teachers, 76
*see also disempowerment*
English as a Foreign Language (EFL),
  15, 22–4, 48, 85, 96, 163, 181, 207
  learners of, 9, 110, 124
  teachers of, 19, 56, 182
  users of, 59, 134
English as a global language, 5, 11,
  13–15, 23–4, 30, 46, 48, 76, 85,
  110–11, 114–15, 125–6, 135–6, 139,
  146, 151, 155, 186, 188, 194–5
  global intelligibility, 32–38, 132,
    156, 176
  global appropriacy, 52
English as a Lingua Franca (ELF), 6,
  8–14, 18, 19, 33–37, 40–49, 51,
  54–58, 66, 84–9, 91–2, 96
English as a Second Language (ESL),
  22–4, 66, 95, 116, 137, 195, 205
  contexts, 26, 27, 163, 207–8, 210
  learners, 110
  teachers, 186–8, 191, 195
  varieties, 84
English as an additional language,
  114, 115, 128, 207
English as an International Language
  (EIL), 6–15, 17, 22, 40–1, 43, 48,
  51–2, 54, 59–60, 64, 85, 88, 110–11,
  134, 151–64, 169, 173–4, 178,
  180–81
  curriculum, 7, 114–128,
  learners of, 12, 131, 136, 142, 146,
    160–161
  users of, 58, 136, 142, 144, 146
  teachers of, 140–41, 152, 160–64
English for Specific Purposes (ESP),
  30, 80